WAGON DAYS

Lawrence Winkler

Note for Librarians: A cataloguing record for this book is available from Library
and Archives Canada at www.collectionscanada.ca/amicus/index-e.html

"Covered Wagon" cover image by Jeff Allen
Cover design by Jenny Engwer, First Choice Books

ISBN – 978-0-9916941-9-8

Printed in Canada ♻ on recycled paper

 FIRST CHOICE BOOKS

firstchoicebooks.ca
Victoria, BC

10 9 8 7 6 5 4 3 2 1

Wagon Days

For Chief Joseph

Foreword Ho

'The Old West is not a certain place in a certain time, it's a state of mind. It's whatever you want it to be.'

Tom Mix, early western film actor

The American West was a notion, not a nation. It was a process, not a place. Or maybe it was, but it was no way to live. The exact boundaries of the Old West were where white men ran up against an alien continent, in space and time, on an ephemeral frontier. The collision annihilated native populations, and spawned completely new myths and metaphors. The borderlands were not an inferior stage of Western Civilization, awaiting the enlightening influence of the East, but a complex novel universe demanding clarity. It was the paradigm for a country that would eventually emerge from its conflicts.

The most formidable American western experience lasted less than fifty years, but its radical transmutation was more turbulent and consequential than many longer histories in other parts of the world. It was a pressure cooker cauldron of mineral, vegetable, animal, and human synergy. The minerality was elemental- radium, mercury, lead, copper, neon, iron, sulfur, uranium, carbon, oxygen, silver, arsenic, chromium, phosphorus, and gold. Bitterroot was sustenance and symbol. The native animal and human life of the West was

1

displaced, replaced, and exterminated- sixty million bison to make way for European bog animals, billions of passenger pigeons for nothing, and ninety percent of aboriginal native Americans, out of an original population of possibly a hundred million, by accident and design. One of my patients was once asked by a student what his occupation was.

"I'm an Indian." He said. "I've been an Indian my whole life."

In 1750, the American colonies had a million people, and the West was the wilderness beyond the Allegheny Mountains. A hundred years later, there were twenty-three million citizens of the United States, and the West went all the way to the Pacific. The white frontiersmen who invaded the howling transformed and were themselves transformed by an unfamiliar, unforgiving horizon. Survival demanded a delicate adaptation. It cost some settlers their manners, and others their minds. Western savagery was measured by the degree of Eastern civility. The first frontier icon of the American West, struck the balance perfectly. Daniel Boone was a Revolutionary War veteran, early Kentucky settler, trailblazer, Indian killer, buffalo eater, bear wrestler, and a gentleman. *I was happy in the midst of dangers and inconveniences.*

Manifest Destiny was the arrogance of the age, at the price of a cowboy hat and change. Along with the homesteaders and hunters came pioneer women, gunfighters and lawmen, wagon trains and railroads, soldiers and explorers, miners and gamblers, newspaper editors and entertainers, preachers and lawyers, and the occasional dentist and doctor. They arrived through and to everything that heaven, earth, water and fire could punish their arrogance with- droughts and floods and blizzards and prairie fires and insect swarms and winds and financial crises, and epidemics. The wooden structures they built caught fire or rotted.

It was the hardship that created the myths, and the bigger the hardship, the bigger the myth. There were all kinds of ways for a man to die- slow from exposure or starvation, or fast, from a bobcat or a bear, or a brave or backwoodsman. The combination of aggression and alcohol and ammunition was brutal, often lethal. The cruelty of frontier life wove colourful slang and tall stories and comedic catharsis into a folktale tapestry, which grew into big legends, changing fast. The frontiersman lived a fevered phantasmagoria of fable, a coarse charming realm beyond conventional laws and logic, where the Eastern rules didn't apply. *The grasshoppers were so thick you could barbecue them like steaks.* The Old West was a place of magic and wonders.

The light that filtered through the Paramount prism of the Saturday afternoon matinees in my old hometown theatre brought Canyonland arches and Joshua trees, the Big Empty, and the giant men that filled it- Indian scouts and confidence men and calvary captains and bank robbers. What happened on that silver screen of my youth lit fires inside me, of curiosity and incredulity, admiration and awe, and disgust and disapproval.

There is a Tocqueville conceit, possessed by all foreign visitors, that one can read America by travelling through it. Late in the summer of 2013, I set out to find the Old West, what it had been, and what had replaced it. Whatever it had been, the last gasp of it likely came out of Mary Hemingway's lungs, when she discovered the vanishing point in her front hallway in Ketchum. The heart and soul of the town was its big annual festival parade of Lewis freight wagons. I wanted to see it, and type on Hemingway's Royal Typewriter, in the den of his own private Idaho. Robyn and I spent two weeks driving the loop, around through what ever we could reach of what else we could find, in Montana, Wyoming, and Idaho, before heading back to Vancouver Island, through Washington.

The quest for my own wild panorama would turn wheels of fortune into a movable feast of *Wagon Days*. And if this don't get your fire started, your wood's wet.

*   *   *

Come Hell or High Water
Nanaimo, British Columbia

'Life's hard. It's even harder when you're stupid.'
John Wayne

Radium. For a brief moment, there was silence on the other end of the line.

"Huh?" was how it began. That had come out of Richard, who I hadn't seen for almost a decade, although it was about to happen.

His exclamation had been in response to the answer I had provided, to the question he originally posed.

"You ready for some mean gin and tonics on the dock?" The first westerns had four standard scenes- a bar, a stagecoach, a holdup and a chase. Ours got stuck outside the bar.

"I can't drink." Which was about where the silence began.

"I'm sorry." He sounded like he had dialed a wrong number. "Why not?"

"Because of the antibiotics." I said. That was the cause of the second long pause.

"What'll happen?" He asked.

"You'll need a bucket and mop." I said.

Richard was a Royal Canadian Mountie and, for that matter, so was his wife, Carolyn. We had met them in Mexico twenty-five years earlier, on our honeymoon, before they were married. Richard had tried to get me bus tickets in English, before I demonstrated how much easier it was in Spanish. We shared many *Dos Equis* in a cantina where you made sure you sat with your back to the wall.

Richard and Carolyn had fallen apart briefly, until we got them together for a reunion in the basement suite we were renting, in a house in Vancouver. They went on to their own honeymoon, three young sons, and an occasional reminiscence with the instruments of their reacquaintance. The one we were planning was long overdue.

Richard and Carolyn were camped out at their cottage on Christina Lake, a long crescentic mountain ellipse of inland glacial water in the middle of the BC Rockies.

"Come for a long weekend." Carolyn said. But Robyn and I knew it would take another long weekend to get there and back, and we had to plan our visit carefully.

"I know." Robyn said. "Let's take a short trip back through the States on the way home. We could see Montana."

My wife is from New Zealand. Her sense of distance is not highly developed. When she first came to visit my parents on Lake of the Woods, just over the Manitoba border into Ontario, she asked if we could take a short drive to Toronto. I told her that this would not be possible. The short excursion she wanted us to take on this trip, *back through the States on the way home*, through Idaho and Washington, with Montana thrown in, would be a reenactment of the original crossing of the American West.

"If you climb in the saddle, be ready for the

ride." I said.

"It'll be fun." Said Robyn. It would be fun, I thought. No matter if our pilgrimage through frontier country turned into either a wretched ordeal or a wondrous adventure, it could also turn into a book. Maybe even this one. I was already visiting the places that had captured my imagination on the big Paramount Saturday matinee theatre screen in my hometown, when admission was a quarter, and a *Rowntree* Cherry Blossom or a roll of black currant fruit pastilles was a dime. Thirty-five cents would get you Roy Rogers and Dale Evans, Gene Autry and the Lone Ranger, and Indians and horses and cattle and outlaws and posses and buffalo and US calvary and rattlesnakes and stagecoaches and sagebrush and saloons. Which brought me back to the source of Richard's disappointment, and mine.

Other than what I did at work most days, I had only been in a hospital as a patient twice before, the first for a tonsillectomy at the age of four (I still remember how good the *Jell-o* tasted, whatever that red flavor was), and the second to have my appendix out, forty years later. But this last time beat me up a bit. I had held off as long as possible, under the deluded impression that physicians are supposed to be endowed with some higher form of immunity from these more common maladies, until I was doubled over in agony on our sofa, at the end of a long day treating ailments that seemed far less serious than mine, listening to Robyn threaten me with death, unless I agreed to be driven to our

7

hospital emergency department. The best thing you can do for death is ride off from it. Robyn took me into a collegial corral of amusement.

"That fast enough for you." Said a good friend, one of the emergency physicians. I had been ushered through an airport-sized waiting room, full of plague and pestilence. Business class.

"You need a scan." He said, after examining my abdomen.

"The radiologist is coming in." Said the technician, not much later.

"What for?" I asked.

"You." She said. And there he was in the flesh, leaning on the machine as I made my exit from it, grinning like coyote at a gopher wedding.

"Classic." He said.

"Classic what?" I asked.

"Classic diverticulitis." He said.

"That's an old man's disease." I said. He didn't say anything.

"Bullshit." I said, but it was too late. I got admitted, and my surgeon, another colleague far too overjoyed at the prospect of looking after me, appeared in my doorway as a silhouette at 3:30 in the morning. He brought travel photos and stories, of my colon, all annotated and primed, to enable my incarceration in his step-down unit.

"I don't think I'll have to operate." He said. "This time." I spent four days on the surgical ward, infused with gorillacillins and transitional diets to nowhere. He let me out the day before he was heading to Portugal.

"Any good wines I should try over there?" He

asked. I told him. He wrote me out a prescription for metronidazole.

"Take this for two weeks." He said. "Of course, as an internist, you know about its disulfuram effect." I had momentarily forgotten. As long as I was taking this antibiotic, no alcohol could pass my lips, or I would become violently ill.

I forget what I called him. He left smiling, and I left it at that.

We both knew that what had occurred, could recur, at any time. Five months later it did, and I was once again on the dreaded regime of abstemious antibiotics. Notwithstanding how devastating it already was, for an author to be unable to drink, it was increasingly unclear whether I would be well enough, or how unwise it would be, to cross the border into the land of mercenary medical care, in my current state of infirmity. *They'll take your house.*

There was another complication on the horizon. One of the planned stops, *back through the States on the way home*, was a hajj to the last home of one of my minor deities, the place where he blew his brains out. Hemingway had lived in Ketchum, and Ketchum was in the news. The Beaver Creek Fire had become a state-wide inferno visible from space, the smoke filled and obscured the sun in Sun Valley, homes were evacuated, wolves were chasing sheep trying to escape, and Salmon, Idaho was becoming Smoked Salmon, Idaho. If the rains came, there would be floods. My medical office assistant, Bonnie, offered me an alternative to our planned diversion.

"You could work if you don't go." She said.
"I plan on being dead in Montana." It was decided. We were going. Come Hell or High Water. We all got pieces of crazy in us, some bigger pieces than others.

'Some may never live, but the crazy never die.'
Hunter S. Thompson

*   *   *

'Good judgment comes from experience,
and a lotta that comes from bad judgment.'
Cowboy proverb

For Robyn and I to find the Wild West, we had to head east, across the Georgia Strait. A turkey vulture turned a lazy sky circle above the *Jesus Loves You* sign, as our own turned into the ferry terminal. We camped out in the back of the boat, hot sun shining on our faces, making us sleepy. I awoke to a lost generation, holding out their dominant hands, in supplication to the signal, missing on the open water. The way they looked past me, spoke to my age, and irrelevance. But it felt good to be invisible to the socially obsessed, reclining in my chaise lounge on the side of the gene pool, watching the blood in the water. Connections are more important than connectivity. Always drink upstream from the herd.

We landed on dusk, and a big harvest moon over Mount Baker. Robyn drove through vast expanses of big cookie-cutter tract houses. The Asian immigrants that had created the monster home had more use for floors than fields; yard space was just another relative that wouldn't have a room to sleep in. We drove through the yellow light of downtown Langley, to the place had once secured the south bank of the Fraser River against the Americans.

In 1827, the Governor of the Hudson Bay Company was a worried man. The boundary between the British and the American possessions of the transmontane West had yet to be decided, and George Simpson feared that Fort Vancouver, his fur trading outpost further south than John Jacob Astor's Fort Astoria in Oregon Country, might be lost, if the final border jumped north from the course of the Columbia River, to the 49th parallel. He ordered the creation of Fort Langley on the south bank of the Fraser, in an attempt to consolidate British claims to both sides of the river. Of the twenty-four men that James McMillan arrived on site with to begin construction, five were incapacitated with gonorrhea, and another had some other, apparently more exotic form, of 'venereal disease.' All the horses were crippled, exhausted, or dead. The brambles were seemingly impenetrable.

Despite the setbacks, the remaining nineteen men had, by early September, built two bastions and a palisade worthy enough *to command respect in the eyes of the Indians, who begin, shrewdly, to conjecture for what purpose the Ports and loopholes are intended.* By 1830, Fort Langley had become a major anchorage for the export of cedar lumber and shingles, and salted salmon in barrels of the same wood, to the Hawaiian Islands.

But the 'Birthplace of British Columbia' would not be destined for anything greater. Traders from Boston controlled most of the maritime fur transactions, travelling along the coast by boat, and the strong competition kept the price of pelts much higher than Hudson's Bay was paying elsewhere. Also, the indigenous Stó:lō people living along the Fraser were not particularly interested in hunting or trapping, since they were quite self-sufficient on salmon, and not in serious need of European goods, except for some guns in the first year to fend off a short-lived, largely symbolic, threat from another tribe. Finally, the Fraser was not as navigable as Simpson had imagined. After the river forked with the Thompson River, the powerful rapids and sheer cliffs convinced him that the passage would be *certain Death, in nine attempts out of Ten.* Parts of the journey from the north would have to be made overland, to bypass the Fraser Canyon and Hell's Gate.

Fort Langley barely survived the threat of

Russian invasion in the early 1850s, the threat of American invasion in 1857, the boom and bust of the 1858 Gold Rush and Fraser Canyon War with American miners, the removal of its military and capital administrative functions to New Westminster in 1859, the loss of Hudson Bay Company monopoly, and Canadian Confederation in 1871. Shipping was lost to paddle wheelers, and the first train.

In 1921, a sawmill brought some measure of blue collar prosperity to the struggling town, until redundancy and aging machinery shut it down for good, just over seventy years later.

Which is why Richard and Carolyn were able to find affordable housing, in what had become a vestigial Vancouver bedroom community, and why Robyn and I, would have a place to stay the night, before beginning our long drive to Christina Lake the next morning. Our wagon sailed under Dr Benjamin Marr's ancient columns of horse chestnut trees along Glover Road, until we reached the correct four-digit house number, on the pink and green trim we recognized as Carolyn's favourite colours. There were two eights in the address. Some day the overseas Chinese will swoop on it. Carolyn and Richard's eldest son, Kyle, was still at the house, working as a lifeguard at a local pool. He had waited up for us, and wondered why we were late.

"Your mother wrote the turnoff as Highway 1, rather than Highway 1a." I said. "We were halfway into Vancouver when I figured it out."

It didn't matter. Kyle offered us a glass of wine,

and then some fruit juice, when I told him of my infirmities. We spoke of the intervening years since we had seen his parents, his university aspirations in kinesiology, and the impact of technology of every aspect of life. He brought out his mobile phone, and introduced us to Siri, an artificial intelligence program that Kyle claimed could 'answer all your questions.'

"Go ahead." He said. I started big.

"What are Maxwell's Equations?" I asked. Siri didn't seem to know.

"Try again." Kyle said.

"What is the meaning of life?" I said. Siri choked.

"He doesn't know everything." Said Kyle, to my obvious relief.

It was late, and we had a long drive ahead of us next day. Kyle showed us downstairs, to grandmother Grace's bedroom, and bid us goodnight. Robyn fell asleep almost instantly, but the light distracted me outside our window, and my abdominal cramps, which ebbed and flowed in synchrony, with the irregular far off Doppler haunted herald horns from passing trains in the night. The first signal of the last of the Old West, would be the last thing I remembered, on the first of our Wagon Days.

*   *   *

'The biggest troublemaker you'll probably ever have to deal with watches you shave his face in the mirror every morning.'

Cowboy proverb

"Head towards Hope." I said. It was the answer to Robyn's question about how to get to Christina Lake, and the ultimate theme of the journey.

The grey waters of the mighty Fraser gave way to the large pink metal raspberries of the Abbotsford roundabout, and the village sign that marked our turnoff onto the bucolic pleasures of Highway Three. *Experience Hope.* But we had no time to stop for something so small. We drove by Hell's Gate, past the salmon-clutching grizzly statue above the prairie dogs in Manley Park, and along the rows of rusted tractors and vintage cars through Keremeos, some with patty pan squash stuck in the parabolic hollows, where their headlights used to be. There was hot buttered corn and fresh fruit and ice cream and flowers and recycled antiques for sale, and Robyn and I congratulated ourselves on what a verdant peaceful country we had citizenship in. We had always believed that, unlike what had happened in the American Wild West, where 'the person with fastest horse got the most land,' in the Dominion's march to western settlement, expansion had been carefully prepared by government officials, with much less attendant violence, and a more controlled flood of immigration.

It was all nonsense, of course. Canadian

authorities used hunger to ethnically cleanse and clear the Western provinces for railway construction and settlement, until the aboriginal populations agreed to trade freedom for rations, and move to their new appointed reservations. *Treaty Number Six.*

Once there, ration house food was withheld for so long that much of it rotted while the people it was intended to feed fell into decades of malnutrition, impaired immunity, and tuberculosis and other sicknesses. Thousands died. The first Prime Minister of the country, Sir John A. Macdonald, boasted that the indigenous peoples were kept on the 'verge of actual starvation,' in an attempt to deflect criticism that he was squandering public funds. Within a generation, First Nations bison hunters went from being the 'tallest in the world,' to a population so unhealthy, they were believed to be genetically more susceptible to disease. Government physicians studied the natural history of malnutrition, instead of treating it, in a collusion not that dissimilar to the African-American Tuskegee experiments with syphilis. Canadians became inured to aboriginal marginalization from the mainstream, to terrible housing conditions on the reserves, contaminated drinking water, disproportionately lower educational and higher prison incarceration levels, and sexual and physical abuse at Indian residential schools. Adult 'Registered Indians' were not granted full citizenship until 1960, seven years after I had acquired mine as a birthright. *Experience Hope.*

The small hedges, separating the land yachts masquerading as homes, at the Sunshine Valley RV Resort, were the tragic topiary of the takeover. Robyn and I had been witness to own neighbourhood second growth forest, chipper-shredded into a tin can ghetto of 'lifestyle choice' and 'resort amenities.' Greed may be good, but it is no guarantee of elegance or erudition.

"I need to know the name of the town after Oosoyos." I said. Robyn told me she couldn't find one on the map. We stopped for a gelato in Oosoyos, and sat with a Nelson couple heading to our island, for their own holiday.

"We always stop here for the ice cream." He said. "Its halfway good." I wasn't sure he was referring to the remoteness or the refreshment. We wished each other happy trails, and climbed up into the desert mountains, past signs that spoke of our geography. *Do not pass snow ploughs on right.*

The irrigation systems on the other side were named *Stemwinder*, like they could have been snakes. We drove through Grand Forks.

"Everybody here has four wives." I said.

"Doesn't look like there's much else going on." Said Robyn. We passed Johnny's Motel.

"Looks like a Johnny's Motel." She said.

It was late afternoon, when we turned off into Christina Lake. We had general directions to Richard and Carolyn's but, in our need for more specificity, we stopped at a motel to ask. The Chinese owner on the other side of the counter was speaking loud Mandarin into his telephone mouthpiece. He didn't so much as raise an eyebrow to acknowledge our entrance. We stood in front of him for five minutes, before deciding to try somewhere else. The proprietor had no idea of our destination. Before a Scottish fur trader named the lake after his daughter, the local Indians had called it 'En-Chalm.' *Unknown.* This had made more sense.

Robyn and I finally arrived at the cottage, to a scowl from the old woman next door. She was sweeping the rocks. We slipped quietly into and through the house, to the magnificent end view of a long glacial lake horizon, flanked by pine-dense mountains, blue and green Kokanee perfection. We descended a path toward the shoreline, and out across the water on the tipsy boardwalk, to the floating pavilion on the dock. Here were watercraft and flotation devices and a ski boat and lounge chairs and laughter. A familiar sound echoed across the water, as they turned to the wooden ones we were making. *Pssssht.*

"Hey!" Said Richard. "You made it. You sure you don't want a beer?"

I forget what I called him.

*   *   *

'We'll drink to good health for them that have it coming.'

Larry McMurtry, *Lonesome Dove*

I kept trying to tell myself I had it coming. Most of my physical health, up until now, had been of the mental variety. Claude Bernard had called it homeostasis, in an era when it had been solely defined by the acquisition of an adequate caloric intake, and the avoidance of occupational hazards, pestilence, and death. Life had been for living, and not rationed into trendy quanta of aerobic torment. I had been an adherent of Epicurus, with a highly cultivated aesthetic appreciation for visceral indulgence. One of the rewards for my somatic and political incorrectness would now seem to be a fragile weakness of my colonic wall, which would henceforth be prone to blowing bubbles, sometimes skyward.

As we caught up, in the shade of the pavilion on the dock, I knew that Richard felt my pain, but he didn't have to make quite that much noise, as he opened each new can of *Kokanee* lager. Carolyn and Robyn were mind-melded on the next bench over, and the two youngest boys, Graham and Trevor, were splashing around the gazebo, with their girlfriends.

They had certainly grown since we last saw them, and in just the directions we imagined. Kyle, left behind in Fort Langley, was the thin quiet cerebral one. Graham, the middle boy, more muscular but still wiry, had a head for business. His girlfriend was gunning for a law

19

degree, and MBA, and 'a lot of money.' The youngest was the sleeper. Trevor was a big boy. Like me, he enjoyed his food. I remember a visit many years earlier, when Robyn asked him if he'd like to try some special dip she made. "I'll try it." Said Trev. "And if I like it, I'll have a lot." Carolyn and Richard's sons had the entire waterfront covered. And, for that matter, so did Carolyn and Richard. Both were within counting distance of retirement that, for members of the Force, Luke, meant a very comfortable landing indeed. They planned to eventually sell the house in Fort Langley, and move to Christina Lake. I asked about the neighbour, still sweeping the rocks. She had turned up her radio.

"That's Crazy Colleen." Said Carolyn. "She was put on the planet to ensure that we don't enjoy ourselves too much." Colleen was a chain-smoker with a vascular dementia, whose only purpose in life was to police the activities of the adjacent law enforcement family. We told them of the illegitimate development that had gone up next to us, and the evil triad that were spoiling the wild tranquility of the neighbourhood. Money flows to beauty and then attracts more money, pushing out everything that does not fit.

"Small minds are driven by greed and envy and contempt." Said Richard. "And sometimes the karma works too slow."

Carolyn served up several meters of teriyaki pork tenderloin for dinner. I told Richard he needed a Portuguese Douro to match it, but he didn't have one, and I wouldn't have been able to partake, if he had.

"Why are you doing this trip, Wink?" He asked, between bites.

"Its a path of pilgrimage. " I said.

"To where?" He asked.

"Not so much to where." I said. "As to what."

"To what?" He asked.

"Authenticity." I said. "The American West was *The Sacred Land*- the gold rush towards truth."

"What's the truth?" He asked.

"The achievement of redemption." I said.

"How do you get that?" He asked.

"By living the authentic life, by living in Nature, and by facing death with dignity and courage."

"Sounds very existential." Said Carolyn.

"That's where the truth lives." I said.

"So, what does that have to do with the American West?" Asked Richard.

"All the main characters lived there." I said. "The cowboys and Indians, outlaws and lawmen, miners and loggers, firefighters, railroad workers and wagon drivers, mothers and prostitutes, were all archetypes of authenticity. The cowboys I used to watch on the Paramount theatre screen Westerns were the embodiment of quiet dignity, grace under pressure and courage under fire."

"What's so specially authentic about achieving redemption in that place?" Asked Carolyn.

"Nature." I said. "Earth, wind, fire and water- big sky and sagebrush, mountains and rivers, buffalo and dinosaur bones, grizzly bears and cougars, wolves and coyotes, cattle and horses."

"I still don't get it." Richard said. "What was so special about the American West that made living authentic in Nature, that didn't exist elsewhere."

"It may have existed elsewhere." I said. "But facing death there was transcendent."

"You might get your chance." Said Richard. "You sure you're well enough to go?"

"The best thing you can do for death is ride off from it." I said, and we had dessert.

The next morning Richard took us around the lake in the ski boat, pointing out who lived where, and what had or would happen to them. There were fishing shacks and a cottage with a tree growing right through its roof, and newer mansions where trees and cottages should have been. There were recurring themes of lottery winners and sports team managers and divorces.

"There's still gold fever in this part of the West." I said. In the early afternoon we took a walk through the creek bed, along a row of metal wagon wheels, painted green. Robyn went for a water-ski later in the day.

Just after dark, we gathered on the deck, full moon on the lake.

"How does your story end?" Asked Carolyn

"In tragedy." I said. "Like all authentic lives."

"Where does the tragedy happen?" Richard asked.

"In Idaho." I said. "In Ketchum. On the Wood River."

"Hemingway?" Asked Carolyn. "You're going to end a book about the American West with Hemingway?"

"That's where the real West ended, Carolyn." I

said. "Not with an iron spike in a railway bed, but with two shotgun shells in a front entrance foyer. Hemingway was the last true son of The Sacred Land. His themes were wilderness and war, and love and loss. He was all about hunting and fishing, bullfighting and death, water and alcohol, and warriors and patriotism. Nature was his religion. His mountains extended to Spain and Africa and Switzerland, his rivers to streams in Michigan. He had a 'Hotel Montana' in both *The Sun Also Rises* and *For Whom the Bell Tolls.*"

"Wait just a minute. His own parents disavowed his writing as 'filth.'" Said Carolyn. "He was an alcoholic racist, a homophobe, and an emasculated misogynist."

"And his books were burned in Berlin in 1933, as 'a monument of modern decadence.'" I added. "But he was the final hard-boiled egg of the American West. Nature is where men are without women: men fish; men hunt; men find redemption."

"Do you think leaving your wife to find your brains all over the front entrance of your house is facing death with dignity and courage?" Carolyn asked.

"Hemingway was the end of the West." I said. "I never claimed that he lived up to its ideal."

"So why are you so determined to make this trip?" Richard asked. "With your rotten guts, and massive bush fires and possible flooding to come. Hell, you can't even have a beer for another two weeks, if you even get that lucky."

"Well." I said. "There are a couple of things I can

still have."

"Like what?" He asked.

"Buffalo steaks." I said. "And huckleberry pie."

*   *   *

The Most Beautiful Town in America
Sandpoint, Idaho

'America is hard to see.'
Robert Frost

Mercury. On the morning we left Richard and Carolyn, buffalo steaks fell off the menu. It happened while I was brushing my teeth. The toothpaste made a sound it shouldn't have made, on the way into the sink.

I usually associate the onomatopoeia of 'clunk' with substances much harder than toothpaste and, in this particular instance, the laws of nature held. I opened my mouth and angled the light so as to illuminate the great hole where the clunk used to be. It was so dark it was like three feet into a wolf.

"Well, that's the trip down the drain." Said Robyn.

"There's still huckleberry pie." I said. "We'll find a dentist in Idaho." I looked over at Richard. He had that 'you-should-go-before-something-else-breaks' look.

Robyn and I fired up the wagon, and each other's enthusiasm, and headed south to the Laurier crossing. But we were almost out of gas, and missed the last chance to fill up, before the frontier loomed up too large too soon.

Our eagerness jumped the red light at the border booth.

"You're supposed to wait until it turns green."
Said the sunglasses. I looked around for
bloodhounds.
"Purpose of your visit to the You-knighted
States?" He asked. I almost shared my need for
a dentist.
"Were searching for the American West." I said. I
watched a frown begin to form.
"I want to see Mon-taw-na." Robyn added, in her
Kiwi accent. The frown subsided.
"Y'all enjoy your visit." He said.
"How far to the next gas station?" I asked.
"The Indians have a place about ten miles
along." He said, and waved us through.
Wow, I thought. Not a minute into the Wild
West, and we were already on our way to meet
our first Indians.
It wasn't quite the cultural experience I had
imagined. There was a flat metal sculpture of a
band member in the landscaping, and the gas
was definitely cheaper than what the cowboys
would be offering elsewhere. We pulled up beside
Tribal Trails pump No. 5, to a sign of
unanticipated discrimination. *Canadian credit
cards please pay inside.* I had to leave my card
with the nice lady at the till. Robyn asked me
what that was all about.
"Apparently we need a reservation." I said. But
almost everything else went as planned, except
for a brief moment of hesitation I had, outside
the washroom doors. It took me a minute to
figure out if I was a *sma?m?im* or a *sqel'ql'tmix^w*,
until the pictures helped me understand that I
was the one with the turkey tail.

"Is there anything else we can help you with today?" Asked the nice lady at the till. "We kill our own chickens." We were good for dead chickens, and I thanked her for her concern. "Have a nice trip, Mr. Winkler." She said. And she was sincere. And I fell in love with Americans all over again. Unlike the 'what's in it for me' attitude of Canadian service, I always had a feeling that, in the States, when they told you to have a nice day, they meant it as a benediction, and not an order.

The scenery got wonderful as well. Our wagon followed the grand curves of a primitive road, under pines and hanging moss, beside the slow rapids sparkle of the Kettle River. A black railway ribbon kept pace, strobe-like through the branches, on the left. The only road signs were divine and devotional. *The key to Heaven is shaped like a cross.*

The reason for this only became gradually apparent. Beyond the melons and antiques, every homestead was having a permanent impermanent yard sale, every highway was up for adoption, and every county shop would leave you guessing. We crossed the Columbia River, and a large bulldog on a water tank. *If it's grouchy, feed it.* George Simpson hadn't worried for no reason. The serene had turned to shabby, and depressing.

"Rough around the edges." Robyn said. The Country Hills Rental Community had been vacated, the mini-storages had been maximized, the transience had become intransigent, the transients had become transitory, and the hole

27

where my tooth used to be had become transcendental.

We entered Chewelah, *A Place for all Seasons*, and parked across from the park, next to the God fearing Brothers Auto Sales. *Anyone who angers you conquers you.*

"Hell of a way to sell an automobile." I said. There was a lovely market set up in the park. It was an oasis, like Washington parks should be. We wandered around the stalls of garden vegetables and knickknacks, and over a bridge with a metal wagon wheel, painted green. On the other side was a verdigris bronze helmet, on a verdigris M-16, on a verdigris pair of boots. *In memory of all veterans of all wars.*

"Wilderness and war, and love and loss." I said. "The Sacred Land. We're on the right track."

I drove the wagon onto the short cut Flowery Trail into the mountains, to Usk, through the pine beetle brown bone yard of the Colville National Forest, to Colville. *This community supports our troops.* Robyn asked me if I knew where I was going.

"Today I'm wingin' it." I said. "Tomorrow I know where we're going."

"Who gave you the day off?" She asked, as she would.

We came down off the eastern side of the mountains, across a small plain and river crossing, and through a small settlement to the other side. *Kick ass America- Remember?*

According to the map we had crossed into Idaho.

"No welcome?" Robyn asked.

"Maybe they don't want us here." I said. But

then they gave us a sign. *Welcome to Idaho.*

"That's it?" Asked Robyn. "Where are we headed anyway?"

"We're going to the most beautiful town in America." I said. "Two years ago both *USA Today* and *Rand McNally* named it the country's 'Most Beautiful Small Town.'"

Our path drew an asymptote along Lake Pend Oreille, one of the nation's deepest and the state's largest, forty-three miles long, in a basin surrounded by the Selkirk, the Cabinet, and the Bitterroot ranges.

The wagon took a hard left across the railroad tracks and up in the hills just south of town.

"We must be staying up here." Said Robyn.

"Yup." I said, and swerved off the road, onto a driveway that curved around to a huge citadel, so confused by its many architectural influences, that Robyn let out her breath in a low whistle.

"Looks like they ran out of block." She said. It was like a small stone village in Umbria, with Spanish ironwork and West Coast cedar post and beam, and Scottish castle and Austrian chalet and Tibetan monastery. Some of the drywall had escaped to the exterior. The front door was a carved masterpiece. I rang the gong. The carved masterpiece opened to a statuesque blonde of no less resplendence.

"Welcome to Talus Rock." She said. "I'm Rebecca." I bet she was. She motioned us inside, and inside gave nothing away to the outside. Open plan hardwood floor to copper ceiling windows, punctuated with old growth fir beams and creations in stained glass, river rock fireplaces with horseshoes and Moose antlers, and a loud echo of opulence and fuck-you money, that reverberated up and beyond the three-story curvilinear staircase.

"This is Elsa, my assistant." Rebecca said, sweeping her hand open to another vision of long flowing black hair and doll's eyes and estrogenic lips. The bimbosity pyrotechnics went high beam. Rebecca showed us to our room, the 'Rio,' although the elk antler on the bedside table, the East Indian elephant painting over the bed, and the Transylvanian feel to the bathroom, suggested more Babel than Brazil. She asked if we had any questions.

"Whose your dentist?" I asked. She gave me a quizzical look.

"Seriously, Rebecca." I said. "I need a dentist." We returned downstairs and she found us three potential leads to explore, and a recommendation for dinner afterwards.

"You simply must go to *41 South.*" She said. "I'll make you reservations, for seven."

And Robyn and I left, to see America's most beautiful small town.

*   *   *

Boss Spearman: It's a pretty day for making things
right.
Charley Waite: Well, enjoy it, 'cause once it starts,
it's gonna be messy like nothing
you ever seen.
Larry McMurtry, *Lonesome Dove*

Of the three dentist offices in Sandpoint, two were closed. Our last chance lived in a refurbished old house across the tracks, in a grove of mature trees, on Ontario Street. The door opened inward, to a small empty waiting room with a fish tank, a stack of *Outdoor* magazines, and the sound of an angry drill, back behind the counter.

The receptionist was plump and pleasant, as you would have expected in any Norman Rockwell experience.

"May I help you?" She offered, and I took her up on it. The short version about the clunk falling out of the hole didn't move her much, but the additional historical features of forlorn foreigners searching for the Old West in the most beautiful town in America, eventually seemed to work.

"He's the only dentist working today." She said. "And he's very busy. Could you come back?" We could come back. I asked if she knew a good place for lunch.

"Y'all like Mexican?" She asked. We all liked Mexican.

"There's a place called Joel's." She said. "They make a mean fish taco." Nothing like the smell of fish and habaneros to endear you to a strange dentist.

Robyn and I headed downtown to Joel's, and got

31

in line. The only road signs were divine and devotional. *Tortas...* *Tostadas...* *Tacos...* *Quesadillas... Burritos...*

A big black home-built car, half Bugatti, half Cadillac, with parabolic headlamps, grille horns, spring fenders, protruding pipes, and a Bentley hood ornament, pulled up to the curb, so confused by its many architectural influences, that Robyn let out her breath in a low whistle.

"Next." Shouted the massive Mamita behind the counter. We ordered the fish tacos.

"Ju are bery lucky." She said. "Ju got the last two." But she was very lucky too.

In August of 1888, a twenty-nine year old author and civil servant named Theodore Roosevelt, writing a book he called *The Winning of the West*, left his New York home and came through Sandpoint, on a caribou-hunting trip. He was heading for the Wild Horse Trail, which went north to the gold fields of British Columbia, the ones that had resulted in the Fraser Canyon War, thirty years earlier. Teddy found a cluster of wooden buildings along either side of the Northern Pacific railroad track, more than half of which were saloons and gambling houses. Of all the men drinking that night, Roosevelt was the one to miss out on a bed in the only lodging house. Someone rented him a shack without telling the owner, who surprised him by returning in the night. It was so dark it was like three feet into a wolf.

A hundred years later, the wolf and the darkness returned to Sandpoint. California computer millionaires, Carl Story and Vincent Bertollini, crossed the bridge 'for its clean air, beautiful scenery, quiet life style, recreation, lack of crowds, low cost of living, low violent crime, but above all, more than 98 percent of North Idaho's population is of the Adamic White Aryan people.' They rode motorcycles and left big tips, and plotted to establish an 'Aryan homeland.' They weren't the first white supremacists to set up shop around Sandpoint. In 1973, the leader of Aryan Nations, Richard Girnt Butler, a former senior Lockheed aeronautical engineer who held patents for tubeless tire repair, moved from California to Hayden Lake, a suburb of Coeur d'Alene, 30 miles down the road from Sandpoint. His 20-acre compound was the epicentre of a global network of neo-Nazis. They held an annual parade, organized 'Aryan Nations World Congresses,' were implicated in plots to overthrow the US government, and often blanketed the surrounding communities with fliers and mass mailings of racist hate. The goal was the establishment of a whites-only 'national racist state' that would include Idaho, Montana, Wyoming, Oregon, and Washington.

Story and Bertollini brought new money and bigoted enthusiasm to the cause, and a higher level of computer-savvy sophistication to the promotional advertising. Their group, the 'Eleventh Hour Remnant Messenger,' spent ten dollars for each 6x3 foot poster of 'Adam's Pure Blood Seedline,' which they mailed out to nine thousand Idaho addresses in September of 1998. The following year they sent out an additional three mailings, *Who are the real hate mongers?, The Seven Year Tribulation of Daniel and Revelation,* and, my personal favourite, *The Wannabe's That Want To Be and Shall Never Be: -- SATAN'S JEWS!*

You can pretty much guess the content. Let me see if I can get this right:

Jews are Satan's Chosen People, out to dominate God's people, the Christians. Like blacks, orientals, and other races, Jews do not have souls. Satanic Jews control Hollywood movie production, radio, television, newspapers, Congress and churches. They want to 'mix the white race with other peoples by encouraging multiculturalism, immigration, and relocation of these other peoples to North Idaho,' and advocate Separatist bashing and belittling the Aryan to deceive the vast majority of Adamic White Aryan people. WWII was the result of a Jewish plot to destroy whites, and the masterstroke was getting the Japs to attack Pearl Harbor. America, dominated by Satan's Jews, had become 'the great whore' described in Revelation 19.

How does this devious Jewish conspiracy work? *Human Rights Task Forces report to the Southern Poverty Law Center, which reports to ADL, which reports to B'nai B'rith, which, together with the US government, answers to the United Nations, overseen by the New World Order which, in turn, reports to Satan's One World Order, Jewry --Communism, Enslavement of Planet Earth.*

And the 'final' solution (my quotes)? *The new 'Mystery Babylon,' New York City, will be 'nuked and burn Forever and Ever.' World War III will result in the migration of the White race from*

America to Israel. The War of All Wars! between the White race and the Jewish, Satanic non-race will lead to Armageddon, or World War IV, resulting in the victory of the White race and the unending reign of Jesus Christ over his White people. And they all lived happily ever after.

Vincent Bertollini even ran for mayor of Sandpoint as a write-in candidate, listing his qualifications as *30 years of High Technology Corporate Executive Management experience,* his *unquestionable fiscal policies,* and his *fairness and honesty in business dealings.* His 16-point platform consisted of a declaration that *Christian prayer will be restored at all Public Meetings and daily in the Sandpoint School system,* and a promise that *Diversity and Multi-Culturalism will be challenged at every front as being wrong and not in the interests of the citizens of Sandpoint.* He lost.

Meanwhile, the white boys were busy making a racial hero of Richard Butler. They produced a video called *My Side of the Story,* which opened with the American flag superimposed on photos of bald eagles, the Lincoln Memorial, and a Little League baseball game. Kate Smith sang *God Bless America,* in the background, until the patriotic montage faded into a tour of the Aryan Nations chapel.

But God's people were so busy going after the Satanic Jews, they missed the two Indians that had snuck up behind them. Jason and Victoria Keenan had been harassed at gunpoint by some of the seedier seedlings of their Adamic adherents. The lawsuit they filed won a combined civil judgement of $6.3 million from Richard Butler and the Aryan Nations members who had attacked them. The 2001 ruling bankrupted the organization and forced them to give up their Hayden Lake property, and disband. Bertollini bought Butler a new house, but there was one last sweet terminal event that would postpone the nuking of New York indefinitely.

"How did ju like jor tacos?" Asked Mamita.

We liked them fine.

'Conflict follows wrongdoing as surely as flies follow the herd.'
Doc Holiday

* * *

'If you find yourself in a hole, the first thing to do is stop diggin'.'
Cowboy Proverb

The holes in American Old West dentistry were deep and dreadful. Like three feet into a wolf. Dental trauma was an everyday part of life. In an era of poor nutrition and worse chewing tobacco, there were few toothbrushes, and plenty of pebbles in the food. Good preventative care didn't exist. There were no x-rays, so there was no way to see into the jaw. Western dentists had no electricity. The only way to inspect the mouth was during the day, with mirrors to direct sunlight into the back of the throat. There was no anesthetic and, although ether and nitrous oxide and morphine had been introduced back East, no Wild West dentist would have met their acquaintance. And few Wild West dentists had real qualifications. Most were barbers or blacksmiths, or shingle charlatans. To the cowboy with a problem, it didn't much matter. Abscesses, broken teeth, wisdom teeth, and jaw infections caused such intense pain that people took any chance to get relief. Tooth problems couldn't wait. Luckily for me, in the most beautiful small town in America, after my fish taco lunch, I didn't have to.

The most famous Old West dentist had been John Henry 'Doc' Holliday who, on March 1, 1872, at the age of 20, had met the requirements for the degree of Doctor from the Pennsylvania College of Dental Surgery.

Doc Holliday was 5 feet 10 inches tall, and weighed about 160 pounds. He died of tuberculosis, at the age of 36. His last words, for a man of such distinction, were rather unremarkable. *Damn this is funny.*

His friend, Wyatt Earp, who had once seen him place a ten thousand dollar bet on a single card, described him well.

'Doc was a dentist, not a lawman or an assassin, whom necessity had made a gambler; a gentleman whom disease had made a frontier vagabond; a philosopher whom life had made a caustic wit; a long lean, ash-blond fellow nearly dead with consumption, and at the same time the most skillful gambler and the nerviest, speediest, deadliest man with a six-gun that I ever knew.'

My Sandpoint dentist, back in the grove on Ontario Street, was 5 feet 10 inches tall, and weighed about 160 pounds. He had ash-blond hair. But he was dressed in a blue jumpsuit, like a pilot, and wore sunglasses, like I had just caught him on the ski fields on Schweitzer Mountain, above the town.

"Damn this is funny." He said, looking at the x-rays his technician had just handed him. He had introduced himself as Bob, seemed quite comfortable calling me by my nickname, and didn't flinch from the smell of fish and habaneros. He pronounced roots as 'ruts.'

"Well, Wink." He said. "A long time ago, someone cut two of the ruts off this back molar, and now you've chipped out a chunk of what was left." My life flashed before my eyes, and my VISA card branded my backside, inside the wallet in my back pocket. I prayed for rain. *Never ask a barber if you need a haircut.*

Water began to circle around in the porcelain sink next to me, *swirling like water round a stone.* Chief Joseph spoke to me directly. *For a short time we lived quietly. But this could not last. White men had found gold in the mountains*

38

around the land of winding water.

"Luckily for you, the tooth is still structurally intact." Said Bob. "I wouldn't crack nuts with those ruts, but it should be OK. I'm just going to grind the sharp bits off, so it doesn't cause you any problems. This won't hurt, because the other guy killed the nerve when he cut off your ruts." The muzak played Handel, and I gave thanks. He was done in a few minutes and, with a flourish, ushered me out of my chair, like a barber would have done.

"How much do I owe you, Bob?" I asked, my back pocket still scorching my butt a bit. He waved me towards the plump and pleasant receptionist, and goodbye, like Doc Holliday would have done. *Why should I obtain by force that which I can obtain by cheating?*

"She'll take care of you." He said.

Robyn had been waiting patiently. She joined me at the counter.

"That'll be forty dollars." Said the receptionist. My VISA card danced with joy. Doc Holliday's cousin had been Margaret Mitchell, who had written *Gone With the Wind*. And so were we.

"I know where the shops are." Said Robyn. We headed downtown. Big colourful murals decorated the most beautiful small town in America. *Welcome to Sandpoint.* The themes were trees with elaborate rut structures, and sun and clouds, and local activities like logging and skiing and cycling and hiking and farming and stump ranching and hunting and fishing and the Kalispel *Sand Place* Indians. There were narrow brick alleys held together with graffiti and puddles and power lines. Flower boxes of begonias and geraniums lined the shops. The Art Deco theatre marquis, across from the second-hand bookstore advertised a choice of two features. *Romantics Anonymous French Comedy*, and *The Hunt for the Pend Oreille Paddler*. The Sand Creek mall deserted itself, as the rain came down.

A small statue outside commemorated David Thompson, the greatest land geographer who'd ever lived. He had come out from England in 1784, at the age of 14, committed to a seven-year apprenticeship in the remote northern Hudson Bay Company fort of Churchill, copying the personal papers of explorer Samuel Hearne. It was here he lost his left eye. Thompson became a fur trader and, in 1797, joined the North West Company, to survey the Canada-U.S. boundary along the water routes from Lake Superior, to my hometown on Lake of the Woods. A decade later he had crossed the Rockies and mapped the Columbia basin, establishing the first trading posts in Montana and Idaho. In response to John Jacob Astor's plan to send a ship around Cape Horn, to establish his fur trading posts of Fort Okanagan and Fort Astor, Thompson was recruited to navigate the full length of the Columbia River, passing The Dalles barrier with less difficulty than Lewis and Clark, and claiming the country for Great Britain. George Simpson's disappointment with the loss of everything below the 49th Parallel, would have nothing to do with the intrepid efforts that David Thompson had applied. Despite a career of mapping almost four million square kilometres of North America, a fifth of the continent, Thompson would die in Montreal in 1857, at the age of 86, his accomplishments forgotten, his reputation among the First Nations as Koo-Koo-Sintm, *The Stargazer*, fading into one-eyed obscurity. There were few Canadian contributions to the American West that were as farsighted and visionary.

The sun broke back through the clouds, and Robyn and I took a long walk along the Pend Oreille shoreline, looking back at the lakefront resort decks, full of diners and wedding celebrants. As we drove across the causeway, the adjacent railroad bridge produced three *Northern Pacific* locomotives, pulling a hundred cars of momentum, and the long reflected resonant blasts of horn, bouncing wounded herds of history, behind us.

Dingdingdingdingdingding...

Robyn and I waited under the moose muzzle and antlers over the fireplace in the bar, until they could seat us on outside on the deck, overlooking the lake. A peregrine falcon soared above our sunset through the pines, the Cobb salad, and the vegetarian strudel.

It was another wedding venue in Sandpoint, and a group of adjoining tables was celebrating. The bride's family was celebrating. The groom seemed less committed, and his children were busy with the condiments, salting and peppering their new family's drinks, when no one was looking. We left, as the sun hit the horizon.

Back at Talus Rock, we made arrangements with Elsa to leave early next morning.

"There's yogurt in the fridge." She said. "Where are you heading?"

"Mon-taw-na." Said Robyn. Elsa looked puzzled.

"Montana." I said. The puzzlement subsided.

"Have a nice trip." She said.

On September 8, 2004, the leader of Aryan Nations, Richard Girnt Butler, died in his Idaho home, from heart failure. Kate Smith sang *God Bless America,* in the background. Just before his one last sweet terminal event, Butler and his traveling companion, porn star Bianca Trump, famous for her explicit interracial sex scenes, had been arrested on an outstanding forgery warrant. Wilderness and war, and love and loss.

Out in the vast great room, was the other traveler, Bluetooth talking to his laptop. He paused long enough to wave goodnight. I asked him where he was from.

"New York." He said.

"Why?" I said.

"That's where I get my nuclear energy." He said.

I didn't tell him how close he was to Forever and Ever.

Dingdingdingdingdingding...

*   *   *

Ghost Riders in the Sky
Philipsburg, Montana

Woodrow F. Call: Why not go up to Montana? It's a cattleman's paradise to hear Jake tell it.

Gus McCrae: Sounds like a damn wilderness if you ask me. And we're a shade old to start fightin' Indians all over again,don't you think?

Woodrow F. Call: I wanna do it, Gus. I wanna see that country, before the bankers and lawyers all git it.

Larry McMurtry, *Lonesome Dove*

Lead. We did get an early start next morning, but not a well-rested one. The castle lights had been on all night outside our window, the plumbing had made weird castle noises, the concrete castle floors had been cold, the toilet paper too far away from the bog and, downstairs in the open kitchen, Babylon boy had been playing happy landings with the ceramic plates and the granite countertops. *Aaargh.* The scream that came out of the downstairs bathroom, from the young girl I surprised on opening the door, could have been prevented, if she had locked it. Goodbye, Talus Rock.

The road took us down, past several garage sales signs. There were others. *First Church Christ. Accepting new patients- same day appointments. Beyond Hope Resort.*

"I haven't been down this street." Robyn said.

"You have now." I said, turning onto the

causeway north.

Another long Great Northern train came out of nowhere, and bore down on us, before diverting into the sky.

"He's going over." Said Robyn. And three locomotives and their iron horses sailed over the bridge above us. Our own path rose into the mountains, and through another warning. *Game Crossing.*

"You game?" Asked Robyn.

"Better to be a has-been than a never-was." I said. And all the mountainous magnificence of Lake Pend Oreille emerged through the pines on our right. After a few miles, we came to a pullout, with a teepee, and a marker.

"The Upper Pend d'Oreilles camped here before it was paved." I said. "Thirty to forty teepees every summer. They caught big three-foot squawfish and built willow frames, to smoke them on. They made cedar baskets, and filled them with huckleberries collected off the mountain trails. Stallions and mares and new foals were pastured down there on the bottom, because their horses could eat the rush hay when it was green."

"Where did they come from?" Robyn asked.

"Originally from British Columbia." I said. "Before they were pushed onto the Flathead Reservation in Montana. They made their clothing from rabbit pelts and deer hides, embellished with dyes and beads and porcupine quills, and traded buffalo hides for other things they could use. Their weapons and tools were made of flint, shaped by rocks. In the winter they lived in lodges constructed from cattails, woven into 'tule mats' that were attached to a branch frame, to form huts. That's why they called themselves the Ql'ispé, the Camas People (after the wild hyacinth bulbs which provided the carbs in their diet), which we anglicized to *Kalispel.*"

"What did their French name mean?" asked Robyn.

"Pend d'Oreille meant 'hanging from ears,' a reference to the large shell earrings they wore. There are a lot of French names where we're going. Coeur d'Alene means 'lonely heart,' Chief Joseph's Nez Percés over yonder had 'pierced noses,' and the Grands Tetons reminded the early French trappers of large breasts.

"The French seemed to have had an obsession with anatomy." Robyn said.

"Mais, bien sûr." I said. "As you'd expect."

"Whatever happened to the Indians here?" Asked Robyn.

"There was this little matter of the Swan River Massacre in 1908." I said.

"As you'd expect." Said Robyn.

"As you'd expect." I said.

Lake Pend Oreille ran into the Pend Oreille River, which ran into Spirit Lake. Past the Squeeze Inn, we encountered other subtle signs of Idaho receding, and Montana approaching. *Full Gospel Fellowship. Cash for guns. Do not even think about it.*

The only traffic consisted of four vehicles, three of which were stuck together. The RV dragging the half-ton truck with the three-wheel ATV in its bed, tailgated an old Ford pickup, whose driver had a straw hat and a strand in his mouth, and wasn't in any hurry to face the morning.

"He should have washed his face before he got on the highway." I said. Robyn blew past them, hell-bent for Mon-taw-na. The pines turned to aspens and birch, and the road grew uneven, and narrow.

"God, a corner." She said, taking her first of many. The kind of rocks she always spoke about loading in the back for her garden began to mock her from beyond the gravel. She asked why the fences had disappeared.

"They have guns instead." I said. There were animals, real and imaginary- wild turkeys and deer, and a fake owl.

"Go back." I said. "I want a photo." But there was no stopping her.

"You have those deer in your garden." She said. "Get over it."

"OK." I said. "No problem. I'll just dwell on it all day." But I didn't, because our Wagon Days had just crossed the inflection point. *Welcome to Montana.*

Thompson Falls, named after our one-eyed stargazing Canadian mapmaker, had the Hotel Black Bear, the Mangy Moose, the Mother Lode Casino, and the Rex Theatre. *More shows coming soon.* It was Robyn's turn to want to stop.

"You can see rivers, or you can see shops." I said. We kept going. *Watch for bighorn sheep ahead... Welcome to Wild Horse Plains...Dew Duck Inn...Congregation of God... Welcome to*

Paradise. Among the signs were roadside grave markers.

A long train of three locomotives, and graffiti on every boxcar, pulled ahead of us. *Dingdingdingdingdingding...*

Robyn and I entered the Flathead Indian Reservation. It was dry, and treeless, and hot.

"So this is where they forced them to move." Said Robyn.

"Long way from huckleberry pie." I said. The road tasted of blood and salt.

It led to Dixon, and a parade. The fire truck, and a rust and gunmetal pickup, with a missing grille and punched-in bumper and buffalo skull hood ornament, blocked the route. A red and white Dodge Ram 250 rolled by, with bald tires, saddle and stirrups and sombrero on the cab roof, and shy young Indian kids and a commemorative banner, hanging off the back and sides. *Douglas Morigeau 1951-2012. I Drive Your Truck.*

The Mission Valley Honor Guard marched by the *ICE* and *Miller High Life* signs of the Dixon Bar, wearing white gloves and belts, red cravats and shoulder braids, and blue pants and baseball caps or berets, the bald eagles on their white shirts clutching two American flags each.

A half-ton bed of spherical white and peach and tan and green-striped orbs- cantaloupe and honeydew and cassava and watermelon, was honor-guarded by a bald old man, with a potbelly and a cane. *Dixon Melons.*

Old wooden pallets lay strewn in front of the derelict and abandoned square western storefront, which looked like it had been constructed out of old wooden pallets. *New and Used.* Two rusted gas pumps spoke of fuel challenges in Dixon. I asked the brown man next to me.

"There's a gas pump about five miles up the road, at the Mercantile in Moiese." He said. He pronounced it *moy-EESE*, where I had always imagined it as *MOY-zee*, but he had the reservation where I had made the mistake.

Back on Vancouver Island, we often treated natives from further north. One day a patient of a buddy of mine arrived in town, and offered to take him out to dinner. He asked is there were any good restaurants. My friend suggested a place called *Montana's.* Which was about where the silence began.

"Montana's." He said. "That's a cowboy place. I'm an Indian."

But here, in a place called Montana, the Indians wore moustaches and sunglasses and boots and chaps and cowboy hats, and lived in long dry grass, and second-hand trailers. *The cowboy must never shoot first, hit a smaller man or take unfair advantage.*

*   *   *

Gus McCrae: Pretty, ain't they?
Pea Eye Parker: I reckon
Gus McCrae: Let's chase 'em. You want to?
Pea Eye Parker: Shoot us one for our supper?
Gus McCrae: No, I mean chase 'em just for
        the sport of it.
Pea Eye Parker: to run them off?
Gus McCrae: You don't get the point, do you
        Pea? I mean chase 'em,
        because before long, there
        won't be any buffalo left to
        chase.
        Larry McMurtry, *Lonesome Dove*

We arrived at the *Welcome to the Moiese Mercantile* gas pump, plumb on unleaded empty. There were *Huckleberry-shakes* and *Buffalo-burgers* painted on the wall of the Burger 'B' Drive-in. A rooftop rubric cubic air conditioner whined above the pennants lining the roof slope, like the used car lot from Hell which, from the heat-stroked vehicles lining up outside for gas, it could have been. A life-sized barbwire buffalo greeted us with his legs apart, and his head and horns lowered. I got a similar reaction from the bacon fat goatee and sunglasses and punched-in Stetson, who cut his black and blue Dodge 4x4 in front of me.

What our story lacked so far was an ironic, unexpected event, which would propel the hero into a full-on punched-in black and blue conflict. I looked at Bacon Fat, and took a long, hard think. Never approach a bull from the front, a horse from the rear, or a fool from any direction. I left Robyn with the wagon in the lineup, and defused my cowboy in the Indian shop across the dust. Inside were 'huckleberry products,' and a refrigerator full of dead buffalo-buffalo jerky $33/lb, burger meat $10.99/lb, burger patties $11.99/lb, and buffalo stew meat and steaks for apparently no charge. I returned to refuel, and Robyn and I went inside to pay for the gas.

The antique owner behind the counter wasn't in a talking mood, but I quizzed him anyway.

"How long does it take to drive through the Bison range?" I asked.

"Three hours." He snorted. "On a good day."

"Is this a good day?" I asked.

"It ain't hot." He said.

"We have to be in Philipsburg for the Vaudeville tonight." I said.

"It ain't hot." He said, again. I wasn't sure he was referring to the remoteness or the refreshment.

In the end we decided that we had come all the way to Montana to see buffalo.

"Let's go see some buffalo." Robyn said. And we drove the few hundred feet to the entrance, under the elk antler arch of the National Bison Range. *Established 1908.*

"Same year as the Swan River Massacre." Said Robyn. But I was already studying the public warning. *Bison are unpredictable and can be very dangerous. They appear to be slow moving and docile but are really very agile and can run as fast as a horse. Bulls are especially dangerous during the breeding season from m d July through August.* There was no 'i' in *mid*. But there would be, in *Kiss your buffalo-gored ass goodbye.* We bought tickets inside the kiosk. I asked the ranger how long it would take to drive it.

"Depends on how long you take." He said, giving less than our Moiese Mercantile Methuselah.

"You are about to experience the ultimate American self-drive safari." He added. "Stay in your vehicle." He pronounced vehicle with hard 'h,' and made us feel like we were entering Jurassic park.

The first part of the safari was sedate. Robyn and I climbed from open grasslands and scrub, into rutted switchbacks of tall yellow grass and sedges, punctuated by lightly wooded hills, with pines in the pubic places, and dust everywhere else. Big blue skies opened onto eroded mauve mountains, their fingers of white clay hoodoo cliffs guarding arroyos below, some still carrying the rare winding river, sleeved with green.

"Buffalo country." I said. Robyn pointed out a pronghorn, camouflaged in the grass. The black patch on his jaw, gave him away as a male.

"Fastest land mammal in the western hemisphere." I said. "First described for us by Lewis and Clark. Big heart and lungs, and hollow hair. They can run high speeds longer than African cheetahs, fifty-five miles per hour for a half a mile, likely because they originally evolved to outrun the American cheetah."

"There is no American cheetah." Said Robyn.

"There isn't now." I said. "And, despite the fact we call it an antelope, with thirteen distinctive kinds of gait, including one that reaches nearly eight yards per stride, it can't jump. They'll fly

51

under any rancher's fence, but can't get over one, which is why some landowners have removed the bottom wire from their enclosures."

"Their heads are like those of giraffes." Robyn said.

"It's true." I said. "Like giraffes, their skin covers the skull, but in the pronghorn, becomes the keratinous horny sheath that sheds and regrows every year. They're interesting in other ways as well. Unlike deer, they have a gallbladder, and are able to eat plants that are toxic to domestic livestock. They migrate every year, across the lava fields of the Craters of the Moon to the Continental Divide, over 160 miles, true marathoners of the American West. You can pretty much predict the behavior of our male friend here, who is very possessive and marks his territory with scent gland musk from the side of his head, vocalizations, and by challenging intruders. The girls are comprised of three strategic groups. *Sampling females* visit several males for a short time before switching to the next one, at an increasing rate, as oestrus approaches. *Inciting females* precipitate conflicts between males, and then mate with the winners. *Quiet females* remain with a single male, in an isolated area. Courting males approach with soft vocalizations, waving their head from side to side, and displaying their cheek patches, like a high school dance."

"So, how are they doing?" Asked Robyn.

"Better than some. Not as good as others." I said. "Originally there were twelve species of antilocaprids in North America, dropping to five when the Indians came across the Bering Land Bridge. Now there is only one. By the 1920s, there were only 13,000 pronghorns that hadn't been shot. They're back up to half a million, but blue tongue disease from sheep, poaching, livestock grazing, road and barrier construction, and habitat loss are killing them off again. At one point their migration corridor is down to two hundred yards wide."

As happy as he didn't look, the mule deer doe, in the splattered shade under the pines at the top of the rise, was miserable. Her ribs projected through the mange of what was left of her hide, her eyes were half closed to the flies, and the only thing in any way upright were her large ears, radiating heat and despair. A barbwire barrier ran behind her, through the trees. *Let me be by myself in the evening breeze, Listen to the murmur of the cottonwood trees, Send me off forever but I ask you please...*

"I didn't think there were supposed to be fences through here." Robyn said.

"Death and worse happened here." I said.

There had been over sixty million bison in North America before Columbus arrived, ranging in a big triangle all the way from Great Bear Lake in northern Canada, down to Durango and Nuevo León in Mexico, then east, almost to the Atlantic tidewater.

They had come off their ancestral lineage from water buffalo and African buffalo ten million years ago, as the Eurasian *steppe bison* that decorated the ancient cave paintings of Spain and Southern France. The European bison descended from steppe bison that had migrated from Asia to North America and back again, where they crossbred again with their steppe bison relatives. Some of these crossbred with the ancestors of the modern yak, and some of them crossed back over the Bering Land Bridge, to become the giant longhorn bison, which was annihilated in the megafauna Quaternary extinction. Two smaller bison subspecies eventually evolved into our North American *Bison bison* buffalo, about ten thousand years ago.

The Native Americans used them, but they never domesticated them. Every animal was a four-legged grocery, dry goods and hardware store. For eight thousand years the Plains Indians dried and pulverized the meat, mixed it with berries and bone marrow, and packed it in buffalo skins. Pemmican was an order of magnitude more nutritious than fresh meat, and lasted until the next season. Tanned buffalo hides were sewn with bone buffalo needles into moccasins and leggings, buckets and cooking vessels, shields and boats, and shelters and bedding. Bone and horns also provided spoons and spikes, drills and scalers, and knives and axes. Children slid down snow banks on jawbones and ribs. Its hooves were made into glue, its shit was turned into heat, and its spirit was transubstantiated into religion and ritual. When the Red Man finished with a buffalo, he had used it all.

The Indians ate, dressed in, talked to, fought for, and died by the sacred buffalo. Their battles occurred over hunting territory, and the last, the one that ended the old life forever at the slaughter that was Wounded Knee, was fought in magic bulletproof shirts and a ghost dance trance.

> The whole world is coming
> A nation is coming, a nation is coming,
> The Eagle has brought the message to
> the tribe,
> The father says so, the father says so,
> Over the whole earth they are coming,
> The buffalo are coming, the buffalo are
> coming.

The Native Americans used them, but they never domesticated them. They have a 'wild and ungovernable temper,' weigh over a ton apiece, and can jump six feet vertically (unlike the pronghorn) and charge at forty miles an hour when agitated. At that speed, their hump, which they use as a snowplow in the winter, is a lethal weapon, and their horns, which face forward, can destroy almost anything in their path, including most fencing systems, including most razor wire.

Before the arrival of the horse in 1600, the only way the Indians could kill bison, was to deceive them, into running off cliffs, like unsuspecting lemmings. They worshipped the rare white buffalo, as a sacred colour. Then came white soldiers and settlers, and their cattle, and guns, and railroads, and the Great Slaughter. The Indians watched, horrified, as the iron horses on iron spikes, sprayed lead bullets out of every

train window, leaving trails of tens of thousands of one ton animals, and blood and salt, with every passing. *Dingdingdingdingdingding...*
The white men called it 'sport.' Piles of buffalo bones, fertilizer instead of food, soared skyward.

'The buffaloes I, the buffaloes I
I make the buffaloes march around
I am related to the buffaloes, the
buffaloes.'

Sioux Proverb

The US Army held a campaign in the late 1800s to exterminate bison, as a way to control tribes that depended on them. In the two years between 1872-1874, white hunters killed over three and half million. The winds of the continent were rotten with the stench of their extermination, ordered by General Sheridan as 'the only way to bring lasting peace and allow civilization to advance.'

Domesticated cattle contributed tuberculosis and brucellosis and other bovine diseases to their path towards extinction. The same germs, guns, and steel that Jared Diamond had identified as the cause of the deaths of nearly all the original American human inhabitants, were the cause of the deaths of nearly all the original American buffalo as well.

The future came wearing cow leather shoes and machine-woven pants. Buffalo were in the way of the cowcatchers, interrupting trains, knocking over telegraph poles, stampeding crops, eating grass. Where never was heard, was heard McDonald's.

At one point in the 1800s, the number of bison had declined to as low as 541 animals. Well-meaning ranchers, in an effort to bring them back, polluted the remnant gene pool with cattle, producing *cattleos* and *beefalos*, and other horrendous hybrids. Only the females of the first generation are fertile. According to mitochondrial DNA analysis, which can only track maternal lineage, there now may be as few as 12,000 pure bison left in the world. *You don't get the point, do you Pea? I mean chase 'em, because before long, there won't be any buffalo left TO chase.*

We stopped in what shadowy shelter we could find, from the vertical glare of the midday sun, for the remains of the vegetarian strudel, leftover from the most beautiful small town in America. The heat was merciless, and Robyn and I were the only source of sympathy and water, for miles.

Our wagon continued higher into the ether, emerging over a montane landscape of yellow haze and purple sage. A patchwork valley lay below, quilted trapezoids of lichen green and ashen grey, with thin ribbons of dark green pine forest along the river, between us and the Bitterroot Mountains on the other side of the horizon.

"They're named after the flower." Said Robyn. "And the roots that the Indians ate, when the buffalo disappeared." We had been in the National Bison Range for over two hours, and had yet to see a single buffalo.

"Maybe they're hiding." She said. "Or sleeping

somewhere."

"Maybe" I said. "They usually graze for a couple of hours, rest and cud chew for awhile, move to a new location, and then do it all over again. They cover about two miles a day, depending on the vegetation, water, bugs, and whether they're rutting or not." We began singing, to encourage their appearance. *Oh, give me a home. Where the buffalo roam, where the skies are not cloudy all day, where never is heard a discouraging word...*

But we were getting discouraged. Nothing, it seemed, could entice them to show themselves. I began to wonder if the National Bison Range wasn't the National Bison Rip-off. I began cursing.

"There's no #@! bison in these stinkin' hills. I've seen more buffalo at the ranch down the road from our place on the island." I said. "Just because you hang a sign on a pine post..." And then they came.

They came at first as brown and bearded and humped and horned silhouettes against the sun dazzle and dust, in single file across the path in front of our wagon. They came as the sixty million would have come, heads down, tails up, hammering the ground with their hooves, and substance, and significance. The males came with their shaggy penises almost touching the ground, red eyes fixed on their females. They came like before they had become mascots and coins and seals and flags and logos, and other symbols, before their heads appeared on the walls of the Royal Canadian Mounted Police in Richard and Carolyn's office, or a dozen other legislatures or city halls or universities or sports team locker rooms or military bases, or the US Department of the Interior. They came like they had created the first thoroughfares of America, and they had, in seasonal migrations between feeding grounds and salt licks, following watersheds and ridge lines to avoid the lower summer muck and winter snowdrifts. Their hornings had shaped the genes of pines and cedars, in the wounded aromatic emissions that repelled the voracious insect swarms of the autumn. The trails of their hooves were followed by the Indians, into hunting grounds and warrior paths, traced by explorers and pioneers, paving the way for the railroads to the Pacific. It was the buffalo that mapped the course of the rail beds through the Cumberland Gap, and across the Ohio and Wabash Rivers. And the railways repaid them, through the windows.

A large bull paused in front of us, and fell and rolled laterally and forward, into a small depression in the dust, leaving his scent in the wallow. And then he rose, unlike so many of his ancestors, and moved. Oh, how he moved. Into the sunny slopes of long ago.

*   *   *

'I could kick you for givin' him all them ideas about Montana.
Now we're gonna suffer for the rest of our damn lives.'

Larry McMurtry, *Lonesome Dove*

I steered down the remaining ruts of the refuge, from the montane to the mundane. Just before the elk antler arch exit, an SUV flew by, throwing gravel in every direction I tried to avoid it. I got my cowboy up again, and chased him to the Mercantile, ready for the ironic and the unexpected. Unleash the hounds.

"OK." Said the bacon fat goatee and sunglasses and punched-in Stetson driver. "I'm sorry." I wondered what had happened to all the real bad guys, but I had to let him go. We made a pit stop, to similarly courteous signage. *Please do not throw trash in the toilets- it is extremely difficult to remove.*

The wagon turned south, through small Montaw-na towns. There was Adlee, with *58 kinds of licorice*, and Evaro's *Buck Snort Bar*, and *Skull Church*, with an honest-to-God skull where the cross should have been. Rolls of hay, like gigantic wheels of cheese, spun by. *Big sky. Thick steak. Full belly.* We passed the promise of a *Testicle Festival*, and travel plazas to nowhere. Buckshot had gone ahead, through road signs that asked perfectly logical questions, if we had planned on staying. *Do you have defensible space?* Further along, there was a *House for Sale.* The nothing around it went forever.

"What are they thinking?" Asked Robyn, correctly. That would be there for a while.

We turned off the Missoula highway across a small wooden bridge, and followed a pretty winding stream east, into a Chinese rock garden, until we didn't, turning off, and north, and up. The gravel became coarse and sparse and gone, and the two wide ruts merged into one narrow trough of potholes. And then some. And then some it got stupid.

The name of the road should have given it away. *Secret Gulch.*

"I wonder what the secret is." said Robyn, lurching and swinging around the steering wheel *in thirteen distinctive kinds of gait, including one that reaches nearly eight yards per stride.*

"Stay out." I said. "Would just about cover it."

We passed a wooden shack, abandoned to all appearances, and time. An old couple emerged onto the porch. I wasn't sure they were waving, or waving us down.

"What do they do all day?" Robyn asked. But our preoccupation with survival would soon dwarf any more trivial musings. We climbed into a tapering constriction of precipitous switchbacks, up the pine-studded rock face of a mountain, with a view of the sun on the plains in the distance, and a black void on the edge of our starboard tires. The back left one kept trying to jump to its death. We had solved the mystery of Secret Gulch. The track held no more torment.

"Are you sure this is the way?" Asked Robyn. I told her I was sure.

"We need a sign." She said. And we got one.

Road closed. Cave Gulch detour 5 mi.

"You must be joking." I said, to no one in particular.

"Let's turn around." Robyn said. "While we still can." It was usually at this point in any of our off-road adventures, that I paused, analyzed the situation carefully, and came to a completely erroneous decision.

"Remember that mushroom-picking logging road you found on Mount Arrowsmith, that turned into the trail of tears?" She asked. I was reminded. We had almost gone off the cliff. But I had learned from that experience and, most of all, I learned that this was my chance for redemption.

"Let's keep going." I said. "It can't be that far now." And it wasn't, if you were a crow. But we were a Toyota, and our powers of flight were more modest. The switchbacks got sharper and shorter. The lurching and swinging became bouncing. If you looked out the window and up, you could almost see God, exactly like if you looked out the window and down. We turned a corner, to a Florida license plate, and a bumper sticker. *Honk if you love Jesus.* We loved Jesus, until he got the hell out of our way.

"Well, honey." I said, pulling out all the stops. "If he can make it, so can we."

"He hasn't made it yet." She said. "And it's not clear where either of us are going. We need a sign." I pointed.

"That's a broken tree trunk." She said. But beyond the broken tree trunk was a clearing, and in the clearing was a patchwork of old wooden shacks, and next to the clearing of old wooden shacks, was a sign. *Garnet. Elevation 6000 ft.*

"This better be good." Said my one true love. This better be good, I thought.

I had researched Garnet as 'Montana's best preserved and least visited ghost towns.' So it came as a complete surprise, when we pulled into a parking lot full of vehicles that looked like they had just rolled off the factory lot. Not a scratch, not a speck of dust. SUVs, 4x4s, camper vans, and RVs. Whole Asian families were getting out of RVs.

"RVs?" Said Robyn. "How did RVs get up here?" It was a question that demanded an answer, and we set off to find one, and see the ghost town, of course. In our enthusiasm, we took a short cut down to the where most of the ghosts had lived, off the main trail. A ranger met us at the bottom.

"You need to stay on the path." He said. I told him we had, fortunately, straight up the mountain, and asked him how whole Asian families were emerging from RVs in the parking lot, when they should be dead.

"You came up the south face?" He asked.

"Apparently." I said. "Didn't everybody." He hesitated, in breaking the good news.

"Hell, no." He said. "Wallace Creek Road comes from north of here, up near Missoula." I glanced over at Robyn. It wasn't pretty.

"So how do we get to Philipsburg from here?" She asked. He hesitated, in breaking the good news.

"Whew, Philipsburg." He said. Not an auspicious

beginning. "Wow. You'll have to go north, then east, then south."

"Big state, Montana." I said.

"Tall too." He said. "You're over a mile high." But that was something we already knew.

Our path of pilgrimage had taken us up, into the gold rush towards truth and redemption. Some archetypes of the authentic American West weren't cowboys and Indians, but miners and mining communities. Ophir holes and gopher holes and loafer holes. Hidden at the edge of the high desert in the Front Range, on the sheltered forest dirt floor of First Chance Creek in Granite County, was a ghost town named for the ruby-coloured semi-precious stone first mined here, until the granite gave up its secret. The yellow metal in California and Colorado had been easily extracted by placer mining, washing it out of the sand and gravel with water, until it ran out. By 1870, the miners had migrated towards the Garnet Mountains, with their rockers and sluice boxes, but most of the gold would be stubborn and hiding, in quartz veins, beyond the extracting and smelting techniques that had not yet arrived on the poor roads, which had still not arrived. The silver mines began to draw the miners, until the repeal of the Sherman Silver Purchase Act of 1893 shut them down, and the diggers trickled back to Garnet

In 1895, Dr. Armistead Mitchell set up a stamp mill to crush the granite, and Sam Ritchey hit a rich vein of gold, at his Nancy Hanks mine, just west of town. The boom was on.

By January 1898, a thousand people lived in

Garnet. There were twenty mines, four stores, three livery stables, two barbershops, a union hall, a butcher shop, a candy shop, a doctor's office, an assay office, and a school with 41 students. Four hotels had been opened with rooms ranging from one to three dollars. The poor miners who could not afford that price could sleep in the window-less attic for a quarter. It was the free-flowing liquor that lubricated Garnet, poured from its thirteen famous saloons, and the brisk business in its bawdy houses.

But there was no Official Community Plan. Garnet was a haphazard hamlet, built by miners and entrepreneurs more eager for the riches below the ground than above it. Buildings had been hastily erected without foundations, on existing or future mining claims. They were small and easy to heat, and flammable. Less than seven years later, it was all over. In 1912, fire destroyed half the buildings and, when WWII restricted the use of dynamite for domestic purposes, the ghosts had come to Garnet.

There were still scorch marks on some of the wooden buildings, but the surviving square-faced storefronts and boardwalks and cabins were well preserved and well kept. Robyn and I leaned on the bars of the saloons, and felt them lean back. A cracked record lay wounded on the old Victrola in a forlorn corner of one, missing a triangular arc of its music, a pizza slice of its past. The dull metal plates of gilded ghosts waited on the wooden tables in darkened dining rooms, for the no one that would ever sit in the wooden chairs, and the nothing that would ever come again, from the chipped enamel pots in the shadows.

We left past another sign on an actual road, heading north to go east, to go south.

Safety zone- no shooting. The ravages of Western pine beetle were rusting out the forests, all the way down to the purple sage.

"The winters don't get cold enough to kill them." Robyn said. We went by Camp Utmost, and pink rock outcroppings, slanting up on angles out of the ridge. Whatever ground level was, we were the only traffic, in the middle of, except for the river that ran through it, nowhere.

"Makes you wonder where everybody went." I said.

The day was draining away to the west, and the race to get to Philipsburg before dark, had commenced. Helmville went by, and the empty Copper Queen Saloon. The hay bales shapes were long and flat, like the road before us. We turned onto Highway 271, too many numbers to have vehicles, a route of Black Angus and sage. Dead trees, chain-sawed to their trunks, were densely nailed with and antlers and animal skulls.

An open wedding wagon went by, decorated with pennants and garlands, pulled by two Clydesdales trimmed with blossoms. It was full of white cowboys hats and moustaches and suspenders, and dancing girls, with bows and pompoms in their hair, carrying bouquets of flowers and pink parasols. White hats waved in the air as Robyn and I drove by.

We were sprinting against the sun, almost setting now on our right. Three ATVs were parked hard up against the front of a house, as we blew through Maxville, at warp speed. And then, as Philipsburg announced its proximity, blackness pulled up like a wraith behind us, and the dusk became an explosion of cobalt and carmine and purple stroboscopic white lightning. We pulled off onto the shoulder and watched, helpless, as our Vaudeville plans, evaporated in the large shadow, slowing advancing towards Robyn's window.

*   *   *

'Are magnesium and scorn sufficient to support
a town, not just Philipsburg, but towns of
towering blondes, good jazz and booze the
world will never let you have until the town you
came from dies inside?'
Richard Hugo, *Degrees of Gray in Philipsburg*

"License and registration." He held himself back behind her window, like no Canadian Mountie would have felt the need. Even from where I sat, I could tell he was made of Kevlar and brass and lead, and caution. She handed over the documents. He retreated to his black *Mad Max* Mariah, the blackest flat black matte blackest thing I'd ever seen. The windows were tinted, like the heavy water in a nuclear reactor. A full ten minutes later, he returned the way he came.

Maybe it was our BC license plate.

"Don't worry." He said. "I'm not going to give you a ticket." I tried to reason with him.

"I'm sorry, officer, it was all my fault." I said. "You see, I was getting her to hurry, so we wouldn't be late for the Vaudeville in Philipsburg." I could see him reconsidering.

"I get so confused between kilometres and miles per hour." Said Robyn. "Here in Mon-taw-na." He tried not to smile.

"Slow it down." He said, and waved us on...*the tortured try of local drivers to accelerate their lives.*

We arrived down Broadway, the main street of Philipsburg, nearly the only street of Philipsburg, wide enough for a cattle drive.

"Probably why they call it Broadway." Robyn said. Frontier buildings of orange brick, with black and white painted signs on square rooflines, *GOLDEN RULE, HARDWARE GROCERIES,* converged on a vanishing point, sidewalks lined with American flags and hanging baskets and lampposts and angle parking. In the centre of town was a single traffic light, suspended on wires arising from the four points of the compass. *You walk these streets laid out by the insane, past hotels that didn't last, bars that did...*

"There it is." I said. And there it was, in all it's Georgian gingerbread glory, creams and forest greens and lichens and pinks and rusts, and spheres and squares, and angles and triangles, dentate and Dorian, rising into the big sky. *The Broadway Hotel.* I had written the owner, Sue, and asked her for a 'quiet place to write.' Her hesitant email suggested the kind of difficulty that was now taking place in the downstairs brewery. She had written something about giving us 'the crosscut room.' The keys were outside the back door, in an envelope. A large loud lady, from a similar utility vehicle, was storming about outside the locked entrance, something about her reservation.

"I didn't actually cancel it." She fumed. We offered to let her in.

"I'll wait right here." She said. And we crept by her, and down the hall to our room. It was small, and all the sharp implements on the wall were a bit intimidating. There was a big circular saw, and two crosscut saws, and a handsaw. A ceiling fan twirled above our heads.

"A man doesn't want to lose his balance in the night." I said. But it was clean and cozy, and topical, as Philipsburg had been logging as well as mining before we arrived. We had just enough time for a quick meal before the Vaudeville began, across from the crosscut, at the Silver Mill. *One good restaurant and bars can't wipe the boredom out... and the girl who serves your food is slender and her red hair lights the wall.*

The tin embossed ceiling was bottom lit by suspended lamps. The girl who served our food was slender and her red hair lit the wall. My steak was served with a slice of orange. It was big enough to take half back to the crosscut room, and saw it up for the next day. We made the Vaudeville show, and it was entertaining enough, but there were more authentic diversions outside the theatre- *a dance floor built on springs.* The few tourists that weren't still in the playhouse, were checking out the sapphire and silver shop windows. *Buffalo Elk Venison Jerky... Try a Bung-Hole Driver only $5. Yep, only available here!*

We returned to the Broadway to meet Sue in the rich red reading room, with the big floral centrepiece, and western memorabilia, and books. English Sue, who had married Jim, and had shared his dreams and offspring and, when everything went sideways, inherited the hotel that had ruled their lives, for twenty-five years. We asked about the large loud lady.

"She cancelled her reservation." Said Sue. "I put them up in the house, but no matter what I do, they won't be happy. *The principal supporting business now is rage.*

I asked about the possibility for future companionship in Philipsburg.

"The gene pool is rather small." She said. *the best liked girls who leave each year for Butte.* Like the buffalo, I thought. *Say your life broke down. The last good kiss you had was years ago...Isn't this your life? That ancient kiss still burning out your eyes?*

And I left her and Robyn, to whisper secret veins of quartz in foreign accents.

One last walk around the town, before I began sawing logs in the crosscut room. Two smokers sat outside the White Front Bar. It was for sale, like everything else had been for sale in Philipsburg. *The 1907 boom, eight going silver mines... Hatred of the various grays the mountain* sends, *hatred of the mill... two stacks high above the town, two dead kilns... in collapse for fifty years that won't fall finally down...*

A mewing cat, imprisoned on the high balcony of a deserted building, cried out to me, or anyone, ghost rider in the sky.

There were big Montana muffins for breakfast next morning, and coffee with Sue. She told us to check out the jail, and the noose, still hanging from the rafters. *The jail turned 70 this year. The only prisoner is always in, not knowing what he's done... The old man, twenty when the jail was built, still laughs although his lips collapse. Someday soon, he says, I'll go to sleep and not wake up. You tell him no. You're talking to yourself.*

It was a sunny Sunday morning in the rest of the town, and it shone on the tipi and caboose and the log cabin with its chains-awed ogres outside. *You might come here Sunday on a whim.* A church bell rang. *Only churches are kept up... Isn't this defeat so accurate, the church bell simply seems a pure announcement: ring and no one comes? Don't empty houses ring?*

We said goodbye to Sue, and fired up the wagon. A-plowing through the ragged sky and up a cloudy draw. *The car that brought you here still runs. The money you buy lunch with, no matter where it's mined, is silver... all memory resolves itself in gaze...*

*   *   *

Vigilante Trail to the Paradise Room
Three Forks, Montana

'Get the water right down to your socks
This bulkhead's built of fallen brethren's
bones
We all do what we can We endure our
fellow man
And we sing our songs to the headframe's
creaks and moans'
The Decemberists, *Rox in the Box*

Copper. The water, if that's what it was, mirrored a reflection of the hill above it, on its surface. Except for the scattered green of it. There was no green in the reflection. The water was here because of the earth that was here, and most of that wasn't anymore. What had been a natural bowl sitting high in the Rockies, straddling the Continental Divide, the 'Richest Hill on Earth,' over a brief 125 years, became the most poisoned ground in America. The gold and silver mined here was almost ploughed aside by the advent of electricity, which exploded the world demand for copper. And where Robyn and I were standing, was where it all came out of the ground.

The tourist brochure had understated it a bit. *Butte's urban landscape includes mining operations set within residential areas.* There was only one congressman, in a state as big as Italy, and he had given away 44,000,000 acres of land to the Northern Pacific Railroad alone. The name of the game in Montana was, and still is, extraction. Between 1880 and 2005, the miners of Butte pulled out more than 9.6 million metric tons of copper, 2.1 million metric tons of zinc, 1.6 million metric tons of manganese, 381,000 metric tons of lead, 87,000 metric tons of molybdenum, 22,200 metric tons of silver, 90 metric tons of gold, and 22 billion dollars... *set within residential areas.*

The magnitude of the magnates, the three Copper Kings that championed the extraction, was evident on the land, thirty miles and 120 years away from our arrival in Butte that morning.

William Andrews Clark had begun to develop the silver and gold mines and mills before copper appeared on the radar. By 1876, Butte had a thousand inhabitants, and Clarke went on to wealth, and a desire to become a US senator which his newspaper, the *Butte Miner,* promoted. The members of the Montana legislature he bribed in 1899, didn't get in the way. The second Copper King, Marcus Daly, had arrived in 1876 to inspect the Alice Mine for the entrepreneurial Walker brothers from Salt Lake City. Four years later he sold his interest and bought another mine, with investment money from several San Francisco moguls, including the father of William Randolph Hearst. In 1883 he filed a town plan for 'Copperopolis, but eventually took the advice of his postmaster, and named in Anaconda. By the time that financiers William Rockefeller and Henry H. Rogers, two principals of John D. Rockefeller's Standard Oil, teamed up to form the giant Amalgamated Copper Mining Co. In 1899, the air of Butte was filled with toxic sulfurous smoke. Daly responded with the construction of the tallest masonry structure on the planet, the 585-foot Anaconda smokestack, and smelter, the world's largest nonferrous processing plant. The third Copper King, F. Augustus Heinze, had fought the dominance of Amalgamated but, when Daly died in 1900, the banker that picked up his widow, convinced him to sell out, creating a monopoly. The Anaconda Copper Mining Company, true to its name, swallowed everything in its path, expanding into the fourth largest company in the world by 1920. *It doesn't matter how big of a ranch you have...or how many cattle you brand... or how much money you've got... the size of your funeral is still going to depend on the weather.*

The Copper Kings are long under the last ground they extracted, leaving a legacy of discarded towns, rivers that will forever run red, and a generation of old men on respirators. They owned the greatest mother lode the earth had ever seen, at the time the world wanted and needed it most- the world's biggest silver mine, one of the biggest gold mines, nearly a million acres of timberland, and freely cut on another million owned by the public. They bought the Montana legislature for ten thousand dollars a vote. They had people they didn't like shot by national guardsmen, or hung from their railroad trestles.

For a Sunday morning, the casino was doing a roaring trade. We drove through Anaconda quietly, past the JFK Bar and Big Jim's Steakhouse and the Grizzly Den Motel.

The sun was shining, and the sky was clear and blue when we arrived into Butte. The only thing that told us it was Butte was the 'Butte' sign on the side of one of the old black mine head frames, and the names of the streets, on the steep hills into town. Galena. Copper. Granite. Mercury. Quartz. The tallest structures on Montanan Street were the closed church steeples, and the open ironies. I passed the Abundant Life Fellowships, and parked, to find one of my own.

"You sure its open?" Asked Robyn. "It's Sunday."

I wasn't sure, but it was open. We went inside the M&M Cigar Store. It wasn't full and it wasn't empty, and it used to be both. Behind the counter was the usual coloured neon *Bud Light...Lite... Budweiser... Pabst Blue Ribbon.* Baseball caps hung above the bottles in front of the mirrored bar, providing an illusion of plenty. A baseball game, America's other pastime, went on obliviously on televisions, in high corners of the saloon. The sound of gambling machines spilled into the space, and away with the hopes of their patrons. *Dingdingdingdingdingding...*

Suspended ceiling lamps and wall sconce lamps, and an elderly man with glasses, manning the off-track betting booth in the back, dimly lighted the place. I migrated to his story, and history. Jack had been a miner, laid off in 1980, when ARCO Atlantic Richfield, which had bought Anaconda and its mines only three years earlier, closed them all down because of lower metal prices.

"Three hundred miners lost the last 3500 dollars they had." He said. "Investing in the new jobs they were promised. Don't get me started." But it was too late for that.

The mines of Butte had attracted workers from around the globe- immigrants from Cornwall, Ireland, Wales, Lebanon, Canada, Finland, Austria, Serbia, Italy, China, Syria, Croatia, Montenegro, Mexico, and all areas of the US. They brought their food into the ground, Cornish pasties, Slavic *povitica*, Scandinavian *lefse*, boneless pork chop sandwiches, huckleberry pie, and their politics back out. Butte became the 'Gibraltar of Unionism.' By 1886 there were 34 separate unions, representing six thousand workers. Violent strikes were inevitable. In 1892, the one in Coeur d'Alene prompted the miners of Butte to mortgage their buildings in order to send disorder support. The Western Federation of Miners was established in Butte the following year, and the Butte Miner's Union became Local Number One of the new WFM. In 1903 the Socialist Party of America won its first victory west of the Mississippi when Anaconda elected a socialist mayor, treasurer, police judge, and three councilmen. After 1905, Butte became a hotbed for the IWW 'Wobblies,' the Industrial Workers of the World. None of this mattered to the Anaconda Company, who lynched an IWW board officer in 1917, and ordered company mine guards to shoot 17 strikers in the back as they tried to flee, in the Anaconda Road Massacre of 1920.

Organized Labor hadn't occupied all the moral high ground. Their unions boycotted Chinese businesses in Chinatown, and the Chinese Exclusion Act stopped further immigration in 1882. Solidarity was an incompletely uniform and inegalitarian commodity.

But vice was equitable, and all-inclusive. In its heyday, Butte was one of the largest and most notorious wide-open copper boomtowns in the American West, where anything was obtainable. In 1893, Butte boasted 16 gambling dens and 212 taverns, including the M&M, and is still one of the few cities in the US where possession and consumption of open containers of alcoholic beverages is allowed on the street. When the miners emerged from below the city on a subzero day, their bodies emitted a puff of smoke, like they were appearing on a magician's stage. *The ladies are very fond of this smoky city. There is just enough arsenic there to let them have beautiful complexions.*

Its famous red-light district, the 'Line,' or the 'Copper Block,' was centred on Mercury Street, where elegant bordellos included the famous Dumas Brothel, near what is now Butte High School, *Home of the Bulldogs*. Behind the brothel was the equally notorious Venus Alley, where 6000 prostitutes plied their trade in small cubicles called 'cribs,' a mattress and washbasin in a single small room. When Carrie Nation came to town, one of its working ladies kicked her to the ground. A hermaphrodite named Liz the Lady charged for a peek below, but everyone could look up at the 90-foot Blessed Virgin Mary statue of *Our Lady of the Rockies*, built and lit by floodlights, dedicated to women and mothers everywhere, on top of the Continental Divide, overlooking the town. The brothels only closed in 1982.

I asked Jack if he thought his years of mining had left him anything durable.

"Silicosis." He said. "And hate."

The civic administrators of Butte were clearly putting on a new kinder, gentler face, *with just enough arsenic to let them have beautiful complexions.* The 'thousands of historic commercial and residential buildings from the boom times, which, in the Uptown section, give it a very old-fashioned appearance' had resulted in Butte's 'recognition and designation in the late 1990s as an All-American City... In 2008 Barack Obama spent his last Fourth of July before his Presidency campaigning in Butte, taking in the parade with his family, and celebrating his daughter Malia's 10th birthday.' Bill Murray owns the Copper Kings baseball team. Butte is the home of the National Center for Appropriate Technology. An EPA operation for the environmental cleanup has made Butte and environs that largest Superfund site in the country. Jack Nicklaus designed the 'Old Works' Golf Course, a big reclaimed championship venue 'hole-in-one' for the effort.

Which brought Robyn and I to the Berkeley Pit, the one big hole in Butte, and the serenity of the water, if that's what it was. *Take 5 in our beautiful picnic area.* The cute little rust bucket mining cart at the entrance was full to the brim with columbines and carnations and pansies and other recent immigrants. It cost two dollars to get in to the south wall observation deck, lined with barbwire.

There were buttons to press, for information. *Berkeley Pit is the largest pit lake in the You-knighted States. It is one of the biggest tourist attractions in the area. In its time, Berkeley Pit was the largest truck-operated open pit copper mine in the country.* All the things you'd expect the buttons to say, but none of the things they needed to say. Like the thousands of homes that were destroyed to excavate the pit. Or like when ARCO shut down the pit in 1982, it also shut down the water pumps in nearby mines, which caused the toxic stew acidic heavy metal pit lake of arsenic and cadmium and mercury sulfate to form and rise, and like how its still rising, and like in 2020, it will overflow and start to run downhill- 30 billion gallons of poison. Or like how, for more than a century, the Anaconda smelter released 36 tons of arsenic every day, 1540 tons of sulfur, and huge quantities of lead and other heavy metals into the air; like how mine tailings were dumped directly into Silver Bow Creek, creating a 150 mile plume of downstream pollution; or like how livestock and agricultural soils had been contaminated, all the way down the Deer Lodge Valley; or like, nothing was done about the unsafe tap water in Butte and no serious effort was made clean up Berkeley Pit until the 1990s. *There is now life in the pond- water striders and a new iron-eating algae, discovered in 2000...* Or like the flock of

342 migrating snow geese which selected the pit lake as a resting place, and dissolved on contact. The broadcasts across the water, if that's what it was, are designed to scare them away.

Butte is the hometown of Evel Knieval Days, but that doesn't seem as dangerous anymore. The fourteen passengers and crew of the airplane crash into Holy Cross Cemetery, arrived at death and devastation in Butte, four years before Robyn and I did, more slowly. The books and movies about the town are telling- *The Killer Inside Me, Runaway Train, Lonesome Dove, Sold Me Down The River, The Last Ride, Don't Come Knocking, Red Harvest, Empty Mansions.* Robyn and I were headed south, to another kind of ghost town, but we would need to pass through one more Butte copper tragedy, on the way. The giant letter 'M' of Montana Tech was carved into the hillside, upstream from the highway signs leading out of town. *Adam and Eve's lingerie at next exit... Drink it. Drive it. Crash it. Can you live with it?* In Whitehall we discovered that we could play Keno at the town pump. The locals were pulling weeds by hand.

"They've got time." Said Robyn. A *Mad Max* black Mariah flew by us, in the haze through which the Tobacco Root Mountains rose, on our left. Real flocks of birds flew and landed, in flocks. Rare swaths of green and the cheese wheel hay bale progeny of their nurturing, contrasted against the yellow and blue of the rest of Montana. Homesteads of dust and rust and dereliction, windmills with missing vanes, took us from earth and water to earth and fire. And water again.

The town was named Silver Star, and there was one on the weatherworn shack on the edge of it. It said 'Open,' and 'Gifts,' but we didn't find either. What we did find were rows of massive double-spoked metal wheels, twenty feet and more in diameter, and the western script explanation along the highway.

> *These Sheave Wheels from the Speculator Mine were used to hoist the bodies of the 168 miners who died in the Granite Mtn Disaster, June 8, 1917. It remains the worst metal mining tragedy in US history. The Granite Mtn Shaft was burned out so rescue was through the Speculator, connected underground.*
>
> *Photos are welcome, but please stay away from Wheels or machinery.*

At the time of the disaster, the Butte copper mines were operating at full wartime production. An electric cable was being lowered into the Granite Mountain mine, paradoxically as part of a fire safety system. When it fell, a foreman went half a mile below the surface with a carbide lamp to inspect the damage. He ignited the oil-soaked insulation on the cable with his lantern. The fire quickly climbed the cable, ignited the timbers, and turned the shaft into a chimney. Flames and smoke and poisonous gas spewed through the labyrinth of underground tunnels, including the connected Speculator mine. Approximately 168 miners died in the ensuing blaze, most from asphyxia. Some did not die immediately, but survived for a day or two. Some wrote notes while they waited to be rescued. A few managed to barricade themselves within bulkheads, and were found after as long as 55 hours later, but many others died in a panic to try to get out. The rescue effort was frustrated by carbon monoxide, which stole the air supply. A fan, used to prevent the fire from spreading, worked for a short time but, when the rescuers added water, the water evaporated, creating steam that burned those trying to escape. Most of the victims were too mutilated to recognize.

In Montana, logs and haystacks and cattle brands and ingots bore witness, to the moral supremacy of hardware. The price of extraction was Big Sky high.

'And you won't make a dime On this gray granite mountain mine
Of dirt you're made and of dirt you will return
So while we're living here Let's get this little one thing clear
There's plenty of men to die, you don't jump your turn.'

The Decemberists, *Rox in the Box*

*　　*　　*

'People love westerns worldwide. There's something fantasy-like about an individual fighting the elements. Or even bad guys and the elements. It's a simpler time. There's no organized laws and stuff.'

Clint Eastwood

Our route took us south, towards the no organized laws and stuff. We passed through purple flowers, and Twin Bridges. There was the Blue Anchor Bar, and a mural of the Twin Rivers Fishing Co. *Lewis & Clark fished here.*

Outside the Ruby Valley Gun Club was a big truck with a gun rack and a bumper sticker. *I hunt with a Labrador retriever.* Which may have partially explained the three deer carcasses on the side of the road, beyond the 'Happy Trails' sign, dead as a can of corned beef. *Some trails are happy ones, Others are blue. It's the way you ride the trail that counts, Here's a happy one for you.*

Visitors fall in love with Montana in the summer. Snow can fall any month and usually will. Eighty per cent per move away within five years of purchase. Some of the ones that stay may be found in the taverns, like the Sump Saloon and the Stockman's bar in Sheridan, *Heart of Ruby Valley...this community supports our troops*, and Chick's Bar in Alder. In May 1863, a party of Crow warriors forced a group of prospectors, heading towards the Yellowstone River, to retreat to Bannack. Their return would change their lives, and the course of American and World history, when Bill Fairweather, joking he might find 'something to buy a little tobacco with,' stuck a pick into the ground near Alder Creek. Robyn and I followed the 'This way' sign out of town, and the Vigilante Trail towards Virginia City. Miles of silence and emptiness, in all directions, eventually arrived at a two-storied log roadhouse, with hitching posts and a veranda and balcony around the back.

"Robber's Roost." I said. "The hangout of the Innocents."

"Who were they?" Asked Robyn.

"Montana's most notorious criminal outlaw gang." I said. "During the height of their activity during the gold rush of the 1860s, there were over a hundred of them, and as many men were killed resisting their holdups. Watchmen in the mining camps and gambling dens would tip off the Innocents about gold shipments, but it was its leader that made the gang most unusual."

"What about him?" Robyn asked.

"Henry Plummer." I said. "He was the sheriff."

"Were they ever caught?" Asked Robyn. The first westerns had four standard scenes- a bar, a stagecoach, a holdup and a chase.

"Oh, that was coming." I said. "In spades."

A big-bellied motorcycle couple parked their bike in front of the next marker. Sage, and the wagons and railroad ties and the steam machinery that extracted the gold ore that made their wealthy widows possible surrounded ghost mansions of sunburned wood, surmounted by cupolas and widow's walks and weathervanes. The chapel between Nevada City and Virginia City was closed. *Cowboy Church Services.*

Most of the story of Virginia City occurred within one year. On May 14 1863, just after Bill Fairweather's discovery of 'something to buy a little tobacco with,' in Bannack, Henry Plummer was made its sheriff. Henry had come out from Maine to the goldfields of California, eleven years earlier, at the age of nineteen. He did well. Within two years he owned a mine, a ranch, and a bakery, and within three, was the sheriff and city manager of his town, and had lost an election as the Democratic nominee to the State legislature. In 1857, he shot the husband of a woman he was having an affair with, and was sentenced to ten years in San Quentin. However, he was pardoned after serving only two because, like Doc Holiday, he was suffering from tuberculosis, and because of his 'good character and civic performance.' Two years later, he shot William Riley, a San Quentin escapee, while trying to make a citizen's arrest. The killing was accepted as justified, but Plummer was advised to leave the state. After he cut down another man in a gunfight in Washington Territory, Henry decided to get out of the violent towns of the gold rush, and return to Maine. He got as far as the dock for the Fort Benton steamer on the Missouri River, when he was offered a job by James Vail, to protect his family from Indian attacks at the mission station in Sun River, Montana. Plummer accepted, as did Jack Cleveland, a horse dealer who had known Henry in California. Unfortunately, both men fell in love with Vail's sister-in-law, Electa Bryan, at the mission. Fortunately, she accepted

Plummer's proposal of marriage. Unfortunately, Cleveland forced Henry into a gunfight in a crowded saloon in Bannack, and was killed. Fortunately, the residents not only deemed it an act of self-defense, they elected him sheriff. Or maybe it was unfortunate.

On June 16 1863, another township was formed a mile south of where Bill Fairweather's pickaxe had landed. It was initially called Verina, after Varina Howell Davis, the first and only First Lady of the Confederacy. The Civil War was raging and, despite the fact that the town was in Union territory, the local resident loyalty was thoroughly confederate. A territorial officer from Connecticut objected to the name registration, and recorded it instead, as Virginia City, not making total sense, since Virginia had seceded, still a Dixie city in a Yankee territory. Within weeks Virginia City was a gold frontier boomtown, bereft of law enforcement, and full of saloons and uneducated fortune hunters wearing firearms as standard attire.

The first Episcopal communion service in Virginia City welcomed Baptists, Methodists, and Lutherans to the Lord's Table. Thomas J. Dinsdale, late of Oxford, was being paid two dollars per child a week for teaching school, before he found better employment as editor of the *Montana Post*. By contrast, in Virginia City alone, $600,000 worth of gold was being extracted every week. In today's dollars, that was the equivalent of $30,000,000 per week or $1.5 billion a year, all of which was threatening to go to the Confederacy. Abraham Lincoln, to ensure that this new wealth would flow instead into Federal coffers, immediately removed the gold towns from the old Dakota Territory, and into the newly formed Idaho Territory, consisting of the present states of Wyoming, Idaho and Montana, with its capital at Lewiston. He appointed W. W. Wallace as the Governor and his friend, and one of the founders of the Republican Party, Sidney Edgerton, as Chief Justice.

It was still a lawless free-for-all, and Henry Plummer was earning his pay, and possibly more. The only court system available for the residents of Virginia City were the informal miners' courts, limited to the resolution of small disputes, and not set up for major crimes. The fiasco of a trial of the perpetrators of the murder of J.W. Dillingham was typical of the time. Like the dentistry, it was held outside, more because of the fact that every resident took part, than the ambient light. In the end all three defendants were released. The first, Charley Forbes, was freed after a sentimental speech he made about his mother. The other two, Buck Stinson and Haze Lyons, were convicted and sentenced to be executed. However, at what would be a very public hanging, friends of Stinson and Lyons convinced the crowd to vote again. Two attempts at counting were made. In the first, those voting 'hang' were to walk uphill, while those voting 'no hang' were to walk downhill. This method was rejected for reasons that are still not clear. The next attempt had four men form two gates and the gathered citizenry would cast their vote by either walking through the 'hang' gate or the 'no hang' gate. The condemned mens' friends simply walked through the 'no hang' gate repeatedly, casting enough multiple fraudulent votes that enabled the two murderers to walk free. *People gotta talk themselves into law and order before they do anything about it. Maybe because down deep they don't care.*

Thomas J. Dinsdale, late of Oxford, paid two dollars per child a week for teaching school, wrote: *Another powerful incentive to wrong-doing is the absolute nulity of the civil law in such cases. No matter what may be the proof, if the criminal is well liked in the community 'Not Guilty' is almost certain to be the verdict, despite the efforts of the judge and prosecutor.*

Robyn and I walked by the marker of the hanging that made Montana. *Site of trial and hanging of George Homer Ives December 21, 1863 - Most extraordinary trial in history.* This one was also held outside, for three winter days. George Ives was a bold and brutal member of the Innocents, and had killed a young German immigrant named Nicholas Tbolt.

But there had been a new development since Dillingham's murderers had been freed. In late December, while Sheriff Plummer was away, a group of local residents spawned the formation of a secret *Vigilance Committee*, with an established set of 'regulations and bylaws.' It was a Neighbourhood Watch, with guns and ropes. The founders consisted of Unit commander Sergeant James Williams, Field commander James Liberty Fisk, Nick Wall,

Wilbur Fisk Sanders, Alvin V. Brookie, John Nye, a sadistic executioner named John X. Beidler (who delighted in strangling rather than hanging his victims), and Paris Pfouts, an anomalous secessionist Freemason, who later became Mayor of Virginia City.

Before long, the Montana Vigilantes had more than one thousand members, almost all of them Republican Mason Unionists. Almost all of their victims were non-Mason, Democrat Secessionists. Confederate conspiracy theorists still charge that the Vigilantes were formed more for the purpose of diverting gold to the Union cause, than for establishing justice. *Virginia City gold won the war for the North.*

The Committee called their enemies 'villains,' and galvanized the population by inventing the myth of the 'road agent,' the hypothesis that a 'secret society' of thieves, tipped off by townspeople in league with them, waylaid unsuspecting travelers, miners and transporters of gold and supplies, murdered them, and made off with their property.

While the vigilantism was still in its initial stages, Clubfoot George Lane, a former horse thief reformed as a boot-maker at Dance and Stuart's store in Virginia City, concerned about the increasingly arbitrary manipulation of what was passing for justice in Virginia City, rode off to Bannack to inform Sheriff Plummer of the George Ives trial, aiming to convince Henry that Ives deserved a civilian tribunal.

But while the sheriff was still away, the Vigilantes hung Ives, and two of Plummer's deputies arrested Lane as 'a road agent, thief, and an accessory to numerous robberies and murders on the highway.'

"If you hang me." Said Clubfoot George. "You will hang an innocent man." But the Vigilante Committee found him guilty anyway, and sentenced him to death. Lane appealed to his employer at the boot store to confirm his innocence. Dance said he couldn't vouch for his other activities.

"Well, then." Asked Lane. "Will you pray with me?"

"Willingly, George." Said Dance. "Most willingly." And *suiting the action to the word, dropped upon his knees and, with George and Gallagher kneeling beside him, offered up a fervent petition in behalf of the doomed men.* As Clubfoot George was led out to the gallows, he turned to a friend who had come to see him executed.

'Good-bye, old fellow." Said Lane. "I'm gone." And *without waiting for the box to be removed, he leaped from it, and died with hardly a struggle... perfectly cool and collected... thought no more of hanging than the ordinary man would of eating his breakfast.* He was buried in an unmarked grave in Boot Hill cemetery, with the other executed men, and 'fellers that pulled their triggers without aiming.'

The Montana Vigilantes summarily executed people using, as the sole evidence, the testimony of others facing their own imminent executions. At one point the Committee assembled a force of over 500 men, and sealed off Virginia City in order to catch gang members. Over the next month, the movement degenerated into a campaign of terror that still haunts the state. The vigilante committee arrested and passed sentences, from execution to flogging to banishment. Twenty-four men were hanged, some in the basement of Joe Griffith's general store, the last having done nothing more than express an opinion that several of those hanged previously had been innocent.

Before one man was hanged, he told the crowd that sheriff Henry Plummer was the ringleader. Suspicions had already been raised, when two residents who had been held up claimed that they had recognized him during the robberies, and when another had confronted him about the danger of the roads, Henry had offered to return some of his money. Plummer was arrested, and attempted, unsuccessfully, to bribe his captors.

The gallows on which Henry was hanged had been built by his own request during a previous case. On January 10, 1864, over five thousand people assembled to watch him and the other alleged gang members meet the rope. He was hanged without the drop, and the noose placed behind the head, not to the side, which would have broken his neck and caused an instantaneous death. With his preexistent tuberculosis, he likely died from a slow and agonizing suffocation. The two youngest members of the Innocents were spared, one sent back to Bannack to tell the rest of the gang to leave, and the other to Lewiston, to do the same. There were river steamers there, that could take them to the Oregon coast, at Astoria. Whether the historical revisionists and the Freemason conspiracists like it or not, the large gang robberies of gold shipments ended with the deaths of Plummer and the others.

On May 26, 1864, Lincoln establish the Montana Territory, carved from the Idaho Territory he had preciously chopped from the Dakota Territory, in order to establish a territorial court, and restore order. The capital moved from Lewiston, to Bannack, and then a year later, to Virginia City, with Martha Jane Canary.

'In 1865 we emigrated from our homes in Missouri by the overland route to Virginia City, Montana, taking five months to make the journey. While on the way, the greater portion of hunting along with the men and hunters of the party; in fact, I was at all times with the men when there was excitement and adventures to be had. By the time we reached Virginia City, I was considered a remarkable good shot and a fearless rider for a girl of my age. I remember many occurrences on the journey from Missouri to Montana. Many times in crossing the mountains, the conditions of the trail were so bad that we frequently had to lower the wagons over ledges by hand with ropes, for they were so rough and rugged that horses were of no use. We also had many exciting times fording streams, for many of the streams in our way were noted for quicksands and boggy places, where, unless we were very careful, we would have lost horses and all. Then we had many dangers to encounter in the way of streams swelling on account of heavy rains. On occasions of that kind, the men would usually select the best places to cross the streams; myself, on more than one occasion, have mounted my pony and swam across the stream several times merely to amuse myself, and have had many narrow escapes from having both myself and have had many narrow escapes from having both myself and pony washed away to certain death, but, as the pioneers of

those days had plenty of courage, we overcame all obstacles and reached Virginia City in safety.
Mother died at Black Foot, Montana, 1866, where we buried her.'

Calamity Jane's mother had died of 'washtub pneumonia.' By the time she buried her, the placer gold had been all but extracted, and the miners were moving towards Helena, and Garnet. By the 1870s Montana was experiencing a sort of *Pax Vigilanticus*, due to its reputation for summary execution and the migration of most of the criminally undesirable. The Montana Vigilantes became an admired group in Montana history. Their secret motto, *3-7-77*, is still on the badges, patches, and car door insignias of the Montana Highway Patrol.

By the time that Robyn and I tread the boardwalks of Virginia City, it was a different kind of highway robbery. The cowboys emerging from the Star Bakery were morbidly obese waddlers, holding out their dominant hands, in supplication to the signal, missing on the open plains. Swayback horses, hitched up for the 'pony rides,' beside the parked SUVs, were secret casualties. No more buffalo would pass before the blown out windows of the rusted Pullman cars. They, and the wagon days of the Wells Fargo stagecoaches, had become the empty shell casings of a more authentic era. The Fairweather Inn had a vacancy. Metal tills inside the general stores, with their scrolled embossing, rang up silence. Red, white and blue stars and bars drooped from their banners.

The bare-breasted paintings that hung over the bottles, inside the bars, suffocated beside the *Cowgirls are Forever* signs and moose heads. Sun-bleached skulls and antlers hung nailed to square wooden facades, and a lone white tipi stood against the thyme and sage, and the big blue sky above the ashen ridge. I asked the trolley car driver if there was a place for a picnic. He grinned through his sunglasses.

"Best picnic spot in the world." He pointed. "Down by the crick."

Robyn and I drove up past the Brewery, with the wagon and Old Glory outside, and turned down into a gulch. There were big old trees for shade, a babbling stream for coolness, and soft grass and rocks and birdsong for contemplation. And there was one picnic table, which I claimed with our French picnic basket. Robyn had made steak sandwiches from the Silver Mill leftover steak, crosscut sawn from the sinew of the Philipsburg night before.

In 1907, a former vigilante showed the residents where George Lane was buried. The exhumed remains included a petrified clubfoot. *It was initially kept in the courthouse, but later moved to the Thompson Hickman Museum in Virginia City,* becoming *one of the Museum's most important exhibits.*

We left Virginia City with a homemade ice cream, like the one that Sheriff Plummer would have had. *The colder it gets, the harder it is to swaller.*

*　　*　　*

'The bigger a man's gun the smaller his doodlewick.'

Calamity Jane

Robyn and I had thought the *Big Sky* boast on the license plates was a Montana myth, until it opened up before us. We were looking farther and seeing less of anything but heaven and earth. *I wanted to be the first to view a country on which the eyes of a white man had never gazed and to follow the course of rivers that run through a new land.* The grey ribbon went to infinity, through a fabric of gold and dotted green, and the hazy purple crenulations along the fringes of our vision. We rode in the direction it was going. Those who had written the history of the Old West hadn't paid more much attention to the women that had come through it. But there were three that, in their own unique way, defined the eras they lived in. All three had the wanderlust, two had ordinary lust, and one had a drinking problem.

Calamity Jane was afflicted with alcoholism, but *her vices were the wide-open sins of a wide-open country – the sort that never carried a hurt.*

Her father died, soon after they left Virginia City. Jane took over as head of the family, loaded up the wagon once more, and took her siblings to Piedmont, Wyoming. She took whatever jobs she could find, a dishwasher, a cook, a waitress, a dance-hall girl, a nurse, and an ox team driver. In 1870, she signed on as a scout at Fort Fetterman, Wyoming. Jane claimed that she served under General George Armstrong Custer, but she claimed a lot of associations and adventures that remained unsubstantiated and, in some cases, were contradicted. One verified story was her swim across the Platte River, and a ninety-mile ride at top speed while wet and cold, to deliver important dispatches for General Crook's detachment on the Big Horn River. The closest she probably got to Custer was during the 'Nursey Pursey Indian Outbreak' of 1872, near present day, Sheridan, Wyoming, although she likely didn't meet him. One of her claims was the manner in which she acquired her nickname.

'It was during this campaign that I was christened Calamity Jane. It was on Goose Creek, Wyoming where the town of Sheridan is now located. Capt. Egan was in command of the Post. We were ordered out to quell an uprising of the Indians, and were out for several days, had numerous skirmishes during which six of the soldiers were killed and several severely wounded. When on returning to the Post we were ambushed about a mile and a half from our destination. When fired upon Capt. Egan was shot. I was riding in advance and on hearing the firing turned in my saddle and saw the Captain reeling in his saddle as though about to fall. I turned my horse and galloped back with all haste to his side and got there in time to catch him as he was falling. I lifted him onto my horse in front of me and succeeded in getting him safely to the Fort. Capt Egan on recovering, laughingly said: "I name you Calamity Jane, the heroine of the plains."'

But in 1904, the Anaconda Standard published a quote from Captain Jack Crawford, who had served under the generals that Jane claimed to have taken orders from ...*never saw service in any capacity under either General Crook or*

General Miles. She never saw a lynching and never was in an Indian fight. She was simply a notorious character, dissolute and devilish, but possessed a generous streak which made her popular. Others maintained that she had obtained her sobriquet as a result of her warnings to men that to offend her was to 'court calamity.' While she worked as a scout at Fort Russell, Jane also found 'on-and-off' employment as a prostitute at the Fort Laramie Three-Mile Hog Ranch.

In 1876, Calamity Jane settled in Deadwood, South Dakota, where she worked, on occasion, as a prostitute for Madam Dora DuFran, and later, as a cook and laundress, for the same patron. She became friendly with Wild Bill Hickok. She later claimed that he fathered her daughter, and that she attacked his murderer with a cleaver, although this is likely fabrication. Hickok, for his part, was not as enamoured with Jane, and apparently went to great lengths to avoid her. Jane lived in the Deadwood area for some time, and at one point she saved several passengers of an overland stagecoach by diverting several Plains Indians who were in pursuit. The driver, John Slaughter, was killed during the pursuit, and Jane took over the reins and drove the stage on to its destination at Deadwood. In late 1876, Jane nursed the victims of a smallpox epidemic, with much kindness and compassion.

In 1893, Calamity Jane started to appear on stage in buckskins, in Buffalo Bill's Wild West Show, as a storyteller. Unlike Annie Oakley, her performances involved no sharpshooting or roping or riding, merely the recitation of her adventures, *which metastasized with each telling*, in colorful but clean language. But she began to live up and down to her name, about six months after her participation in the 1901 Pan-American Exposition. Depression and drinking had driven her colorful language increasingly profane, and ended her career as a stage performer. She died of pneumonia in 1903 and, in accordance with her dying wish (and possibly as a final piece of mischief from his friends), was buried next to Wild Bill Hickok in Mount Moriah Cemetery, overlooking the city of Deadwood.

The second woman was made an honorary fireman in Virginia City. Like Doc Holliday and Sheriff Henry Plummer, and the buffalo, she had tuberculosis, and like Calamity Jane, she loved travel, and men, and exaggeration. Like me, she wanted to be a writer, but other things got in the way.

Adah Isaacs Menken was the highest earning actress of her day. Her origins were obscure, but her real name was likely Ada C. MeCord, born in 1835, in New Orleans, of Auguste Théodore and Magdaleine Jean Louis Janneaux, both mixed race Louisiana Creoles. Ada was raised as a Catholic, fluent in French and Spanish, and danced in the ballet of the local French Opera House as a young girl. After a performance in Havana, where she was crowned 'Queen of the Plaza,' Ada left dance on the stage, for the stage, first in Texas. She married a musician named G.W. Kneass. This lasted less than a year. In

1856 she married another musician Alexander Isaac Menken, who took her home to Cincinnati. Here, she converted to Judaism, and changed her name, adding an 'h' to her first name. She published poetry and articles on Judaism in The Israelite in Cincinnati, and in the Jewish Messenger of New York. Although divorced by Menken, she never abandoned her adopted religion. In 1859, she married a popular Irish-American prizefighter named John C. Heenan, by whom she had a son, who died soon after birth. She met Charles Blondin, famed for having crossed Niagara Falls on a tightrope, and the two had an affair on a vaudeville tour across the country. Adah had suggested she would marry him if they could perform a couple's act above the falls but Blondin refused, saying that he would be 'distracted by her beauty.' In 1862, Adah married Robert Henry Newell, a New York humorist who had published most of her poetry. In 1866 she married a gambler, James Paul Barkley, whom she left while pregnant. She went to France without him, and gave birth to Louis Dudevant Victor Emanuel Barkley; the baby's godmother was the author George Sand. Louis also died in infancy.

Adah's career path had a similar trajectory. Early reviews remarked on her 'reckless energy.' She cultivated a bohemian and at times androgynous appearance. Her first New York play, *The French Spy*, was highly disregarded. The New York Times described her as 'the worst actress on Broadway,' and the Observer was only slight more complimentary. *She is delightfully unhampered by the shackles of talent.* Her business manager, Jimmie Murdock, knew she had little acting ability, but offered her the 'breeches role' (that of a man) of the noble Tartar in the melodrama *Mazeppa*, based on a poem by Lord Byron. At the climax, the Tartar was stripped of his clothing, tied to his horse, and sent off to his death. The audiences were thrilled with the scene, although the production used a dummy strapped to a horse, which was led away by a handler giving sugar cubes. Menken changed the stunt. Dressed in nude tights and riding a horse on stage, she caused the sensation that would bring her success. She went on to play the role in San Francisco and Paris and London. Here, she responded to critics of her costume by remarking that it was 'more modest than ballet or burlesque.' Nonetheless, the controversy made it into the pages of *Punch*.

> 'Here's half the town - if bills be true -
> To Astley's nightly thronging,
> To see the Menken throw aside
> All to her sex belonging,
> Stripping off woman's modesty,
> With woman's outward trappings -
> A barebacked jade on barebacked steed,
> in Cartlich's old strappings!'

Adah attracted a crowd of male admirers, including Charles Dickens, the humorist Tom Hood, and the dramatist Charles Reade. She had affairs with the English poet Algernon Charles Swinburne, and Alexandre Dumas, the French novelist more than twice her age.

In 1867, as she reentered England, her

tuberculosis entered her abdomen. She was forced to stop performing, and her fame and fortune evaporated into pain and poverty. She returned to Paris, where she died the following year, at the age of 33. *I am lost to art and life. Yet, when all is said and done, have I not at my age tasted more of life than most women who live to be a hundred? It is fair, then, that I should go where old people go.*

Her only book, *Infelicia,* a collection of 31 confessional free verse poems, heavily influenced by her Judaism and her association with Walt Whitman, was published several days after her burial in Montparnasse cemetery. Most were about a woman's struggle to find a place in the world.

My own true love was struggling with whatever had entered her eyes. The semitrailer that passed, while she was rubbing them, just about blew us off the road.

The big sky had filled with cotton cloud billows, and the prairie was rising into hills of sage and conifer. We had driven past the Lure Me Inn, at Ennis, and the Water of the Gods Hot Springs, in Norris, and the biggest American flag I had ever seen. Just outside of Harrison was another indication of where we were. *We eat beef in Montana.* I teased Robyn about her pronunciation. *Mon-taw-na.*

"It sounds more beautiful when I say it." She said. *There's two theories to arguin' with a woman. Neither one works.*

We arrived at the Lewis and Clark Caverns towards the end of the afternoon, just before they closed, and just in time for the last tour. Our guide was a bulky girl, with so many multiple piercings along the margin of her left ear, she must have needed to sleep on her right side. I asked her how she liked being a park guide.

"It's hard to get a good job in Montana." She said. But she was good at what she was doing, and ushered us through the constricted apertures and large caves of the monument.

"It starts off small but it doesn't last." She said.

"Like me, when we were first married." I said, before a well-placed elbow found my ribs. We followed a steep descent into molten minerals, moulded into extraterrestrial intraterrestial organic organ pipes and pillars, icicles and waterfalls and coral gardens and cathedral candelabras, wedding cakes and treacle and skeletal skyscrapers. Our echoes entered the largest cavern at the bottom, moments before we did. It was magnificent.

"We call this the Paradise Room." She said. "You can see why."

The sky was still black and angry when we emerged, but the storm had let everything go when we were underground, and our tires were like rattlesnakes, hissing all the way down the mountain.

The wagon landed on the open plains again. Just on dusk, we arrived at a junction. *If you come to a fork in the road, take it.* We would do even better. We were heading to three of them.

*   *   *

'We have an unknown distance yet to run, an unknown river to explore. What falls there are, we know not; what rocks beset the channel, we know not; what walls ride over the river, we know not. Ah, well! We may conjecture many things.'

John Wesley Powell, Old West soldier and explorer

We drove into the town at the headwaters of the longest single river in North America. All the way to the Gulf of Mexico, Three Forks was where the waters of the Jefferson, Madison, and Gallatin converged to form the Missouri. Meriwether Lewis gave them their names in 1805. *Both Capt. C. and myself... agreed to name them after the President of the United States and the Secretaries of the Treasury and state.*

The third woman was twelve years old when the Mennetaree tribe captured her here, five years earlier. They had named the local hostelry after her. *Sacajawea Hotel.*

The magnificent white palace of the plains also had three stories, with a row of three dormers across the top floor, and a wrap-around veranda with hanging baskets and double Dorian columns around the bottom. A flagpole with a big stars and stripes shot straight up out of the equilateral triangular Palladian atop the entrance to the lobby. We climbed the stairs. Inside, a sign outside the restaurant advertised *Tonight- Snow Crab- All You Can Eat.* It had come a long way, like us.

And so had Meriwether Lewis and William Clark and Sacajawea, when they arrived in 1805. It was a strange convergence that night- the

Commonwealth couple, the Discovery Corps, and crustacean corpses. The main thing we had in common with the Lewis and Clark Expedition was that no one of any geographical consequence was eating snow crab in Three Forks.

We had all come because of what had been eating Thomas Jefferson in 1802. It was a book by a British-Canadian explorer, named Alexander Mackenzie. *Voyages from Montreal* was eating Jefferson's brain.

The Pacific Northwest had always been the last temperate *Terra Incognita* of the continent, an expanse of geology too large to lay claim to and, in the same space and time, a crossroads of cultures. After LaSalle's exploration through the guts of it, in 1682, the French established a chain of posts along the Mississippi, from the Great Lakes to New Orleans.

Almost a hundred years later, Thomas Jefferson was the Minister to France of the new United States. He met John Ledyard in Paris and discussed an expedition of exploration to the Pacific Northwest. He had just read Le Page du Pratz's *The History of Louisiana* and, more intensively, Captain James Cook's *A Voyage to the Pacific Ocean*, and was on fire to discover a practical route through the Northwest to the Pacific coast.

In 1787, the French explorer Pedro Vial gave a map of the upper Missouri River and locations of 'territories transited by Pedro Vial' to Spanish authorities. Early in 1792 the American explorer Robert Gray, discovered a big river on the Pacific coast, and named it after his ship, the *Columbia Redivida*. Later in 1792, George Vancouver explored over 100 miles of it, into the Columbia River Gorge.

Alexander Mackenzie's book convinced Jefferson that Britain intended to gain control of the lucrative fur trade on the Columbia River, and that he needed to secure the territory as soon as possible. But everything west of the Mississippi was still unknown to non-natives, except for the existence of the Rocky Mountains, that the upper Missouri seemed to flow from them, and that the large Columbia River entered the Pacific on the other side of them.

In 1803 the US acquired a considerable piece of promise in the Louisiana Purchase, and Jefferson seized his chance to jumpstart his push to the Pacific. Because of his poor relationship with his opposition in Congress, he used a secret message to ask for funding the first American expedition to cross the western United States. Different disguised explanations were provided to British, French and Spanish diplomatic officials.

Jefferson commissioned a Corps of Discovery, and a U.S. Army Captain its leader. He chose a frontiersman, Meriwether Lewis, to be the Captain Cook of uncharted America, rather than a 'qualified scientist,' because *It was impossible to find a character who to a complete science in botany, natural history, mineralogy & astronomy, joined the firmness of constitution & character, prudence, habits adapted to the woods & a familiarity with the Indian manners and character, requisite for this undertaking. All the latter qualifications Capt. Lewis has...* Jefferson sent him to study North American geography in his library at Monticello, navigational instrument use with astronomer Andrew Ellicott, and medicinal cures under the tutelage of physician Benjamin Rush. Lewis chose Lieutenant William Clark as his second in command. In October of 1803 they met at the Falls of the Ohio, near Louisville, and received Jefferson's departure instructions.

> 'The object of your mission is to explore the Missouri River, & such principle stream of it, as, by its course and communication with the waters of the Pacific ocean, whether the Columbia, Oregon, Colorado or any other river may offer the most direct & practicable water communication across this continent for the purpose of commerce.'

There were scientific and economic secondary objectives, to study plants, animal life, geography, and other natural resources, and to engage the Indians in such a way as to establish sovereignty. The U.S. mint prepared a series of special silver Indian Peace Medals, with a portrait of Jefferson inscribed with a message of friendship and peace, for distribution to the nations they met. The expedition was supplied with knives, blacksmithing supplies, cartographic equipment, flags, gift bundles, medicine, black powder and lead for their flintlock firearms, and an advanced .44 caliber air rifle, powerful enough to kill a deer. They carried a description of Moncacht-Apé's transcontinental route a century earlier, which neglected to mention the need to cross the Rockies. This resulted in an unfortunate mistaken belief that they could easily carry boats from the Missouri's headwaters to the Columbia.

The Corps thirty-three members of trained at the Camp Dubois winter staging area in Indiana Territory, near Wood River, Illinois, until their departure at 4 pm, May 14, 1804. The Spanish in New Mexico had already been informed of their true intentions, and sent four armed expeditions of fifty-two soldiers, mercenaries, and Indians from Santa Fe northward, intending to imprison the entire party. When the Spaniards reached the Pawnee settlement on the Platte, they learned that the expedition had been there but Lewis and Clark were covering 80 miles a day and they were too late.

The only member of the Corps to die, Sergeant Charles Floyd, succumbed to the rotten guts of acute appendicitis on August 20, 1804, and was buried on a bluff on the river where Sioux City now stands. The Sioux called themselves the Lakota, and were there before the city. They had a reputation for hostility, and had proudly boasted of the almost complete destruction of the once great Cahokia nation, along with the Missouris, the Illinois, the Kaskaskia and the Piorias tribes, that lived in the upper Mississippi and Missouri river basins. Determined to block free trade on the water, Clark described them as the 'vilest miscreants of the savage race.'

They were in a particularly vile mood when Lewis and Clark arrived, anticipating a retaliatory raid from the Omahas further south, for killing 75 of their braves, burning 40 of their lodges, and taking four dozen prisoners. When the Teton Sioux under Black Buffalo, received gift offerings before their rivals, the Partisan tribe, the resulting tensions required more tribute, including tobacco, and lubrication with a bottle of whiskey, to negotiate further westward passage. *Never follow good whiskey with water, unless you're out of good whiskey.*

The Corps of Discovery stopped near present day Washburn, North Dakota, and built Fort Mandan to overwinter in. Here, they were visited by nearby Hidatsa tribes in numbers, and interviewed prospective trappers who might be able to interpret or guide the expedition up the Missouri River in the spring. On November 4, 1804, Clark wrote in his journal. *A french man by Name Chabonah, who Speaks the Big Belley language visit us, he wished to hire & informed us his 2 Squars were Snake Indians, we engaged him to go on with us and take one of his wives to interpret the Snake language.*

Toussaint Charbonneau was a Quebecois trapper, who had either purchased his two wives, or won them gambling. One was named Otter Woman but it was the other, Bird Woman, pregnant with her first child at the age of eighteen, who would be of the greatest value, because of her fluent Shoshone, and her gentile presence, which served to emphasize the mission's peaceful intent.

When she went into a difficult labour on February 11, 1805, Charbonneau suggested that crushed rattlesnake rattles be administered, to speed the delivery. Lewis just happened to have some, and Sacajawea delivered a healthy baby boy named Jean Baptiste Charbonneau, who Clark nicknamed 'Pompei.'

The Corps left Fort Mandan in April, in *pirogues*, poled against the current and sometimes pulled from the riverbanks, following the Missouri to its headwaters.

On May 14, Sacajawea rescued items that had fallen out of a capsized boat, including the journals of Lewis and Clark, who named the river in her honor. She encouraged the Shoshone to barter horses, and provide guides to lead the expedition over the Rockies. The trip was so hard that they were reduced to eating tallow candles. On their descent, over the Continental Divide at Lemhi Pass, Sacagawea helped the Corps find camas roots to help them regain their strength. She became dangerously ill at Maria's River, but recovered by drinking from the sulfur mineral spring that fed it.

The group carried on down the Clearwater River, the Snake, and the Columbia, past Celilo Falls. As they approached the mouth of the Columbia River, Sacagawea gave up her beaded belt of blue beads in trade for a fur robe for President Jefferson.

The Discovery Corps spent its second bitter winter, on the Pacific coast near Astoria, building Fort Clatsop. The decision had been put to a vote, which had included Sacajawea and

Clark's slave, York, the first time in American history a woman and a slave had been allowed suffrage.

In late March of 1806, the expedition started its return through Idaho, collecting 65 horses to cross the Bitterroot Mountains, still covered in snow. Lewis and Clark split into two teams. Lewis' dog was stolen by Indians, and retrieved. Blackfoot tribes tried to steal his weapons, and two braves were killed in the melee. Clark had half his horses stolen by the Crow in the night, but no one had seen them do it. In July, Sacajawea took the Corps through Gibbons Pass and the Rocky Mountains, and across the Yellowstone basin at Bozeman Pass, which would later be chosen as the optimal route for the Northern Pacific, to cross the continental divide. On August 11, 1806, as the two parties reunited, one of Clark's hunters mistook Lewis for an elk, and shot him in the thigh. A month later they had arrived in St. Louis, and made Jefferson's history.

Clark invited Charbonneau and Sacajawea to settle there, and enrolled Jean-Baptiste in the Saint Louis Academy boarding school. In 1810 Sacajawea gave birth to a daughter, Lizette, and two years later, on December 20, 1812 ...*the wife of Charbonneau, a Snake Squaw, died of putrid fever.*

The expedition she had guided, comprised of the first Americans to cross the continental divide, to see Yellowstone and enter into Montana, that had produced 140 first accurate maps of the area, recorded the whereabouts, lifestyles, customs, activities, social codes, and cultures of at least 72 native American Indian tribes, established legal title to their indigenous lands under the Doctrine of Discovery, and recorded more than 200 plants and animals new to science, would be largely forgotten, scarcely appearing in history books, even during the United States Centennial in 1876, until today.

By any measure, the room we had booked was tiny, so tiny in fact, that there was no way the large bellies we saw, gorging on Alaskan king crab in *Pompei's Grill* downstairs, would have fit through the door, or on the bed. We asked for a room we could move in, but the desk clerk had to track down the manager, who was possibly a Crow brave, because no one had seen him in the night. We wandered outside for the sunset, backlighting the sky with a blazing radiance. *Red Cloud.* A motorcycle gang, a Discovery Corps of subdermal ink and transdermal metal, had taken over the veranda.

"I'm allergic to pigs and bull." Said one particularly vocal member. But they were out of crab in *Pompei's* by the time we were seated, and that's what Robyn and I were left with for dinner. She had the pulled pork, and I had the Bison burger. It was my first taste of buffalo.

I don't really know what Sacajawea would say about the trail she left, or the paradise room in the hotel they named after her. But that buffalo burger, in the restaurant named after her son—that buffalo burger was a hell of a lot better than eating candles.

'I am not a coward, but I am so strong. It is hard to die.'

The last words of Meriwether Lewis

*   *   *

The Last Best Place
Bozeman, Montana

'I'm in love with Montana. For other states I
have admiration, respect, recognition, even
some affection. But with Montana it is love.
And it's difficult to analyze love when you're
in it.'

John Steinbeck, *Travels with Charley*

Neon. The way Calamity Jane came, to get to
Virginia City, had been a dangerous gamble. The
country in between was wild as a corncrib rat.
The trail that was evolving to take her there,
would open up the rest of the Old West and,
finally and truly, link Jane up to General George
Armstrong Custer, through a blazing radiance.
Red Cloud.
Breakfast in bed was mandatory at the
Sacajawea Hotel in Three Forks. The front desk
woke us early, to find out why we hadn't filled in
our official *Breakfast in Bed Special Choices* form
the evening before. As we had been instructed,
when we had checked in. We explained our
preference for coming downstairs to eat in the
dining room, and nothing further had been said.
But that, if it happened, was incorrect, and we
had been expected to fill in our form. We told the
desk that we still wanted to come downstairs for
breakfast and, with some reluctance, agreed to,
on the condition that I give her what would have
been our *Breakfast in Bed Special Choices.*

Imagine our surprise, therefore, when not ten minutes later, our *Breakfast in Bed Special Choices* arrived by themselves. We told the young lady who delivered them that we had been granted special dispensation to eat them in the restaurant. She looked at us quizzically, and withdrew back downstairs. We followed at a safe distance. *If you're sitting at the counter leave your hat on, but if you're sitting at the table take it off.*

It hadn't been worth the effort.

On our way out, we asked how to get to Bozeman?

"Go down Main Street." She said. "Turn right."

Which took us unto into a land of haystacks and wild sunflowers, and black birds with long tails, and blue stripes around their necks.

We followed the Sunflowers to the Madison Buffalo Jump, surrounded by mesas and cactus and sage, and scorching heat. No one was there to collect the five-dollar entrance fee. No one was there to collect the buffalo either, but when there had been, it must have been something to watch. It would have been impossible to distinguish the bison from the Indian impostors in their midst, the ones that panicked the herd into jumping off the cliff, without getting trampled in the stampede. It was a long way down.

The sunflowers took us to Bozeman. We passed an Indian girl, dream-catcher hanging from her mirror. And a billboard. *Life... a beautiful choice.*

The Museum of the Rockies was, according to our Montana guide, a 'must see' destination.

But Jack Horner's dinosaurs were mostly fibreglass casts (the real ones had gone off to the Smithsonian mothership), the outer space exhibit a century ahead of where our heads were at, the winter squash in the outdoor pioneer homestead had been eaten by deer, and the buffalo on the top floor was made of telephone cord and bicycle tires and electric guitars and fire extinguishers. The Indian exhibit was full of screaming white kids. I wondered why progress looked so much like destruction.

I had discovered that my old camera's memory card was full, and back down on Main Street, Jeff and Logan, who found the secret of reformatting it. They recommended the Bacchus Pub for lunch.

"My wife wants to go shopping." I said to the waitress. "What have you got that's fast?"

"Do you want healthy or unhealthy?"

We had one of each. I had the best Reuben in the world, with a Big Sky Moose drool. Robyn had a falafel, with a Madison River Salmon Fly Honey Rye draft. A motorcycle roared by, no helmet, and a red bandana covering his face. Decades earlier, Robert Pirsig, a professor of English composition and rhetoric here at Montana State, had written the definitive guidebook on *Zen and the Art of Motorcycle Maintenance*. It had forced the first step, on my trip around the world.

The waitress returned to inquire after our health. Robyn said she might need a bath.

"Really ready to go shopping, huh?" She said. They both left me alone with the bill.

I wandered down the main drag, looking at the signs of progress.

*Sorry, We're open... Odyssey... John Bozeman Bistro Steaks Seafood...*Robyn and I had heard of the place, but it was a Monday, and closed. We would be eating elsewhere.

I passed under the neon buffalo of *Ted's Montana Grill*, media mogul Ted Turner's steak restaurant. Ted, together with his friend, Tim Blixseth, had built the elite Yellowstone Club, a nearby ski and golf resort for some of the wealthiest people in the country. *Dressed up like a million dollar trouper, Trying hard to look like Gary Cooper (super duper). Come let's mix where Rockefellers walk with sticks. Or umbrellas in their mitts, Puttin' on the Ritz.* It was in bankruptcy because of the recession, and the seventy year old gas line that ran down Main Street, to the Montana Trails Gallery.

At 8:15 on the morning of the 9th of March 2009, an explosion ripped a hole in the heart of downtown Bozeman, leveling five historic buildings that contained thriving businesses, and damaging several more. The director of the gallery, Tara Bowman, was killed. Dozens of plate glass windows were blown out, along with the hopes for a resurgent downtown. The discovery of three more gas leaks didn't help. Ted got off easier than Tim's son, who was issued an` arrest warrant for defaulting on a loan he had taken for another elite mega development planned on the edge of town.

Before there had been an edge, in 1863, John M. Bozeman opened a new northern trail through

the Gallatin Valley, to the goldfields of Virginia City. A year later he founded his town... *standing right in the gate of the mountains ready to swallow up all tenderfeet that would reach the territory from the east, with their golden fleeces to be taken care of.*
Any of the fly rods and reels in *The Bozeman Angler* would have fleeced more gold than I had. *A River Runs Through It.* William Clark would have likely used less expensive gear here in July 1806, at his camp near the mouth of the Kelly canyon.
The old woman staring at the clutter in her antique shop barely looked up.
"That's quite a collection you have." I said.
"Yeah." She said. "I'm just looking it over to see if I can commit any of it to memory." One of the murals off Main Street portrayed an Indian chief overlooking a stagecoach, and a train in a valley of flowers. A river ran through it.
Further along, I was mesmerized by the life-sized standing white stallion twirling on the marquis outside the Gallatin Masonic Lodge, horse whispering of secrets from the same symbol, on the graves of boot hill in Virginia City, and other Old West tombstones we would find. Something happens to a man when he gets on a horse, in a country where he can ride forever. One of the men who rode the path of pilgrimage to authenticity had attended Gallatin Valley High School in Bozeman.

"Authenticity." I said. "The American West was *The Sacred Land-* the gold rush towards truth."
"What's the truth?" He asked.
"The achievement of redemption." I said.
"How do you get that?" He asked.
"By living the authentic life, by living in Nature, and by facing death with dignity and courage."
"Sounds very existential." Said Carolyn.
"That's where the truth lives." I said.

*   *   *

'There ain't never a horse that couldn't be rode...
There ain't never a rider that couldn't be throwed.'

Gary Cooper

Frank James Cooper was born in Helena, Montana in 1901, of English parents. His mother sent him back to a grammar school in Bedfordshire when he was nine. He returned to 'shoveling manure at forty below' on his father's ranch, until his parents moved to Los Angeles. Deciding that he would 'rather starve where it was warm, than to starve and freeze too,' Frank followed them. He failed as a sign salesman, and eventually got a job stunt riding as a cowboy extra at a movie studio, for ten bucks a day plus a box lunch. One of the casting directors noticed him, renamed him after her hometown in Indiana, and made him a star in his first sound picture, *The Virginian*, in 1929. *How was I to know she was a lady? She was with you, wasn't she?*

In 1953, the year I was born, he won the Academy Award for Best Actor for his performance as Marshal Will Kane in *High Noon*. John Wayne accepted it for him. He was sick with an ulcer. *Courage is being scared to death and saddling up anyway.* In 1961, he received an honorary Oscar. An emotional Jimmy Stewart accepted it for him. He was sick with cancer and, when he died a month later, a German newspaper noted that Gary Cooper was 'the symbol of trust, confidence and protection.'

I wandered into Chee's sporting goods store, fully unprepared for the salesman in the hunting room, who was loaded for bear. The room was huge, dimly lit by overhead chandeliers and wall sconce incandescences, and crowded with so many dead species of fur and feather, that double the number may have filled the ark. A grizzly bear stood up behind a counter, mountain goats and raptors near the roof, and heads of the dismembered ungulates filled the spaces in between. Firearms and ammunition and other merchandise of murder were illuminated by spotlights or accompanied by multimedia displays, offerings in the temple of taxidermy.

"Where' ya from?" He asked.

"Vancouver Island." I said.

"I used to be a guide there." He said.

"Really." I said.

"Yep." He said. "Shot a lot of bears in your back

yard." I was sick with disgust. Hunting for food I was a self-acknowledged hypocrite about. Robyn and I had friends that hunted, and gave us meat, in return for our silence. But to simply exterminate a noble sentient creature in the wild, for the same cheap visceral thrill that had come out of the windows of the trains in the Old West, was deplorable.

"Anything grab you?" He asked.

"Hemingway." I said.

"Good man." He said. "Good hunter."

"You know his work?" I asked.

"Nope." He said. "What do you suggest?" *You have two ways of leaving this establishment, my friend. Immediately or dead.*

"Farewell to Arms." I said. He squirmed like a worm in hot ashes. "Gary Cooper played the lead in the 1932 film adaptation. He was a friend of Hemingway's. They used to hunt and ski at Sun Valley together."

"Good man." He said. "He was from here."

"When I was a kid, I had a pet rattlesnake." I said. "I was fond of it, but I wouldn't turn my back on it." *Now turn around and head for the door. Keep movin' and don't do anything sudden with your hands.*

There were different kinds of books, and records and discs, at Vargo's Books and Jazz. The owner was reading one of them, and listening to Miles Davis at the same time. No one else was there.

"You've got a perfect life." I said, on the way out. He smiled, and pointed at the sign, in one of the local book sections. *Montana- The Last Best Place.*

I met Robyn and the end of Main Street, as we had arranged. I asked if she had bought anything. She shook her head.

"You find anything?" She asked. I shook my head as well.

"Let's go check in." She said. And we walked to the wagon.

The bed and breakfast I had booked was an old mansion of one of the first brewers in Bozeman. We found it out near the lone grain elevator and the railroad tracks at the edge of town.

I had written the owners and asked if it was possible to have a room with a minimal amount of train noise. I had read the reviews and the recurrent remarks about locomotives in the middle of the night.

Chris wrote back to tell me that very few people found the train noise excessive, and some even found it hypnotically soporific. I let it lie. *A journey is like marriage. The certain way to be wrong is to think you control it.*

Out near Lehrkind's old derelict brewery, we pulled along the sidewalk, beyond which stood a three-story Queen Anne manor, two wings of brick facade paneled with two shades of green, and railings of the same colour, with white balustrades and scalloped scrollwork. The dentates were red, and some were green.

Verandas hugged the front two sides of the angled mansion. Out of the intersection grew an octagonal shingle-peaked cupola, with a top set of diamond lattice windows. Half-curtains hung from them all. There was a spire on top, a couple of small gargoyles at the roof edges, where you wouldn't have expected them, and creepers on all the surface sunlight they could find, where you would have expected them. An arabesque balcony hung off in the space to our right.

The lawns hadn't been mown for a while. A short walk took us up the California porch stairway. There was a radiant yellow sun inset in the triangular Palladian, above. Potted plants, in various states of vigour, squeezed the veranda shade.

The doorbell, beside the handwritten sign requiring us to remove our shoes, brought no response, even through we were long past the check-in time. We finally found him in the carriage house changing beds, and he became the second interesting part of the experience. *Very imprudent to make your presence known in unsettled country.*

Chris had been a biologist, a Yellowstone park ranger, before he and his partner, now a politically correct euphemistic way of degenderizing relationships, bought the mansion. He thought well of himself, and clearly loved the idea of witty repartee with daily new faces, but you could tell the less savoury elements of running a stagecoach inn were taking their toll. He had become increasingly introverted with each new less-than-erudite experience. I'm not sure his partner was pitching in his share. At two o'clock in the morning Chris had been required to drive out to the airport to pick up patrons that had flown in on a red-eye. His original guest suggestions had evolved into paramilitary ranger rules, and he spoke to you like he was willing to listen only so long, before deciding that any further investment would be a waste of his time. He took our money quickly. *I'd like to buy him for what he's worth, and sell him for what he thinks he is.*

The interior was packed with the period it was built in. Chris showed us a vintage music box, with a large rotating tin wheel, as big and fierce as the rotary saw blade in Philipsburg, punctured with holes at radial intervals. He inserted it into its position, along a row of metal tines, inside its large Victorian wooden cabinet. He cranked the winding mechanism, and a calliope of harmonious tintinnabulation rang out and echoed through the manor.

"I've upgraded you to the Audubon Suite." He said. "In the tower. Near the trains." And then he chuckled. We asked him where to eat. He told us of the Montana Ale Works, just down the street.

"I always send my guests there." He said. "Try the ribs." We left just before dusk. Two barbwire bear cubs and a shears-snipped sheet metal beehive on a tree stood like a tiny tin taxidermy take-off of Chee's, off the crooked sidewalk to our right. The sun was fading. It was as typical an American neighbourhood as you could find anywhere that romance was still more important than reality. The shrubbery encroached over the crumbling sidewalk, a message from the homeowners to keep on moving. American flags cast late afternoon shadows, on the front of the houses. There were mailboxes and gates and dogs, and people on porches, horse whispering quietly.

It was longer that we had been told. There was that uniquely American restaurant phenomenon, a lineup to get in. The difference between a lineup and a queue is that, in a lineup, competitive forces are still at work. It's very stars and stripes.

Our waiter seemed happy to see us, and interested in our trip. He was particularly enthusiastic about Yellowstone, and gave us a list of activities that would have lasted a month. I asked how crowded the park got in September. I knew American national parks were more congested than those in Canada. It was a simple ratio of volume to area. But I had read that, in the month we were visiting, there would be almost three-quarters of a million tourists. I wrote the park service, to ask if the most remote site in the park, the one that didn't take reservations, would be a sure thing or a gamble when we came through. The response was not reassuring. *May not be a problem, as long as you're there by 9 am.* I booked us a bed and breakfast, all the way out the other side of Yellowstone, from Wyoming back into Montana. The proprietress in Gardiner was just as encouraging as Mr. Ranger. *You may have to share the bathroom.*

"It's not crowded at all." The waiter said. And he told us about his secret swimming hole on the Yellowstone River, just a few miles down the road from our Gardiner Bed and Breakfast.

"You'll love it." He said.

Robyn ordered the calamari. I had told her we were a long way from water. It tasted like it had

126

just been caught. I had the ribs.

"Paradise Valley." The waiter said. The same Indian *Valley of the Flowers* whose invasion produced Red Cloud's War, and closed the Bozeman Trail. But in 1866, Nelson Story, a Virginia City gold miner turned cattleman, braved the hostile trail to successfully drive a thousand head of longhorn into Paradise Valley. He had eluded the US Army, who had tried to turn him back, to protect the drive from hostile Indians.

Story's sizeable ranchlands in the Paradise and Gallatin Valleys were ultimately and ironically donated to the establishment of Montana State University, and the contribution, in its Museum of the Rockies, to the cultural history of an entire people. It was some kind of shrine to the Indians whose land he had primed for invasion, a taxidermy temple of the toppled.

The ribs were to die for. Robyn had vanilla crème brûlée for dessert. "Hard to believe this used to the canned peas capital of the world." The waiter said. Indeed.

We arrived back at the mansion at twilight. It was a sunset just like the others we had seen in big sky. Against the silhouettes of the Bridger Mountains and big pines and telephone poles along the railroad tracks, and the last shadows on the brewery's big grain elevator, were laminations of sunflowers, and lamentations of gray clouds and orange and red flames. It was the loneliest sunset in the world. *Red Cloud.*

We turned in, after our baths, under the thick down comforter of the high-back tiger oak bed, surrounded by overstuffed chairs, antique rugs, stained-glass lamps, a leather trunk, and an ornate writing desk, on a protected upper floor with a view of the entire horizon.

Shadowy profiles rolled across the edge of the cobalt sky.

The trains came at intervals through the night. Sometimes it was so quiet you could hear daylight comin.' I had the wildest dream. All night. Evocative. *Dingdingdingdingdingding...*

* * *

Eating Crow
Buffalo, Wyoming

'They made us many promises, more than I can
remember. But they kept but one- They
promised to take our land...and they took it.'
Red Cloud

Iron. Chris wasn't humming next morning, as he
prepared our breakfast. We had asked for it
early, and he hadn't had much sleep. I poured
some coffee, and through an Old West book of
Lyon photographs I'd never seen. There was two
of the Hudson Bay Company trading post in Rat
Portage. Outside the store, in the early morning
light, Indians waited. I showed Chris, over the
stove.
"That's my hometown in Northern Ontario." I
said. "I never thought it had anything to do with
the westerns I used to watch in the Saturday
matinees at the Paramount."
"If you really knew how dirty and raggedy the
Old West was, you wouldn't want any part of it."
He said, dishing out the eggs.
An antique painting of the woman in the hat
wrapped with a scarf, on the Victorian floral
wallpaper behind the breakfast table, looked like
Robyn. We ate quickly, and grabbed our bags.
"Which anniversary is it?" He asked. I had
forgotten about that.
"Thirty-first." I said.
"How'd you like the trains?" He asked. I nodded.
"Don't believe all you hear, spend all you have,

or sleep all you want." He said. "Have fun in Wyoming."

Robyn and I left him, and the edge of town, for the Bozeman Trail. The sun was still above the morning cloud cover, trying to ignite the tan sediment of the mesas. It was a country of sage and juniper, and freedom. *See Grizzly Bears 5 miles*. But not for all.

Gusty crosswinds shook our wagon, as we passed over the Yellowstone River. A skunk had apparently died, not long before we reached the other bank. In a land of logs and elk horns and American flags, we drove through a fire burnout area, and a house on a lone homestead that had been lucky. *Big Timber- wood salvage*. Our map became a metaphor. Crow Reservation Land had cut the Custer National Forest in two, and there was more cleaving to come- fracking in Columbus, and a billboard for *Adam and Eve- your romance superstore- coming to Billings soon*. Three BNSF locomotives pulled a coal train past a van of *Disabled American Veterans*. If you don't meet the devil every now and then, it means you're traveling in the same direction. *Steak ahead...Hunger behind. I am a child not a choice.* Microwave towers crept up over the ridges.

"Those used to be Indians." Robyn said. We passed oil tanks of coal bed natural gas, big *No Smoking* signs wrapped around their curves.

"No peace pipes." I said. There was a momentary shimmer off the plastic tarp of a *Star Ranger* from Jacksonville, Florida. *The time to live and the place to die. That's all any man gets. No more, no less.*

Robyn and I were heading to the graves of two men of the Old West, who got both in spades. The first had been a Civil War hero and in 1866, as a 33 year-old captain in the Second Battalion of the 18th Infantry Regiment, was stationed at Fort Phil Kearny to protect the immigrants traveling to Virginia City goldfields, invading along the Bozeman Trail. Never take down another man's fence. William Judd Fetterman had boasted that with eighty soldiers, he could 'ride through the whole Sioux Nation.' No one had informed the Sioux.

His commanding officer, Colonel Henry Carrington had advanced along the Bozeman Trail ahead of him in June, into Powder River Country, the hunting grounds of the Lakota, Cheyenne and Arapaho. Carrington, with 700 soldiers and 300 civilians, had established three forts along the trail, including his headquarters at Fort Phil Kearny. The fort's construction had been plagued by fifty Indian attacks, and several dozen soldiers and civilians had been killed. The Indians, mounted and mobile, had always appeared in groups of less than a hundred, and stole as many horses as each occasion allowed.

Fetterman's arrival in November put Carrington under pressure, reinforced by an order from General Cooke at Fort Laramie to take the offensive, in response to the 'murderous and insulting attacks.' His first opportunity made Carrington look even less up to the task. Fetterman ended up rescuing him from the hundred Indians trapping his effort to relieve the work detail west of the fort. Two soldiers were killed and four wounded. Carrington's guide, old Mountain Man Jim Bridger, remarked that his troops 'don't know anything about fighting Indians.'

Chastened by the experience, Carrington reconstituted his soldiers and officers into six companies, intensified military training, doubled the number of guards for the wood trains, and kept the fifty serviceable horses he still possessed saddled and ready to sally, from dawn to dark.

When the Indians attacked another group on December 19th, Carrington sent his most cautious officer, Captain Powell, with explicit orders not to pursue them beyond Lodge Trail Ridge, two miles north of Fort Kearny. Powell followed orders, accomplished his mission, and returned safely. The following day, Carrington refused a proposal from Fetterman, to lead a group of civilians in a raid on the Lakota village on the Tongue River, fifty miles away.

But the woodpile doesn't grow much on frosty nights, and the morning of December 21, 1866 was cold enough to freeze the words out of your mouth. About ten o'clock, Carrington dispatched a wagon train, guarded by ninety soldiers, to the nearest source of firewood for Fort Kearny, the 'pinery' about five miles northwest. Less than an hour later, Carrington's pickets on Pilot Hill signaled by flag that they had come under attack. Carrington ordered a relief party of 79 soldiers, and two civilian volunteers. Claiming seniority, Fetterman asked for and was given command. He would finally get his eighty men, and the chance he had been waiting for, to make good his boast.

Once again, Carrington's orders were as clear as the air. 'Under no circumstances' was the relief party to 'pursue over the ridge, that is Lodge Trail Ridge.' The first thing Fetterman did on leaving the fort, was to immediately climb towards the steep hill of snow and ice that was the Lodge Ridge. *If you don't know where you're going, it's a good idea not to use your spurs.*

You can't weigh the facts if you got the scales weighed down with your own opinions, and the most important fact, inaccessible to Fetterman that day, was who was directing tactics on the other side of the Lodge Ridge Trail.

His real name was Maȟpíya Lúta, but that wouldn't fit around the less melodic forked tongues of the white invaders. He was born close by two other forks, on the river that Calamity Jane swam, near what is now the city of North Platte, Nebraska, to equally discordant-sounding Lone Man and Walks As She Thinks. His parents died when he was three, and the future chief of the Oglala Lakota was raised instead, customary among the matrilineal tribe, by his maternal uncle, Old Chief Smoke.

Fetterman was racing to encounter the brilliant radiance of one of the most capable Native American strategists the US Army would ever face, towards the opening gambit of what would become Red Cloud's War.

Before the winter snows would force them to disperse their large encampment on the Tongue River, Red Cloud, and other Indian leaders, had decided to launch a large military operation against Fort Kearny. He assembled almost two thousand warriors north of the Lodge Trail Ridge, more than would be at the Battle of the Little Bighorn ten years later. Cheyenne and Arapaho lay in ambush on the west side of the trail, Lakota on the east. There would be friendly fire collateral damage. Ten warriors were chosen to decoy the soldiers, including a young Oglala named Tȟašúŋke Witkó, who the forked tongues of the white invaders would later call Crazy Horse.

Your life is in the hands of any fool who can make you lose your temper. Fetterman fired volleys at the small group of Indians harassing his flanks and taunting his soldiers. At the top of the ridge, in violation of Carrington's orders, he made the fateful decision to follow the Indian decoys north, rather than turn east to rescue the wagon train. A short time later the flag signal came to Carrington, back at the fort, that the wood train was no longer under attack. He may have thought that Fetterman had successfully routed the Indians by surprising them from the detour he had taken up Long Trail Ridge. But that wasn't what was happening.

Fetterman was out of sight of the fort, pursuing the decoys over the ridge summit with his infantry, sending his calvary further ahead, under the command of 2nd Lt. George Grummond, another distinguished Civil War combat officer, but also a bigamist, who had been court martialed for drunkenness and abuse of civilians. Fetterman made it half a mile further. The decoys gave their own signal, and Red Cloud's ambush erupted from both sides of the trail. *There's no way to get down from a high horse gracefully.*

It was around noon back at the fort, when Carrington heard heavy firing to the north. *Every time you shoot at someone, plan on dying.*

Fetterman's infantry took up position facing outwards in a small circle among some large rocks where, huddled together, he and fifty men were annihilated in desperate hand-to-hand fighting. A mile further on, his thirty horsemen came under sniper fire with bows and arrows, and then charged with spears and clubs. It took twenty minutes for the Indians to kill the infantry, and another twenty to dispatch the calvary, all on foot, using mostly Stone Age weapons. Only six of the 81 soldiers died of gunshot wounds.

Fetterman and his battalion quartermaster, Captain Frederick Brown, committed suicide by shooting each other in the head, at the exact moment that a Lakota warrior named American Horse was slashing Fetterman's throat. *Give me eighty soldiers, and I'll ride through the whole Sioux Nation.* Sometimes you get and sometimes you get got.

The Indians scalped, stripped, and mutilated the bodies of the soldiers, ensuring that they would be unable to partake in the physical pleasures of an afterlife. The next day, as a blizzard was approaching, Carrington found his soldiers, castrated, their eyes torn out and laid on rocks, noses and ears cut off, teeth chopped out, brains taken out and placed on rocks, and hands and feet severed.

The only two civilian volunteers, Wheatley and Fisher, carrying brand-new sixteen-shot Henry repeating rifles which caused a disproportionate number of Indian casualties, had had their faces 'smashed into bloody pulp, and Wheatley had been pierced by more than a hundred arrows.' The last trooper to die in the battle, Adolph Metzger, was an unarmed teenage bugler who had used his instrument as a weapon, until it was battered shapeless. His was the only body that hadn't been mutilated, covered instead with a buffalo hide by his enemies, in tribute to his bravery. Carrington buried the bodies of the Civil War hero, his officers and his men on Boxing Day, in a common trench. Fetterman had never married and left no heirs. His pension was sent to his mother.

What would become known as 'The Battle of the Hundred Slain' was the worst military disaster, with the most casualties ever suffered, by the United States on the Great Plains. An entire US Army command had been exterminated. The mood of the nation built on a belief in their own Manifest Destiny grew sullen, and sour. Over the two years following the Fetterman Massacre, the prosecution of Red Cloud's War would result in a total Indian victory. Red Cloud signed the Treaty of Fort Laramie, which established the Great Sioux Reservation in 1868. The white invaders agreed to abandon their forts and the Bozeman Trail, and to withdraw completely from Lakota territory. *For the first time in its history the United States Government had negotiated a peace that conceded everything demanded by the enemy and which extracted nothing in return.*

Two years later, Red Cloud visited Washington D.C., and met President Ulysses S. Grant. *We eat, we sleep, we rest and soon we'll be all better again.*

But of course, it wasn't to last. Red Cloud's sovereignty over the Powder River country would only endure for another eight years.

In 1874, a US Army reconnaissance mission into the Great Sioux Reservation found gold, in an area held sacred by the local Indians. The General that led the expedition into the Black Hills, would soon have his own 'pretty day for making things right,' just like and a decade after the calamity of Captain William Fetterman. *Well, enjoy it, 'cause once it starts, it's gonna be messy like nothing you ever seen.*

'I have two mountains in that country- the Black Hills and the Big horn Mountain. I want the Great Father to make no roads through them. I have told these things three times; now I have come to tell them the fourth time.'

Mahpiua Luta (Red Cloud)

*   *   *

'The easiest way to eat crow is while it's still warm.'
Cowboy Proverb

Our wagon headed south, off the main Interstate that had cemented the Atlantic to the Pacific, onto the road that had fused the interloper to the indigenous. A lone combine stirred the yellow dust of Bauxauwashee. *Welcome to Crow Country.* They had been his scouts. *Fireworks. No Services.* We took the off ramp. *Exit 510 Casino Little Bighorn......*
It became an overpass. I would have wondered what would be out here in the middle of nowhere, that would require an overpass, but I already knew. We pulled into a big parking lot, full of license plates from all over America. *Just because you're following a well-marked trail doesn't mean that whoever made it knew where they were going.*
"This wasn't just a battle over whether the land was made for buffalo or of gold." I said. This was the final war over the meaning of life. Either we belong to the land, or the land belongs to us, constituent or commodity, existential or exploitative.
"Just a point on our path of pilgrimage." Robyn said. Authenticity and redemption come from living the authentic life, by living in Nature, and by facing death with dignity and courage.
"Remember when Richard asked me what that had to do with the American West?" I asked.
"You said it was *The Sacred Land.*" She said.
"The gold rush towards truth."

"On the shelves beside Hemingway's work desk were two books on General Custer's fall at the Battle of the Little Big Horn." I said. "One more book than on any other topic. The two men whose paths crossed here were the ultimate symbols of the ultimate clash of cultures."

"More than Red Cloud and Fetterman?" Robyn asked.

"More." I said. The first was named Jumping Badger, at his birth on the Yellowstone River, in 1831. *God made me an Indian. If the Great Spirit had desired me to be a white man, he would have made me so in the first place.* Eight years later, on the other side of the germs, guns and steel, a Michigan blacksmith of German descent, had a son.

With his first youthful courage, in a battle between his Lakota and the Crow, Jumping Badger was given one of his father's names, Thathaŋka Iyothaŋka. *Sitting Bull.*

In 1858, the blacksmith's son was admitted to West Point. Over the next three years he came close to expulsion as many times, due to excessive demerits, many from the pranks he pulled on his fellow cadets. Gonorrhoea had sterilized his reproductive potential, but not his charm. Even the officer who graduated last in his class could do well in the Civil War that had just begun. He burst onto his first calvary brigade command, the Battle of Bull Run, distinguishing himself with an aggressive, fearless willingness to lead attacks, at great personal risk. What some claimed as foolhardy or reckless, and he called 'luck' was actually a battle style of meticulous planning- scouting the battlefield, gauging the enemy's strengths and weaknesses, ascertaining the best line of attack, and then satisfied, and only then satisfied, launching his surprise 'Custer Dash with a Michigan yell.' He rose quickly, to brigadier general at the age of 23, the 'Boy General' darling of the press, in his polished cavalry boots, tight olive corduroy trousers, black velveteen hussar jacket with silver piping on the sleeves, a sailor shirt with silver stars on his collar, and a red cravat. His blond German hair, generously sprinkled with cinnamon-scented oil, bounced in long ringlets, under a wide-brimmed slouch hat. His showy style alienated some of his men; others began to wear red neckerchiefs.

On July 3, 1863, Custer led a mounted charge of the 1st Michigan Cavalry, breaking the back of Jeb Stuart's Confederate assault at Gettysburg. 'I challenge the annals of warfare to produce a more brilliant or successful charge of cavalry,' He wrote, despite his loss of 257 men, the most of any Union brigade. He was present at General Robert E. Lee's surrender at Appomattox Court House. General Sheridan, who included a note praising Custer's gallantry, gave the table upon which it was signed as a gift to his wife. The following year, Sitting Bull defended a village against two brigades of over two thousand soldiers. In an attack he led a wagon train near Marmath, North Dakota, a bullet that had entered his left hip, left the small of his back. *In my early days, I was eager to learn and to do things, and therefore I learned quickly.*

After the Civil War, in 1865, Sheridan sent Custer to lead the Military Division of the Southwest on an arduous eighteen day march in August, from Louisiana to Texas, so hot they could have boiled beans with their tears. The five regiments of veteran Western Theater cavalrymen were waiting to be mustered out of Federal Service, but found themselves instead under the vain discipline of an Eastern dandy. Several planned to ambush Custer, but he was warned the night before.

Although the depletion of buffalo herds was driving more and more tribes into the agencies, Sitting Bull had refused to sign Red Cloud's Treaty of Fort Laramie, and continued to lead hit-and-run guerrilla attacks against forts along the upper Missouri. *Look at me, see if I am poor, or my people either. The whites may get me at last, as you say, but I will have good times till then. You are fools to make yourselves slaves to a piece of fat bacon, some hard-tack, and a little sugar and coffee.*

Custer was mustered out of the volunteer service, denied the opportunity for ten thousand dollars in gold as adjuvant general of the Mexican army, and toured instead with President Andrew Johnson's 'Swing Around the Circle' train journey as head of the Soldiers and Sailors Union, in support of his reconstruction policies towards the South.

When the new U.S. 7th Cavalry Regiment was formed at Fort Riley, Kansas, to prosecute the Indian Wars, Custer was appointed Lieutenant colonel. Beyond his familiar red cravat, every conceited component of his costume converted to buckskin. His troopers nicknamed him 'Iron Butt and 'Hard Ass,' for his saddle stamina and strict discipline, and 'Ringlets' for his vanity. After taking part in an expedition against the Cheyenne in 1867, he was court-martialed for abandoning his post to see his wife. Maj. Gen. Sheridan, allowed him to return to duty, before the term of his year's suspension had expired.

On November 27, 1868, Custer led the 7th Calvary in an assault on Black Kettle's encampment. The Battle of Washita River was a massacre. He killed 103 warriors, an indeterminate number of women and children, and most of the 875 Indian ponies. The remaining Southern Cheyenne went onto an assigned reservation.

Three years later, Sitting Bull 'most vigorously' attacked survey parties mapping a proposed railway route through Hunkpapa Lakota lands. The 'Panic of 1873' halted construction, and forced the Northern Pacific's backers into bankruptcy. In August, near the Tongue River, Custer and the 7th Cavalry clashed for the first time with the Lakota. One man on each side was killed.

Tensions increased considerably in 1874, when Custer's discovery and announcement at French Creek triggered the Black Hills Gold Rush. The US government was increasingly pressured to open the Lakota lands to mining and settlement. Towns like Deadwood, notorious for their lawlessness, appeared overnight. The Lakota delegation that met with President Grant in

Washington in 1875, including Red Cloud, attempted to persuade him to honour the existing treaties, and stem the flow of miners into their dominion. Grant offered them $25,000 and resettlement onto reservations. Spotted Tail told him to pound sand. *When I was here before, the President gave me my country, and I put my stake down in a good place, and there I want to stay.... You speak of another country, but it is not my country; it does not concern me, and I want nothing to do with it. I was not born there.... If it is such a good country, you ought to send the white men now in our country there and let us alone.*

In November, the Interior Department of the Grant government set a deadline of January 31, 1876 for all Lakota and Arapaho wintering in the 'unceded territory' outside the Great Sioux Reservation, to report to their designated reservations or be considered 'hostile.' They suspected that not all would comply, and knew full well the one man who wouldn't.

Instead, Sitting Bull created the Sun Dance 'unity camp' alliance between the Lakota and the Northern Cheyenne, Hunkpapa, Oglala, Sans Arc, and Minneconjou and a large number of 'Agency Indians' who had slipped away to join them. He sent scouts to the reservations to recruit new warriors, and generously shared his resources. His reputation for 'strong medicine' developed as he evaded the Americans. Over the course of the first half of 1876, Sitting Bull's Ash Creek camp expanded into the largest gathering of Plains Indians ever recorded. Natives joined him for safety in numbers, to discuss what to do about the whites. By the time he had moved to the banks of the Little Bighorn River, he had created an extensive village 3 miles long, containing more than ten thousand people. *God put in your heart certain wishes and plans; in my heart, he put other different desires.*

On February 1, 1876, the US Army began to track down their 'hostiles.' Six weeks later, Captain Reynolds attacked Wooden Leg's Northern Cheyenne, who fled to Sitting Bull for safety. Custer was supposed to have led the corresponding expedition against the Sioux two days earlier, but was stuck in Washington, subpoenaed to testify against President Grant's brother Orville, among others, who had been involved in Secretary of War Belknap's kickback scandal, supplying troops with defective weapons and hostile Indians with superior ones. It didn't endear him to President Grant. Custer was accused of perjury and disparagement of brother officers, and vilified in the press. Grant gave orders to appoint another officer to command the operation against the Sioux. General Sherman asked Grant to meet with Custer. Grant refused. Custer took a train to Chicago. Sherman ordered General Sheridan to intercept him. Sheridan, together with Sherman and General Terry wrote to Grant accepting Custer's 'guilt' and promise of future restraint, and presented the advantages of Custer's leadership of the expedition. Grant became apprehensive above being blamed if the 'Sioux campaign' failed for ignoring the recommendations of his senior army officers, and gave the green light for Custer to take command. Grant had nothing to lose. Custer had everything to prove.

On May 17, 1876, the 7th Cavalry departed westward from Fort Abraham Lincoln in the Dakota Territory, together with the 17th U.S. Infantry, the 20th Infantry Gatling gun detachment, and teamsters driving 150 wagons and pack mules. He arrived at the mouth of the Powder River, with the rest of Brig. Gen. Alfred Terry's column, twelve days later, to await the arrival of the twenty companies of Brig. Gen. George Crook's column coming north from Fort Fetterman in the Wyoming Territory, and the steamboat *Far West*, loaded with 200 tons of supplies. At Fort Snelling, Custer had said that he would 'cut loose' from Terry the first chance he got.

During a Sun Dance on the Rosebud Creek on June 5, 1876, Sitting Bull had a vision of *soldiers falling into his camp like grasshoppers from the sky.* Twelve days later, Crook's column limped back from the Battle of the Rosebud, to wait for reinforcements.

A week before the clash of civilizations, Sitting Bull fasted, sacrificed over a hundred pieces of flesh from his arms, and had his most intense revelation. *The Great Spirit has given our enemies to us. We are to destroy them. We do not know who they are. They may be soldiers.*

On June 22, Terry ordered Custer and his 7th Calvary of 31 officers and 566 enlisted men to begin a pursuit along the Rosebud, with the option to 'depart from orders upon seeing sufficient reason.' Two evenings later, his scouts arrived at the Crow's Nest, a viewpoint fourteen miles east of the Little Bighorn River. *The earth has received the embrace of the sun and we shall see the results of that love.*

*   *   *

'There are three kinds of men: The ones that learn by reading. The few who learn by observation. The rest of them have to pee on the electric fence.'
                                            Will Rogers

It was a clear and sunny morning, like it had been. The sunrise on June 25, 1876, brought reports of a massive pony herd and Indian encampment in the distance, and news that Custer's own trail had been discovered. He didn't know that the group that had found his tracks was leaving, and hadn't alerted the village. Custer had planned to wait another day before attacking, but his first priority was to prevent a scattered southern escape by any of the tribes, and he decided to carry out an assault on the south end of their camp without further delay. His Crow scouts warned him about the size of the settlement.

"General, I have been with these Indians for 30 years, and this is the largest village I have ever heard of." Said Mitch Bouyer.

Custer's field strategy had soared into the psychological. His initial objective was the capture of noncombatant women, children, elderly and disabled, to serve as hostages and human shields. He had described the tactics in his book, *My Life on the Plains*, published just two years before the Battle of the Little Big Horn.

'Indians contemplating a battle, either offensive or defensive, are always anxious to have their women and children removed from all danger...For this reason I decided to locate our camp as close as convenient to the village, knowing that the close proximity of their women and children, and their necessary exposure in case of conflict, would operate as a powerful argument in favor of peace, when the question of peace or war came to be discussed... ride into the camp and secure noncombatant hostages and force the warriors to surrender... would be obliged to surrender, because if they started to fight, they would be shooting their own families.'

Custer prepared to attack in full daylight, and divided his regiment into three battalions. Major Marcus Reno's companies would be sent west across the Little Bighorn River to launch a direct northern attack on the southern end of the encampment. Captain Frederick Benteen was instructed to head northwest to intercept any attempted escape, and force fleeing noncombatants up the bluffs above the river. Custer would make a wide detour to the east, and capture the women and children at the top. They left at noon.

Major Reno crossed the Little Bighorn at the mouth of what is today Reno Creek around 3:00 pm. He began his charge northwest, without any accurate knowledge of the village's size, location, or its disposition to stand and fight.

The thick bramble of trees along the southern banks of the Little Bighorn not only screened his men's rapid advance across the wide meadow, they blocked any view of the Indian encampment they were racing toward. The scene around the river bend almost stopped him dead in his tracks. Neither was far off. *The river always runs one way, and it runs to something bigger.*

Five hundred yards short of the village, Reno ordered his men to halt and dismount, and deploy in a skirmish line. Every fourth rider held the horses for the others to assume firing positions at ten-yard intervals, officers to their rear and the troopers holding the horses behind the officers. This formation reduced Reno's firepower by twenty-five percent. The soldiers began firing into the camp, killing several wives and children of the Sioux leader, Chief Gall.

More than five hundred mounted Lakota and Cheyenne warriors streamed out en masse to meet the attack, riding hard against Reno's exposed left and rear flanks, forcing the entire regiment to take hasty cover in the trees along the bend in the river. *The very earth seemed to grow Indians.* Reno's assessment that they were present 'in force and not running away,' was not even close. *This is a good day to die. Follow me!...*

I give you these because they have no ears.
The Indians set fire to the brush. Reno's scout, Bloody Knife, sitting on his horse next to him, was shot in the head. His blood and brains splattered the side of Reno's face. "All those who wish to make their escape." Said Reno. "Follow me." He led a disorderly rout across the river toward the cliffs on the other side, immediately disrupted by Cheyenne attacks at close quarters. Reno's bloody retreat, up and onto the same bluffs that Custer had planned for Indian women and children, cost him a quarter of his command. Captain Benteen's column, meanwhile, had been summoned by Custer's bugler with a handwritten message. *Come on...big village... be quick...bring ammunition.* But it came as he arrived from the south to encounter Reno's badly shaken and wounded troops, atop the bluffs now known as Reno Hill, just in time to save them from annihilation.

Rather than continuing on toward Custer's summons, and despite hearing heavy gunfire from the north, Benteen's regiment helped Reno's troopers dig rifle pits with knives, eating utensils, mess plates, pans, and whatever other implements they had.

Around 5:00 pm, Capt. Thomas Weir and Company D moved out against orders to make contact with Custer. They advanced a mile, to a distant view of mounted Native warriors shooting at objects on the ground. They returned to their comrades entrenched on the bluffs, to be pinned down for another day, until General Terry's brought relief on June 27. And news.

Robyn and I read the names on the tall white obelisk. There were no Indian names. On the near slope opposite was a 'Danger' sign with a crude embossed diamond-back rattlesnake, and a concentration of stone markers, scattered like a handful of corn kernels on a dirt floor. One had a badge-shaped black patch and a spate of periods. *G.A.Custer BVT. Maj. Gen. Lt. Col. 7th Cav. Fell Here June 25 1876.*

What happened to Custer on the ridge that day remains in the air among the markers, since none of the 208 men, in the five companies under his immediate command, survived the battle.

We know he rode north in a wide circular detour, hidden from the encampment by the cliffs, planning to sandwich and 'seize women and children' fleeing to the bluffs between his attacking troopers and Reno's command, in a 'hammer and anvil' maneuver.

He came to a crossing which provided 'access to the women and children fugitives,' within 'striking distance of the refugees,' before Indian sharpshooters firing from the brush along the west bank, and hundreds of warriors massing around the bluffs, repulsed and forced him back to Custer Ridge. *If your horse doesn't want to go there, neither should you.*

The young man who helped decoy William Fetterman to his death a decade earlier led the surprise charge that Custer had thought uniquely belonged to him. Whichever way your luck is running, it's bound to change. *The sun doesn't shine on the same dog's tail all the time.* The Indians fielded over 3,500 warriors that day, and Crazy Horse's charge delivered a swarming Lakota and Cheyenne cluster to Custer, completely overwhelming the iron-butted, hard-assed, ringleted boy general glory hunter, and his calvarymen. *No man in the wrong can stand up against a fellow that's in the right and keeps on a-comin'.*

"Hurrah boys, we've got them!" Said Custer. "We'll finish them up and then go home to our station." *Our capacity for self-delusion is boundless.*

Myles Keogh's men fought and died where they stood but pandemonium broke down the command structure everywhere else. Many orders were given, but few obeyed. Soldiers threw down their weapons, dismounted, held or hobbled their horses, or turned them loose. *After that the fight did not last long enough to light a pipe.*

About forty men made a desperate stand around Custer on Last Stand Hill, delivering volley fire. The space was too small to secure a defensive position, too small to accommodate the wounded, the dying, and the dead. With no doubts about prospects for survival, surviving troopers put up their most dogged defense, shooting their remaining horses to use as breastworks for a final stand. *When your horse dies, get off.* There is something about the outside of a horse that is good for the inside of a man. They shot the great majority of the Indian casualties on Custer Hill, far more here than anywhere else. At the end they shot each other, and themselves.

"We circled all around them." The warrior Two Moons said. "Swirling like water round a stone." Indian warriors rode down the fleeing troopers with lances, coup sticks, and quirts. Almost thirty troopers ended up in a deep ravine three hundred yards away, their deaths the battle's final actions. *Deep Ravine Trail... Stay on gravel trail... No smoking... Violators will be fined...Steep grades/Uneven surfaces... Rattlesnakes.* It was, a running fight, a panicked rout, a buffalo run. Indian women ran up from the village, waving blankets to scare off the soldiers' horses, and used stone mallets, ten pounds of round cobble on a rawhide handle, to finish off the wounded.

Crazy Horse's warriors annihilated every man in Custer's command in less than one-half hour, *as long as it takes a hungry man to eat a meal.* The only survivors were a Crow scout, Curley, and Captain Keogh's horse, Comanche.

A Michigan yell and a Hokey Hey.

'One does not sell the earth upon which the people walk.'
                    Tashunka Inyanke (Crazy Horse)

*   *   *

152

> 'Never run a bluff with a six gun.'
> Bat Masterson

In June 2005, the Northern Cheyenne, breaking more than a century of silence, revealed that Buffalo Calf Road Woman, a heroine of the Battle of the Rosebud, had knocked Custer off his horse before he died. Two other women shoved their sewing awls into his ears, to allow his corpse to 'hear better in the afterlife,' because he had broken the promise he made to Chief Stone Forehead, to never again fight against Native Americans.

Custer was found with shots to the left chest and left temple. Heartless and mindless. Tin man. Straw man. Either wound would have been fatal, though he appeared to have bled from only the chest wound, an indication that his head wound may have been delivered post-mortem. His two younger brothers, Thomas Custer and Boston Custer, had both died with him.

Two days later, General Terry found the 7th Cavalry's dead corpses stripped of their clothing, firearms and ammunition, ritually mutilated and scalped, and in an advanced state of decomposition, making identification of many impossible. Most of the bullet holes had been caused by ranged rifle fire. Under threat of attack, they were hastily buried, covered by pieces of tent canvas and blankets, side by side in a shallow grave, where they had fallen. A year later, Custer's remains were recovered and sent back east for reinterment with full military honours, at West Point Cemetery.

The rest had stayed behind with Robyn and I, at the National Cemetery of the Little Bighorn Battlefield National Monument. William Fetterman's headstone was here. A lone tipi overlooked two fields of graves. One cemetery plaque looked toward the battlefield. *The muffled drum's sad roll has beat The soldier's last tattoo No more on Life's parade shall meet That brave and fallen few.* One looked away. *On Fame's eternal camping ground Their silent tents are spread And Glory guards with solemn round The bivouac of the Dead.*

Inside the museum was a dramatic depiction of 'Custer's Last Stand,' the painting commissioned by Anheuser-Busch. Reprints had been framed and hung in saloons across the United States, forever connecting the golden boy and the golden brew in the hearts and minds of bar patrons.

But, if Custer had been as good as he was supposed to have been, why did it all go so wrong? Here is very little neutral ground.

Custer clearly overestimated his own ability, and that of his troops.

Four days before the battle, he had turned down General Terry's offer of an additional battalion, four companies, of the 2nd Cavalry, stating that he 'could whip any Indian village on the Plains' with his own regiment. At the steamer *Far West* on the Yellowstone, he left behind the battery of Gatling guns, provided for his regiment. The heavy, hand-cranked weapons could fire up to 350 rounds a minute, but each had to be hauled by four horses, soldiers often had to drag the heavy guns by hand over obstacles, and they were known to jam. Custer believed they would impede his march and hamper his mobility. Before leaving the camp all his troops boxed their sabres and sent them back with the wagons.

The life of a soldier was a 'glittering mishap.' The 7th Cavalry had been carved out of a few Civil War veterans, returning from constabulary duty in the Deep South. A quarter of the troopers had been enlisted in the prior seven months, were marginally trained, and had no combat or frontier experience. A sizable number were immigrants from Ireland, England and Germany. Many were malnourished and in poor physical condition. Fourteen officers assigned to the regiment (including the regimental commander) and 152 troopers, did not accompany the 7th during the campaign. Twenty-two per cent of its soldiers had been detached for other duty, three of the regiment's 12 captains were permanently absent, two officers had never served a day since their appointment, and three second lieutenant vacancies were still unfilled.

Custer's plan 'to live and travel like Indians; in this manner the command will be able to go wherever the Indians can' had resulted in a rapid march en route to the Little Big Horn, averaging 30 miles a day. His men were tired.

Government Indian agents had provided an estimate of 'hostiles' the Army could expect to face. 'Fewer than eight hundred,' they said, based on the number that Sitting Bull had led off the agency. It was wrong by an order of magnitude, by the several thousand 'reservation Indians' that had joined him for the summer buffalo hunt. More concerned about preventing the escape of the Lakota and Cheyenne than fighting them, Custer conducted an inadequate reconnaissance before launching his attack. He ignored the advice of his scouts, who began to change back into their native dress right before the battle. *If your mind's not made up, don't use your spurs.*

Custer was unable to communicate with his divided force, relying on rifle volleys to bring support to another unit's aid. He assumed that Benteen would have quickly come to his.

Unlike the valley, the heights above the Little Bighorn River were completely unsuited for mounted troops. Direct fire at the Indians through the dense scrub would have been difficult. The exposed terrain to which Custer led his troops actually gave deadly advantage to the bows and arrows of the Lakota and Cheyenne, in the heavy sagebrush below. The large volume of iron-tipped shafts that flew upward over obstacles at the puffs of smoke from the weapons of the troopers inflicted massive casualties. Custer's men were trapped on higher ground. Indian women rushed troopers waving blankets and bright robes to induce panic in the cavalry mounts, forcing troopers to choose between holding their horse's reins or letting go to return fire. Aiming soldiers also had their hands pulled upwards by the frightened mounts, which resulted in weapons discharged uselessly into the air. When horses carrying ammunition packs were driven off, the Indians quickly gained control of them. They systematically stripped dead soldiers of guns and cartridge belts, their firepower steadily increasing as Custer's losses mounted and his return fire became silent.

Also, and paradoxically, the Indians were armed with repeating Spencer, Winchester and Henry rifles, while the 7th Cavalry carried single-shot Springfield Model 1873 carbines, which not only had a slower rate of fire, but also were cursed with an additional fault.

The Army had chosen single-shot rifles over repeating weapons to prevent overuse of ammunition, emphasizing marksmanship to economize on the costs of transporting cartridges along a 1,000-mile supply line.

But the Springfield's copper cartridges expanded in the breech when heated upon firing; the ejector would cut through the copper and leave the case behind, and the rifle would jam. The carbine version used by the cavalry did not come with a cleaning rod that could have been used to clear stuck cartridges. Troopers were forced to extract them manually with knife blades; thus, the carbines were nearly useless in combat except as clubs. Custer's men's were not terribly familiar with the Springfields, as they had been issued only weeks before the battle. Lakota accounts noted his soldiers throwing down their rifles, in panic or anger, or both.

Finally, Custer was in a hurry to redeem himself, from the scandal he had left behind back east. President Grant still had no love for him. *I regard Custer's Massacre as a sacrifice of troops, brought on by Custer himself, that was wholly unnecessary – wholly unnecessary.*

As the country celebrated its centennial, citizens accustomed to battlefield victories and inherent Manifest Destiny superiority, were stunned by the news of the defeat. They were in no mood to recognize the reality of the historic mistreatment of Native Americans defending their traditional lands and way of life against the relentless westward expansion of European-American invaders, aided by the U.S. Army. Custer was a cavalier without fear and beyond reproach, a tragic military hero and exemplary gentleman who sacrificed his life for his country. Frederick Whittaker rushed out a reverential biography the same year of his death. Henry Wadsworth Longfellow wrote an adoring erroneous poem. 'Buffalo Bill' Cody popularized him as a heroic officer fighting valiantly against savage forces, in his Wild West extravaganzas. President Teddy Roosevelt's lavish praise pleased Custer's widow. Marble monuments and memorials sprung up like mushrooms- counties and towns were named after him in six states, as well as a national cemetery, a military camp and reservation, a museum, and a state park and a hill. *No, sir. This is the West, sir. When the legend becomes fact, print the legend.*

From the Indian perspective, the Battle of the Little Bighorn was the beginning of the end of the Indian Wars, their own last stand. Any white prisoners were tortured and killed the night of the victory. Three charred and burned heads were later found in the vacated village near the scene of the big war dance.

Within 48 hours after the battle, the large encampment on the Greasy Grass broke up into an exodus. Many of the Indians slipped back to the reservation, leaving only about 600 warriors still at large, and hostile. Crook and Terry finally took the field with two thousand reinforcements against the Indians in August. In May 1877, Sitting Bull escaped to Canada. Within days, Crazy Horse surrendered at Fort Robinson, and The Great Sioux War was over.

Threatened with starvation under the direction of the Manypenny Commission, the Lakota ceded the Black Hills, their *Paha Sapa*, to the United States.

Sitting Bull remained in exile for four years near Wood Mountain, Saskatchewan, refusing a pardon and the chance to return. The Canadian Mounties Commander, James Morrow Walsh, who explained that the Lakota were now on British soil and subject to British law, had welcomed him. The two became good friends for the remainder of their lives. *There is no use talking to these Americans. They are all liars, you cannot believe anything they say.*

Because of the smaller size of the buffalo herds in Canada, and a growth in tension between the Canadian and the US governments, Sitting Bull, and 186 of his family and followers surrendered to the Americans on July 19, 1881. The Army transferred Sitting Bull and his band to the Fort Yates agency, and then loaded onto a steamboat to Fort Randall, as prisoners of war, for almost two years.

In May 1883, they were moved again, this time north to the Standing Rock Agency in South Dakota. And this is where the story goes strange. In 1885, Sitting Bull was allowed to leave the reservation to join Buffalo Bill Cody's Wild West Show.

He earned fifty dollars a week for riding once around the arena, and gave speeches about his desire for education for the young, and reconciling relations between the Sioux and whites. In the four months he stayed with Cody, his audiences began to view him as a romantic warrior. He gave his money away to beggars.

At dawn on December 15, 1890, back at Standing Rock, Sitting Bull was shot in the heart and in the head by agency native police, in a raid to prevent him from supporting the Ghost Dance movement of magical bulletproof spirit shirts and returning buffalo. He died six hours later, and was buried at Fort Yates in a coffin made by a U.S. Army carpenter.

During the firing, the old show horse that Buffalo Bill had presented to him began to go through his tricks. At the crack of a gunshot, the mount had been trained to raise one hoof. For the faithful at Standing Rock that day, the horse sat upright, held a hoof aloft, and seemed to be performing the Dance of the Ghosts.

'All Indians must dance, everywhere, keep on dancing. Pretty soon in next spring Great Spirit come. He bring back all game of every kind. The game be thick everywhere. All dead Indians come back and live again. They all be strong just

like young men, be young again. Old blind
Indians see again and get young and have fine
time. When Great Spirit comes this way, then all
Indians go to mountains, high up away from
whites. Whites can't hurt Indians then. Then
while Indians way up high, big flood comes like
water and all white people die, get drowned. After
that, water go away and then nobody but Indians
everywhere and game all kinds thick. Then
medicine man tell Indians to send word to all
Indians to keep up dancing and the good time
will come. Indians who don't dance, who don't
believe in this word, will grow little, just about a
foot high, and stay that way. Some of them will
be turned into wood and be burned in fire.'

Wovoka, the Paiute Messiah

In 1909, Red Cloud died at the age of 87 on the
Pine Ridge Reservation, where he was buried.
President Kennedy considered naming a ballistic
missile submarine after him, but the Pentagon
objected that it might be misinterpreted as pro-
Communist.

After litigation spanning 40 years, the United
States Supreme Court, in the 1980 decision
United States v. Sioux Nation of Indians,
acknowledged that the US Government had
taken the Black Hills without just compensation.
The Lakota refused the money offered, and
continue to insist on their right to their land.
The profile of Crazy Horse is returning in stone.
We did not give you our land; you stole it from us.

In 2010, a research team at the University of
Copenhagen, announced their intention to
sequence the genome of Sitting Bull, with the
approval of his descendants, using a hair sample
obtained during his lifetime. So far, no one has

announced a similar plan to clone anything that might resemble George Armstrong Custer. *Hokey Hey.*

'In that desolate land and lone,
Where the Big Horn and Yellowstone
Roar down their mountain path,
By their fires the Sioux Chiefs
Muttered their woes and griefs
And the menace of their wrath.

'Revenge!' cried Rain-in-the-Face,
'Revenue upon all the race
Of the White Chief with yellow hair!'
And the mountains dark and high
From their crags re-echoed the cry
Of his anger and despair.

In the meadow, spreading wide
By woodland and riverside
The Indian village stood;
All was silent as a dream,
Save the rushing a of the stream
And the blue-jay in the wood.

In his war paint and his beads,
Like a bison among the reeds,
In ambush the Sitting Bull
Lay with three thousand braves
Crouched in the clefts and caves,
Savage, unmerciful!

Into the fatal snare
The White Chief with yellow hair
And his three hundred men
Dashed headlong, sword in hand;
But of that gallant band
Not one returned again.

The sudden darkness of death
Overwhelmed them like the breath
And smoke of a furnace fire:
By the river's bank, and between
The rocks of the ravine,
They lay in their bloody attire.

But the foemen fled in the night,
And Rain-in-the-Face, in his flight
Uplifted high in air
As a ghastly trophy, bore
The brave heart, that beat no more,
Of the White Chief with yellow hair.

Whose was the right and the wrong?
Sing it, O funeral song,
With a voice that is full of tears,
And say that our broken faith
Wrought all this ruin and scathe,
In the Year of a Hundred Years.
Henry Wadsworth Longfellow, *The
Revenge of Rain-In-The-Face*

*   *   *

'Always take a good look at what you're about to
eat. It's not so important to know what it is, but
it's critical to know what it was.'
Cowboy Proverb

"Y'all like Indian tacos?" She asked. Her T-shirt
was topical. *I'm so cute I must be Crow.* I asked

163

her what Indian tacos were.

"There kinda like Mexican tacos but we make them with fried bread." She was cute. We had the tacos.

The Trading Post at the bottom of the hill from where Custer last stood, had been an old log cabin military barracks, with metal bars and red, white and blue stars and bars banners on the dormer windows, a cow skull and big wooden stars high on the facade, and a *Buffalo steaks and burgers* cutout buffalo hanging under the porch roof. An elevated log guard tower stood at the end of a row of tipis with long wooden poles, protruding into the sky like abandoned aerials, in supplication to the signal of a lost generation of spirits, missing on the open plains. We approached under a lone cottonwood, past a group of wooden wagons, so faded and dilapidated, I figured they must have been from the battle. An American flag flew over our entrance.

The place was packed for lunch. It was bustling. The Crow had done well, or at least the owner, who rolled through the crowded tables in his ponytail and cowboy hat, and a large flyswatter in the back pocket of his jeans. The cash register played pinball, beside the rack of *Doritos* and *Chitos* and *Frito-lay* snacks and the heat lamp and coffee maker, just inside the café. The Indian farmer with the Mexican straw Stetson and the large Pepsi said grace at the next table, beside the fat white Southerner with a long beard and *Alamo* baseball cap, and pants with both a belt and suspenders. *You can't trust a man that can't trust his pants.* The rest of the Indians at the table were holding out their cell phones, double-checking the courage that was fear saying its prayers. A morbidly obese native policeman in a blue uniform, big gun and walkie-talkie on his big belt, bought two feather-shaped lollipops, out of the bonbon bonnet of the plaster Indian chief.

"We haven't seen this many Indians in one place before." Said Robyn.

"Custer's words." I said. The iPod over the cash register played honky-tonk. *Well I ain't never been the Barbie Doll type, I can't swig that sweet champagne...*

"How did you like your tacos?" She asked. We nodded. They had been like beignets, with lettuce and tomatoes and shredded cheddar and olives and sour cream and salsa. "Is there anything else we can help you with today?" I had a mental image of Curley, Custer's Crow scout.

"No, thanks." I said. "I reckon we should be gettin' up over the hill there." A Michigan yell and a Hokey Hey. I went to the *Bacheé* men's room, and bought a cowboy hat in the Indian shop. Buffalo heads and cow skulls and empty papooses looked down on my purchase.

Robyn and I headed south, through the yellow that is Montana, to the yellow across the state line. *Welcome to Wyoming... Bridges may be icy... No jake brake.*

If lunch had been Indian and buffalo, Sheridan was all cowboy and cattle. The wide main street was empty, like a ghost town. But beyond the bad mural of Buffalo Bill and the brilliant bronze statue of a moustached cowpuncher with his rifle slung over his shoulder (and his exaggerated heavy metal jock strap), was the green and red bucking bronco lassoing cowboy and the green neon cattle brands on the marquis of the Mint Bar. A giant pink neon horseshoe hung on below. Inside, under the embossed tin roof and wagon wheel chandeliers, were three walls of horns and heads, and period photos. A big *Jack Daniels* in yellow neon illuminated a length of stools, firewater full of mid-afternoon patrons, happy as ticks on a fat dog. But we hadn't stopped in Sheridan for the liquor. We had stopped for the leather.

Queen Elizabeth had visited King's Saddlery. At first, we had no idea why.

"Its in the back." She said. "You have to cross the alley." We opened the most unremarkable door, and entered the most marvelous museum mausoleum. Room after room of equestrian equipage and ropes and relics of the Old West were crammed together under dim fluorescent light. Every animal that had ever lived had left its head and horns on the brick walls- elk and moose and deer and bighorn sheep and mountain goats, and gazelles and kudus and ibex and wildebeest and water buffalo, some walls looking in one direction, others in another. A stuffed giraffe looked over at us from a far corner. Regimented rows of saddles from all over the world ran along wall-mounted displays; a sea of skilled awl-worked calfskin and sinew filled in the spaces. And then it just started in my head. *Movin', movin', movin', Though they're*

*disapprovin', Keep them dogies movin'... Don't try
to understand 'em, Just rope an' throw an' brand
'em. Head 'em up, move 'em on. Move 'em out,
head 'em up...Ride 'em in, cut 'em out, Cut 'em out,
ride 'em in... Rawhide.* Indian art and artifacts
hung on and off the walls. The message in the
last room was subtle. *Hippies use back door.*
Back on Main Street, the poster on the Boot
Barn window, down from the *Hair We Are* styling
salon, advertised a *Stinky Boot trade-in event...*
with a skunk climbing out of a cowboy boot. We
drove to the city park to look for the elk and
buffalo, but they may have been aware of the
fate of their relatives on the walls of King's
Saddlery, and didn't come out of their
enclosures.
Robyn and I continued south towards Buffalo,
and got lost, detouring through the native
agency, *swirling like water around a stone.* We
ended up in some 'drug free' school zone, where
a recent migrant from California told us we had
to go back to Sheridan, and take the highway.
"You came a long way to find something that
isn't out here." She said.
"What's in Buffalo?" Robyn asked.
"Even less." She said. But she was wrong.
The Occidental Hotel was in Buffalo. It appeared
at the bottom of the hill, all brick and awnings.
Buffalo was also in the Occidental Hotel. Buffalo
Bill Cody built it. *Founded 1880.* But the town
wasn't named for Buffalo Bill, but for Buffalo,
New York. Furthermore, its restaurant was
called The Virginian. *Fine Western Dining.* I
wouldn't find out why until later. *Why, oh why,*

did I ever leave Wyoming? Cause there's a sheriff back there, Lookin' for me high and low...

Robyn and I walked into over a hundred years ago. Between the wooden floors and high embossed tin ceilings was wainscoted lichen wallpaper decorated with Old West paintings, separated by tall draped windows with *OH* in gothic script in the opaque upper ones over the valences. The lobby was huge and barely filled with settees and cushions, rocking chairs, a clavichord, and books. It was lit by hanging tulip chandeliers, a titanic Tiffany suspended in flame ember and liquid green, electric candles, and several standing opalescent globe table lamps. A fireplace, with a mirror over the mantle ushered us toward the decapitated elk eyes, watching us over the reception desk. The ageless grey-haired owner already knew us.

"Which was the room that Hemingway slept in?" I asked.

"Number four." She said. "But I've upgraded you to the Rose Room." I wanted to sleep where he had, but Robyn like the sound of roses.

"What was he doing way out here, anyway?" She had asked.

"During the early 1930s Hemingway spent his summers in Wyoming." I said. "He hunted deer, elk and grizzly bear, and called it 'the most beautiful country he had seen in the American West.' In November of 1930, after he took John Dos Passos to the train station in Billings, he broke his arm in a car accident. The surgeon who treated the compound spiral fracture sutured his writing arm bone back together with kangaroo tendon. It took a painful year to heal, during which his wife Pauline had his third son, and after which she took him and the rest of the children and left for good. Hemingway married Martha Gelhorn in Cheyenne, where she inspired him to begin *For Whom the Bell Tolls*, his most famous novel, in 1939. It sold half a million copies within months, was nominated for a Pulitzer Prize, and triumphantly re-established Hemingway's literary reputation." Robyn had tuned out my last words.

"What time would you like to book dinner in The Virginian? Asked the grey-haired proprietress. I told her we hadn't decided. She told me to let her know when we had.

The stairs creaked, and the floor did the same. We inserted our key into its opening. A painting of a lady from two centuries before, and a hanging opaque glass lamp, looked over the crocheted rose pillows on the four-pointed post bed. Fresh roses sat in a vase on a side table. The floor sloped away to the Old West. I went creaky walkabout, first to the library of the 'Families of Dinosaurs' poster above the carnivorous dinosaur skull fossil, and then back down the stairs, to the saloon.

Moose and elk and buffalo and deer heads, and horns and pelts lined the three walls that the stained glass and mirrors didn't. It was dark and quiet. Old newspaper articles had become wallpaper in the restroom, around a period porcelain sink and oval mirror. No one was eating in The Virginian. I went back upstairs to get Robyn.

"Quieter than a mouse chewing cotton." I said.

"What about that steakhouse we saw on the other edge of town?" She asked. So we went there. Beyond the wild mustangs and cattle and cowboys on the mural near the bridge. *Buffalo, Wyoming... More than a one-horse town 1884... A creek runs through it.*

It was called the Winchester, and the parking lot was full. Inside was the kind of noise you only hear in American restaurants, the sound of individualism, digging in like wolves after guts, gorging on a good deal. We had to wait. The fastest way to move cattle is slowly.

"You must be getting hungry." Said the girl that finally took us to a table.

"My belly button's rubbed a blister on my backbone." I said. We ordered rib eyes and mushrooms, with potatoes and an iceberg salad 'wedge' with blue cheese dressing, and Moose Drool beer to wash it down.

"How do you like your steak?" She asked.

"Lop off the horns and the tail and put it on the plate." I said. And we waited with anticipation, to experience what had brought all these other Wyoming gourmets to town.

It didn't go well. We were two Moose Drools down the road before the food caught up. Everything was as big as the country, but the potatoes tasted of powder and process and packaging; the mushrooms tasted of tin. The blue cheese dressing had drowned the lettuce wedge, but it may have been an act of mercy. I detected a strong odour of Bovril. The only thing fresh was the beer glass that Robyn had asked to be replaced, because it was dirty. It came hot, fresh out of the dishwasher. My rib eye tasted like it had been salvaged from one of the taxidermy torsos on the wall of the Occidental saloon. And it came with an unexpected bonus.

"What's that?" Asked Robyn. I looked down at a filiform foreign body in my meat.

"Dunno." I said. We called over the waitress.

"What's that?" I asked.

"Dunno." She said. She called over the manager. They went away to decide.

"We think it's a noodle." She said, on returning.

"You don't have noodles on your menu." Robyn said. They offered to bring me another rib eye, but I was full.

It hadn't been the first worm in the Wyoming cattle. In 1892 there was bloodshed, which took the U.S. Calvary to subdue. What would become known as the Johnson County War, or the War on Powder River, the Wyoming Range War, or the Western Civil War of Incorporation, a fight between smallholdings settlers against large well-established cattlemen. It culminated in a lengthy shootout between the local ranchers, a band of hired gunslingers, and a sheriff's posse. Home on deranged.

In Wyoming's early days, land was public domain, freely available to homesteading and stock raising. Large numbers of cattle, turned loose by large ranches, roamed the range. Before roundup, calves were branded, sometimes furtively. *Trust your neighbor. But brand your cattle.* The only way to tell a fake brand was to kill the calf, and examine the inside of its hide, to see if the brand went all the way through. Suspected cattle rustlers were lynched. Herd sizes, and the doctrine of Prior Appropriation, who had been the first to settle the land, determined property and usage.

The largest ranching outfits banded together to monopolize large swaths of rangeland, and discourage new settlers. *No rancher has the right to sell, or own, what God meant to be free. The range must always remain open.* The richest and most influential cattle barons formed the Wyoming Stock Growers Association (WSGA). They overstocked the range and hired detectives to investigate any theft from their holdings. In August of 1883, Johnson County newspapers, owned by the tycoons, claimed that Buffalo was 'the most lawless town in the country,' a haven for 'range pirates' whom 'mercilessly' stole big cattlemen's livestock. *Well the neighbors stopped by yesterday while I was outside choppin' wood, They filled me in on a local news, ain't none of it sounded good, Said, there had been some cattle stealin' by some no count outlaw bands, We'd all been branded rustlers by the big ranchers of this land.*

As the petri dish grew more crowded and noisy, tensions rose between the many small homesteaders and the few large meat magnates. The weather finished off the last of the harmony.

A bad drought hit the grasslands in the summer of 1886. It was so hot you could pull baked potatoes right out of the ground, so dry the catfish were carrying canteens, so dusty the rabbits dug their holes six feet in the air. Maybe not, but white Arctic owls made their first appearance, muskrats built taller and thicker houses, and the beavers were busier than their namesake. A blue haze arrived at the end of summer. It lifted to altitude in October, moving out of the way of the worst winter in Wyoming history.

January brought tornados of white frozen dust, and the *Moon of Cold-exploding Trees.* Cows were so starved it took three of them to make a shadow. Steers were so thin you could read the brand off the other side. Maybe not, but the mercury plunged to fifty below zero, and blizzards blew thousands of frozen carcasses into the rivers. Armed bands of rustlers roamed across Wyoming and Montana. The old buffalo pickers of the plains reappeared, collecting for the fertilizer factory bone yards. Banks failed, stockyards closed. Only the men with the bark on came back. *Well, it was us against the cattlemen and the years just made it worse,*

First the drought and then the tough winter, Johnson County had been dealt a curse.

The big owners of the big herds were in big trouble, and deeply resentful of anyone who might challenge their unfettered right to run their cattle on public land. They appropriated terrain, tightened the water supply, forced settlers off their property, and burnt their buildings. Excesses on public land were excused as self-defense against rustling. Montana and Wyoming 'declared war' on the rustlers.

On July 20, 1889, six cattlemen lynched two homesteaders in Carbon County. Ellen Watson, the 'Queen of the Sweetwater,' hadn't worn enough clothes to dust a fiddle, and may have accepted maverick cows for her favours. Wild Bill Hickok may have got it right. *When you begin a cattle drive you can't expect to say you are finished until you have visited a fancy woman and played some games of chance.* She was hung with her partner, storekeeper Jim Averell. The double lynching enraged local residents.

Emotions revved higher with every additional body found. Agents of large stockholders killed alleged rustlers from smaller ranches. Buffalo sheriff Frank Canton, once a WSGA detective, was rumoured to be behind several of the deaths, and became a virtual prisoner in his own *more than a one-horse town.*

By 1891, a local settler named Nate Champion had become the leader of a new group of small independent Johnson County ranchers, the Northern Wyoming Farmers and Stock Growers' Association (NWFSGA). When they announced plans to hold their own roundup, the WSGA told them to cease all operations, and formed an assassination squad under the old Buffalo sheriff, Frank Canton. After hanging a horse trade named Tom Waggoner, they declared Nate Champion 'King of the Cattle Thieves.'

In the early morning of November 1, 1891, WSGA paid killers burst into Nate's tiny cabin next to the Middle Fork of Powder River in the same Hole-in-the-Wall country that had once been the hideout of Butch Cassidy and the Sundance Kid. The two members of the five-man squad, which were able to squeeze into the cabin, held pistols on Champion and his visitor, and demanded that he 'give it up.'

Nate stretched and yawned while reaching under a pillow for his own revolver. The intruders fired at point-blank range, leaving powder burns on Champion's face. But all the shots fired had missed. Champion's return fire caught one in the arm and the other in the abdomen, a mortal wound. The rest of the assassins fled, but Champion got a good look at one of them, Joe Elliott. In the public investigation that followed, one of squad members admitted the names of the entire party to two witnesses, ranchers John A. Tisdale and Orley 'Ranger' Jones. Johnson County authorities filed attempted murder charges against Joe Elliott, and local newspapers pushed for charges against the wealthy cattlemen believed to have employed the assassination squad.

On Dec. 1, 1891, both witnesses were murdered. *Then there came the story about the two dry gulch attacks, Ranger Jones and John Tisdale had been both shot in the back.* The resultant uproar in Johnson County and the demand for justice became the focus of the community. Joe Elliott was bound over for trial and, with Champion's testimony, seemed likely to be convicted.

But in Chicago, a hundred years later, I had learned from a group of Texan cardiologists, inquiring about the limited resources in my small regional hospital on Vancouver Island. *You can't run with the big dogs, if you pee like a puppy.*

The cattle barons declared that Buffalo was a

rogue society in which rustlers controlled politics, courts and juries. The WSGA, led by a rough North Platte rancher named Frank Wolcott, secretly planned, organized and financed an invasion of Johnson County. Wolcott had once offered a Texan visitor some carrots.

"Where I come from," The Texan said. "We feed these to the hogs."

"So do we." Said Wolcott. "Have some."

Frank Canton was selected to lead an expedition of fifty-two men, twenty-three gunmen from Paris, Texas, four cattle detectives from the WSGA, Idaho frontiersman George Dunning, Wyoming State Senator Bob Tisdale, water commissioner W. J. Clarke, two statesmen who had organized Wyoming's statehood four years earlier, surgeon Dr. Charles Penrose, and reporters from the Cheyenne Sun and the Chicago Herald.

On Tuesday April 5, 1892, a special private Union Pacific train rode secretly north from Cheyenne. It had one engine, a passenger car, a baggage car, several stock cars filled with horses, and three freight cars loaded with guns, ammunition, dynamite, tents, blankets and wagons. At 3 am, just outside Casper, the men switched to horseback, cut the telegraph lines to Buffalo, and continued north.

The first target of the invaders was Nate Champion. The invaders quietly surrounded his KC ranch, and waited for daybreak. Nate and his three guests had enjoyed a night as fine as a frog hair split four ways, killing a bottle of snake juice, and thumbing through the latest Montgomery Ward catalogue. Two of his visitors were captured as they emerged to collect water at dawn, and the third, Nick Ray, was shot inside the cabin doorway. He died a few hours later.

Champion, besieged inside, kept a tragic journal. *Boys, I feel pretty lonesome just now. I wish there was someone here with me so we could watch all sides at once... Well, they have just got through shelling the house like hail. I heard them splitting wood. I guess they are going to fire the house tonight. I think I will make a break when night comes, if alive. Shooting again. It's not night yet. The house is all fired. Goodbye, boys, if I never see you again.*

Nate was shot as he ran from the burning cabin. They pinned a note to his bullet-riddled chest. *Cattle Thieves Beware.*

"On to Buffalo!" Yelled Wolcott. *Then, last night at supper time riders stopped by chance, They said cattleman and their hired guns just burned the Kaycee Ranch, Two men had died this mornin', shot down in the snow, Now the vigilante army was on the march to Buffalo.*

The fracas had not gone unnoticed, however, and a local rancher, Jack Flagg, rode to Buffalo, where the sheriff raised a posse of two hundred men over the next twenty-four hours. They caught up with the invaders early on the next morning, and trapped them inside a log barn at the TA Ranch on Crazy Woman Creek. One of the WSGA group escaped from the fusillade, and rode hard to reach Wyoming Governor Barber by the next day. Barber sent President Benjamin Harrison a telegram.

> 'About sixty-one owners of live stock are reported to have made an armed expedition into Johnson County protecting their live stock and preventing unlawful roundups by rustlers. They are at TA Ranch, thirteen miles from Fort McKinney, besieged by Sheriff and posse and by rustlers, said to be two or three hundred in number. The wagons of stockmen were taken away from them and a battle took place yesterday, during which men were killed. Great excitement prevails. Both parties are very determined and it is feared that if successful will show no mercy to the persons captured. The civil authorities are unable to prevent violence. The situation is serious and immediate assistance will probably prevent great loss of life.'

President Harrison did what presidents do. He sent the U.S. Calvary to the rescue. The Sixth arrived at the TA ranch on the morning of April 13 and took custody of the WSGA expedition, just as the posse was about to set the barn on fire. *Well the County was in an uproar and every man saddled up to ride, Caught the cattlemen at the TA Ranch and surrounded all four sides, We hailed the house with bullets and swore they were gonna pay, But the cavalry came across the plains and once again they saved the day.*
The Army took possession of Wolcott, 45 other men with as many rifles, 41 revolvers, 5,000 rounds of ammunition, and Frank Canton's gripsack. Inside, they found a list of seventy men to be shot or hanged, ranch houses they had burned, and a contract to pay the Texans $5 a

day plus a bonus of $50 for every man killed.

The invaders were taken to Cheyenne and received preferential treatment. They were allowed to roam the base by day as long as they agreed to return at night. Charges were never filed. The perpetrators were released on bail and told to return to Wyoming for the trial. The ones that didn't flee to Texas went free when the charges were dropped because Johnson County had insufficient resources to pay for the prosecution, said to exceed $18,000. You can't run with the big dogs. *Well, they marched 'em off to Cheyenne, no one went to jail, The cattlemen were all turned loose and the hired guns hit the trail, And I guess the only justice wasn't much to say the least, Last winter me and mine ate mighty fine on the cattle baron's beef.*

Local passions remained high for years following the Johnson County War. The 9th Cavalry of Buffalo Soldiers, to quell pressure from the local population, replaced the discredited 6th Cavalry. Both sides spun tall tales, in an attempt to morally justify their actions. The smaller ranchers accused the Old West's most notorious gunslingers of being under the employ of the invaders, including Tom Horn. Horn had worked as a detective for the WSGA in the 1890s but there was no evidence he was involved in the war.

"Killing is my business." He had said. "Dead men don't steal no cattle." Politics was involved. President Harrison, and the ranchers who had hired the gunmen, were Republicans. The Democrats would sweep Wyoming for a long time after the invasion. In 1888, Teddy Roosevelt foretold the end of the open range.

'In its present form stock-raising on the plains is doomed, and can hardly outlast the century. The great free ranches, with their barbarous, picturesque, and curiously fascinating surrounding, mark a primitive stage of existence as surely as do the great tracts of primeval forests, and like the latter must surely pass away before the onward march of our people; and we who have felt the charm of the life, and have exulted in its abounding vigour and its bold, restless freedom, will not only regret its passing for our own sakes, but must also feel real sorrow that those who come after us are not to see, as we have seen, what is perhaps the pleasantest, healthiest, and most exciting phase of American existence.'

The most notorious event in the history of Wyoming, open class warfare, and the intervention by the President of the United States to save the lives of hired killers, produced much of, but did not necessarily reflect favorably on, the mythology of American West.

The hero of *The Virginian*, a seminal 1902 western novel, took the side of the wealthy ranchers. The 1949 novel *Shane* took the side of the settlers. In the 1968 novel *True Grit*, the main character was 'hired by stock owners to terrorize thieves and people called nesters and grangers.' *Baby sister, I was born game and I intend to go out that way.* Only John Wayne could have been Rooster Cogburn. *Oh, Powder River, you're muddy and you're wide, How many men have died along your shore? When you brand a man a rustler, he's gotta take a side,*

There's no middle ground in this Johnson County war.

Back at the Winchester, just on closing, our waitress handed Robyn a big Styrofoam box to pack her own leftover steak. We put it in the Occidental Hotel fridge, around three corners of creaky floors. Our noisy attempts to retrieve it, before sunrise the next morning, would almost start a second Johnson County War. Never drive black cattle in the dark.

'Time and space – time to be alone, space to move about – these may well become the great scarcities of tomorrow.'

Edwin Way Teale

*   *   *

Wheels of Fortune
Gardiner, Montana

'Eventually one gets to the Medicine Wheel, to fulfill one's life.'

Old Mouse, Arikara

Sulfur. We ate hurriedly before dawn. Crackers, shaped like the animals in our first destination. We had a wheel that would take us from here to there; they had a wheel that would take them from there to the stars.

Robyn and I rescued the leftover Winchester steak from the fridge three creaky hallways away, and humped our packs down Buffalo Bill's groaning Occidental stairs, to the wagon.

Coral cotton fingers, bottom lit by streams of gold, drew the black predawn Wyoming silhouettes onto a mauve highway, through olive grassland and dark green camouflage mountain pie, smothered in grey meringue and powder blue filling. There were pronghorns, and the stink of dead skunk in the middle of the road.

"I hope it's not the meat." Said Robyn. We needn't have worried, for there would have been more in the next town. *Steak night tonight.* "Every night is steak night in Wyoming." I said. We pulled into Ranchester for gas. *Cowboy State Bank.* A bearded beer belly with a baseball cap was asleep on one of the verandas of the Tongue River Apartments. The sultana on his T-shirt spoke of his devotion. *Happiness is raisin kids.*

Robyn began to find the route more exotic than

her antipodean upbringing could accommodate.

"Wombat?" She asked, about the next smudge of road kill.

"Porcupine." I said.

"I never imagined Wisconsin would be like this." She said.

"Wyoming." I said, as we drive by the Branding Iron Restaurant and the Crazy Woman Saloon, in Dayton.

The mountains we ride past will outlast everything we know. Robyn and I ascended the Bighorn Range switchbacks, to white limestone and conifers climbing into sagebrush, lodgepole pines like sentinels on the cliffs, turning into stepped mesas protruding from undulating hills, and then hoodoos, until the Bighorn National Forest highway turnoff, at the top of the world. We could reach up here only two months of the year, around the summer solstice, when enough snow had melted.

The air was ten thousand feet thin, thinner than the ribbon of deserted desert that wound upwards, between the desolate grey pink hills, through their quarry dust to our destination quarry. As we started our uphill hike, another two and a half kilometers, the mountains and forests of the Bighorn came up with the sun to meet us on our right, threatening to push us off the earth's curvature and the plains far below, to our left.

"I've never been where you can feel such an expanse." Robyn said. Large-eared pikas bolted into rock crevices along our path, signaling to each other. *Beeep...Beeep...* The chipmunks were less afraid, more inquisitive, almost courageous. They had said their prayers, and perhaps there was something in it for them, the spirits of the warriors from before. There were ink-spotted plantain lilies. That's what I would have called them anyway. We came past a copse of tall skinny pines in a field of crumbling stone chess pieces pervaded with fine red filigree, onto a convex rise of loose white rocks, broken like the continuity of what was supposed to be forever here. *Our elders teach us that there is a model of the universe inside ourselves.*

There was a modern spherical astronomical observatory on the far horizon, and a more proximal plaque, courtesy of the conquerors. *Medicine Wheel/Medicine Mountain...This site possesses national significance in illustrating the history of the United States of America.*

"That's one way of putting it." I said. It looked like a wagon wheel, lying on its side.

"What is this thing with you and cartwheels?" Robyn asked.

"Pattern recognition, I guess." I said. We looked over a mound, an eighty foot wide wheel of stones, over two hundred feet in circumference. The hub was a doughnut shape cairn, a dozen feet in diameter and two feet high, connected to the rim by a monolithic radiating footprint of cobblestone lines.

"How many spokes are there?" Robyn asked.

"Twenty-eight." I said. "The same number as the days in their lunar cycle. The same number of rafters as the Lakota used in their Sundance lodges."

"It's a calendar." Said Robyn.

"It's a calendar." I said. "And an observatory of the vanquished. You see the spokes with the stone cairns, extending out beyond the tipi ring tent-peg foundation stones, on the rim of the wheel?" She nodded.

"They're aligned to the horizon positions of sunrises and sunsets on the first days of the four seasons." I said. "The dawn rising of a star is important because it can pinpoint an exact date. This is the day a star is first seen, just before daybreak, after it has been behind the Sun for an entire season. The wheel's star alignments are most accurate for around 1200 AD, so that's how we know when it was built. Since then, there have been slight changes in the Earth's orbit that have caused perturbations. These heliacal stars formed the animal constellation of the Lakota. They marked the summer season as precisely as they could, for their time and technology. The star Fomalhaut rose 28 days before the Summer Solstice, Aldebaran during the 2 days just before the solstice, Rigel 28 days after the solstice, and Sirius 28 days after that, at the end of August, marking the end of summer and the time to leave the mountain."

"It's more than that, though, isn't it." Robyn said.

"It's more than that." I said. "It's a sacred hoop, a symbol of the never-ending cycle of life. Or at least, it was. It had no beginning and no end. Or at least it wasn't supposed to. Different tribes had unique spiritual definitions of the place, and interpreted the significance of the medicine wheel differently. The four directions also represented the four seasons, the four stages of life, the four elements of nature, the four sacred animals, the four sacred plants." *Eagle, Bear, Wolf, Buffalo... Tobacco, sweet grass, sage, cedar.*

"And prayer offerings are still left here, even now." She said. We looked around the mound, over the rocks among the grass, and the hundred of bits of coloured rag and cloth, strips and pompoms and *bouquet garni*, invocations inside, tied to ropes between the posts around the perimeter, flying in the thin air like a sacred hoop of Tibetan prayer flags. Their pleas and petitions, like those on the wind in Tibet, were leaving too late. Heaven, instead of calvary, could only send condolences.

Robyn and I took some time to examine the other individual offerings and oblations tied to the rope rim of the Medicine Wheel. There were buffalo jawbones, hanging webbed dreamcatchers, eagle feathers, and braided and beaded leather wristbands and belts. One of them had a design with a diamond, a heart and a club, and a spade. *Poker is a science; the highest court in Texas has said so... Trust everybody in the game, but always cut the cards.*

Of all the hanging agony on the ropes of ruin at the Bighorn Medicine Wheel, the one that got us with a club in the heart in spades, was the diamond of desolation, a plaster death mask with fur pelt hair, small green triangle in the middle of her forehead, tears streaming from her left eye socket, bloody lacerations cut diagonally under her right, and smashed nose and pink painted lips.

"They were here for seven thousand years." Robyn said. "But a sad soul can kill you quicker than a germ."

*   *   *

'When a cowboy spits in a corner, they'll put up a statue of him.'

Ralph Grant

If the eastern road up the Bighorn had been a series of graded switchbacks, the descent down the western slopes would be a long drop. Robyn and I fell nine thousand feet, plummeting downward on a ten per cent grade, descending so fast past runaway truck ramps, we wouldn't have caught one if we needed it. *No parking.* As if. The ravens were huge, possibly a result of previous consequence.

We drove by the one shop in Lovell. *La De Da.*

Byron billed itself as 'A Great Place to Live.' Robyn and I stopped to photograph its bone yard of wagon chassis. If cartwheels were worth a buffalo nickel, you would have had enough money to burn a wet mule. Garland boasted a talentless chainsaw carver, and a field of droopy sunflowers next door. Plantations of sugar beets took us beyond Heart Mountain, to the town that Buffalo Bill founded in 1895. We drove through Cody to its western edge, and turned off near the *Psychic Readings* sign. The single street of wooden buildings in Old Trail Town held historic treasures. Robyn and I ate the leftover Winchester steak out of its Styrofoam box, and paid to reenter the past. The town had more than a hundred wagons of every description, and twenty-five original cabins with their square planked façades, some with high antlers and cow skulls on high dentate square projections, overlooking the sloped porch roofs held up by tall balustrades, overhanging the boardwalks.

Here was Butch Cassidy's shack brought in from the Hole-in-the-Wall country, the Sundance Kid's shantey hideout from the bank they robbed in Red Lodge, and the log cabin that belonged to Curley, General Custer's surviving Crow scout. Cairns of elk antlers, a crowded livery, beaded Indian relics, and wagon wheel shadows on the walls of the Old West, half the spokes of the Bighorn Medicine Wheel, were in a herder's hurry to get here in half the time. The saloon had authentic hanging chandeliers, a mirrored bar, a cash register ornate as a Chinese pagoda, and the mandatory painting of a naked reclining woman beside the heads of buffalo and bighorn sheep and deer, on the red velvet wallpapered walls. Outside was powder blue on tawny powder, dust and faded wood and sage, and the graves of the three most powerfully poignant mountain men of the American West. *I know who you are; you're the same dumb pilgrim I've been hearin' for twenty days and smellin' for three.* Every one of them would have been someone to ride the river with.

A bronze torso of the first mountain man, all buckskin and beard and mane, stood tall in the wind, under an old tattered American flag, blue and cotton sky and yellow hills in the backdrop. John Colter was born in Virginia in 1774. Before his thirtieth birthday, Meriwether Lewis offered him the rank of private and a pay of five dollars a month, to join his Corps of Discovery. Colter was court-martialled for threatening to shoot a sergeant he had disobeyed, while Lewis and Clark were somewhere else, but was reinstated after offering an apology and a promise to reform. One of the best hunters in the expedition, he was routinely sent out to scout for game, and to find Indians who could guide them further west. Colter was given an honourable discharge on the return to the Mandan villages in what is now North Dakota, to enable him to join Forest Hancock and Joseph Dickson, two frontiersmen headed into the upper Missouri River country in search of furs. It only lasted two months. After they reached Three Forks, and he helped establish Fort Raymond, Colter lit out for the larger wilderness. In the dead of the winter of 1807-08, he traveled hundreds of miles alone, much of the time unguided, in a region where nighttime temperatures in January are routinely –34 °C. He was the first European-American to enter and explore Jackson Hole below the Teton Range, and what is now Yellowstone National

Park. John visited at least one geyser basin, near where Robyn and I were standing in what is now Cody, and probably saw the geothermal areas near Tower Fall as well. He found the Crow, and they found him.

He was treated at his reception, back at Fort Raymond in April of 1808, like he don't got all what belongs to him. His report of a place of 'fire and brimstone' was ridiculed as imaginary, dismissed as delirium, and nicknamed 'Colter's Hell.'

Later that year John was injured in a fight with the Blackfoot, after he had teamed up with John Potts near Three Forks, but it was what happened in 1809, that became immortalized as 'Colter's Run.' While paddling their canoe up the Jefferson River, Potts and Colter encountered several Blackfoot who demanded they come ashore. John did, and was disarmed and stripped naked. When Potts refused to land he was shot. His return fire killed one of the warriors, and their fusillade from the riverbank riddled him to the great beyond. His body was brought in and hacked to pieces. Colter was motioned to leave, and encouraged to run. But he was running for his life, pursued by a large pack of young braves. After several miles John was exhausted, bleeding from his nose, with only one assailant still closely tagging him.

> 'Again he turned his head, and saw the savage
> not twenty yards from him. Determined if
> possible to avoid the expected blow, he suddenly
> stopped, turned round, and spread out his
> arms. The Indian, surprised by the suddenness

of the action, and perhaps at the bloody
appearance of Colter, also attempted to stop;
but exhausted with running, he fell whilst
endeavouring to throw his spear, which stuck
in the ground, and broke in his hand. Colter
instantly snatched up the pointed part, with
which he pinned him to the earth, and then
continued his flight.'

Colter grabbed the dead Indian's blanket, and
continued his run with the pack still in pursuit,
until he reached the Madison River, where he
hid inside a beaver lodge, to escape capture.
Emerging at night he climbed and walked for
eleven days to the fort of a trader on the Little
Big Horn.
In 1810 John Colter helped construct another
fort at Three Forks, but after returning from a
trap line, found his two partners mutilated by
the Blackfoot. He left the wilderness for good,
married a woman named Sallie, and bought a
farm in Missouri. The map he gave William
Clark, later that year, was the most
comprehensive of the region produced for the
next seventy-five years. Colter fought with
Nathan Boone's Rangers in the War of 1812, and
died of jaundice in the same year.
The next statue over, was of a seated man,
aiming a flintlock, elbow on his knee, cord
wrapped around his boot, to steady his aim. Jim
White was the greatest buffalo hunter in the
world. Born in Missouri sixteen years after John
Colter died, no one knew his original name. His
deliberately lost that when he inadvertently lost
his wife, to a rich Spaniard in Mexico, in 1868.
Jim killed him and several others in the fracas

and, with a large reward on his head, walked the seven hundred miles back into Texas. There are three uncertainties in life- woman, wind, and wealth. White got into buffalo hunting, and kept several skinners gainfully employed.

One day a group of ciboleros rode over a hill and scared away the small herd that White was firing on. Mad as a mule chewing bumblebees, he shot the horses out from under four of them. Jim earned a reputation for toughness, *more guts than you could hang on a fence.*

By the summer of 1878, all the Southern Plains buffalo were gone. Jim White was an autochthon, like the buffalo he hunted, with a very hard head, a very uncertain temper, and a very lonely future. He left for the northern buffalo range in Wyoming, and reached the Big Horn Mountains with two big span of mules, two wagons, 700 pounds of lead, five kegs of gunpowder, three 16 pound Sharp's rifles, and an old buffalo skinner named Watson. Here he teamed up with Oliver Hanna, one of General Crook's old scouts. Over the next two winters, the two men hunted, with a contract to furnish five thousand pounds of game meat to the army at Fort McKinney, near Buffalo, just as Buffalo Bill was building the Occidental Hotel. The 4,600 hides they had collected were freighted to the Yellowstone River by ox teams, and then hauled down the river by steamboats. In the fall of 1880, Hanna returned from a quick trip over the Big Horns. He found Jim White dead, shot in the head with his own 50-caliber buffalo rifle, by thieves who had stolen their horses, mules, wagons, guns, hides and furs, and future. *Dying ain't much of a living, boy.*

It was a hard land, and it bred hard men to hard ways. The third statue was of a legendary iron man on a bronze horse, all beard and feathered hat and gun, on a stone pedestal. *No more trails.* He was born John Garrison in New Jersey in 1824, but he deliberately lost his name after striking an officer, after losing his age in order to enlist on a fighting ship in the Mexican-American War. John Johnson was swept away by and to the gold rush in Montana, where he became a 'wood hawk,' supplying cordwood to steamboats. At the age of 23, he took a Flathead Indian wife, and built a cabin on the Little Snake River in Wyoming. One day, returning from a trap line, he found his wife and unborn child dead and mutilated on the cabin floor, killed by Crow Indians.

Johnson began a personal war of revenge against the Crow, a vendetta that would last a quarter of a century. From his dead enemies, he would take a bite of their liver, a supreme insult because the Crow believed an intact organ was vital to arrive in the afterlife. Liver Eating Johnson made a fierce impression on his foes, and redefined the meaning of 'Eating Crow.'

It was a time of tall boots and tall hats and tall tales. Like John Colter a hundred years before, Johnson was ambushed by a group of Blackfoot warriors in the dead of winter on a foray to sell whiskey to his Flathead kin, a trip of over five hundred miles The Blackfoot planned to sell him to the Crow. He was stripped to the waist, tied with leather thongs and put in a teepee with a guard. Johnson broke through the straps, knocked out the guard with a kick, scalped him with his own knife, and cut off one of his legs.

He escaped into the woods, surviving by eating the Blackfoot's leg, until he reached the cabin of his trapping partner, a journey of about two hundred miles.

In his old age he developed rheumatism, and treated his ailment at the DeMaris Hot Springs, near the river below us. Johnson died in 1900, in a veteran's home in Santa Monica, but through the efforts of a seventh grader named Tri Robinson, and his class in Lancaster, California, was reinterred in Old Trail Town in 1974, near the mountains he loved. More than two thousand attended the funeral, 'probably the largest burial service in the history of Wyoming.'

In his time, Liver Eating Johnson was a sailor, a United States Army scout and Indian fighter, a Union Civil War soldier wounded in battle, a gold-seeker, a hunter, a trapper, a whiskey and wood peddler, a guide, a Marshall, the first sheriff of Red Lodge, Montana, a log cabin builder, a seeker of any source of income-producing labor he could find, and the western film inspiration for *Jeremiah Johnson*. Grab what you can and let the loose ends drag.

"You've come far, Pilgrim." He Said.

"Feels like far." Said Johnson.

"Were it worth the trouble?" He asked.

"Eh." Said Johnson. "What trouble?"

'People are always asking me why they don't make
Westerns like they used to.'
                                        Roy Rogers

*   *   *

'Go West, young man, and grow up with the
country.'
                                   John B. L. Soule

I didn't really like the man. Or maybe I never
really liked the idea of him. Life is simpler when
you plow around the stump. But there was no
way of going around him, not for this book,
anyway.
*Welcome to the Buffalo Bill Historical Center...
Please leave these items in your vehicle: Food and
beverages... Large containers and backpacks...
Child-carrying backpacks... Motorcycle helmets...
Weapons. New this year! The Family Rate. Ask
about it at the admissions desk.* When they ask
you to leave your weapons in the car, on the
same line they're introducing their family
discount, you know you've arrived in the
Heartland.
We met the giant behind the admissions desk.
"How long does it take to see the exhibits?"
Robyn asked.

196

"Most people take two to three days." He said. And then he saw the terror in our faces. "There's a wing of Buffalo Bill memorabilia, a wing of Native American artifacts, a museum of armaments..." It looked like he could go on for a bit.

"We have about two hours." I said. "We're driving through Yellowstone today." He looked at us like we were crazy.

"You'll be busier than a stump-tailed cow in fly time." He said. "I'd concentrate on the Buffalo Bill and Native American part. That'll be thirty dollars." And then he saw the terror in our faces. "Make it twenty." He said. We thanked him, and ran so fast by Buffalo Bill's hologram, he turned back into mist.

It is still almost easier to decide what William Frederick 'Buffalo Bill' Cody wasn't, than to define what he was. Bill claimed many jobs- Civil War soldier, Indian wars U.S. Army scout chief, trapper, bullwhacker, Colorado 'Fifty-niner,' Pony Express rider, wagon master, stagecoach driver, and hotel manager, flamboyant showman, Freemason, unofficial American cultural ambassador, and elder statesman. He was also a self-serving exhibitionist, historical revisionist and, as history could well judge, at least as much a hunter of publicity as he had been of bison.

William Cody was born on a farm in Iowa in 1846, but was baptized by his Quakers parent, Isaac and Mary, in Peel, Ontario. At the age of 11, Cody took a job with a freight carrier as a 'boy extra,' riding up and down the wagon train, delivering messages.

Nine years later, he married Louisa Frederici. Two of their four children would die young. In 1867 he contracted to supply the Kansas Pacific Railroad workers with bison meat. Cody killed over four thousand in eighteen months. He and William Comstock had a shooting competition. Whoever killed the most number of animals, would earn the exclusive right to be called 'Buffalo Bill.' Cody won by a score of 68 to 48. In the same year that he received a Medal of Honor for 'gallanty in action' as a Third Cavalry civilian scout, Bill travelled to Chicago to debut in Ned Buntline's original Wild West show, The Scouts of the Prairie. When his friend James 'Wild Bill' Hickok joined him the following season's new performance of Scouts of the Plains, the troupe toured together for ten years.

Then, in 1883, in North Platte, Nebraska, Cody founded 'Buffalo Bill's Wild West,' a circus-like travelling extravaganza of main events, feats of skill, staged races, and sideshows that eventually toured the continental United States and Europe. It came to town on a gigantic billboard.

An Object Lesson

Differing as it does from all other exhibitions, Buffalo Bill's Wild West and Congress of Roughriders of the World. Stands as a living monument of historic and educational magnificence. Its distinctive feature lies in its send of realism, bold dash and Reckless abandon which only arises from brave and noble inspiration. It is not a 'show' in any sense of the word, but it is a series of original Genuine And instructive object lessons in which the participants repeat the heroic Parts they have played in actual life upon the Plains, in the Wilderness, Mountain fastness and in the dread and dangerous scenes of savage And cruel warfare. It is the only amusement enterprise of any kind Recognized, endorsed and contributed to by governments, armies and nations; And it lives longest in the hearts of those who have seen it most Often Since it always contains and conveys intensely inspiring ideas and motives, While its programme is a succession of pleasant surprises and Thrilling incidents.

The show began with a cultural parade on horseback, with participants from all over the world in their most colourful costumes- the US military, American Indians, Turks, Gauchos, Arabs, Mongols, and Georgians.

Bill employed several historical western figures. Gabriel Dumont, Lillian Smith, and Calamity Jane toured with Cody, but one of the most fascinating company members was Annie Oakley. Like Buffalo Bill, her parents had been Quakers, and her father had died from a combination of injury and exposure. Annie spent part of her childhood in servitude with another family in Ohio, enduring physical and mental abuse, so poor she almost had to borrow water to cry with. She referred to them as 'the wolves.' Annie began hunting at the age of nine, sold the game, and soon became known as a crack shot.

In the spring of 1881, the Baughman and Butler shooting act came to Cincinnati. Marksman Frank Butler placed a $100 bet with hotel owner Jack Frost, that he could beat any local fancy shooter. The hotelier set up a shooting match with Annie, then 21, in Greenville, Ohio. After missing his 25th shot, after losing the match, Frank won Annie. They were happily married for the rest of their lives.

Both sharpshooters joined the Buffalo Bill's Wild West in 1885. Standing only five feet tall, using a .22 caliber rifle at 90 feet, Annie could split a playing card edge-on and put five or six more holes in it before it touched the ground. In a performance before Queen Victoria and other crowned heads of state, at his request, she knocked the ashes off a cigarette held by the Prince of Prussia, the future Kaiser Wilhelm II. Some later mused that, if Annie had shot the prince instead of his cigarette, she may have prevented the First World War. In another shooting contest in 1922, at the age of sixty-two, even after numerous spinal operations after a railway accident, and wearing a steel brace after a car crash, Annie hit a hundred consecutive clay targets straight from the 16 yard mark.

When she died of pernicious anemia four years later, her husband Frank stopped eating. He died twenty days later. When Sitting Bull had first met Annie Oakley, he was so impressed with her marksmanship that he offered a photographer sixty-five dollars for a photo of the two of them together. The admiration was mutual. Sitting Bull adopted her as a daughter, and called her Watanya Cicilla, *Little Sure Shot*, a name she used throughout her career. After Annie's death, it was revealed that she had given her entire fortune to charity. Her adoptive father had taught by example. *The white man knows how to make everything, but he does not know how to distribute it.*

The meeting of Sitting Bull and Annie Oakley would have not occurred without chance, and the chance would not have occurred without Buffalo Bill. Cody knew that his show could not claim to represent the Wild West, without representative Indians. The Native Americans knew that performing in Bill's shows offered their best chance of preserving their heritage, resisting the assimilation the Bureau of Indian Affairs was determined to inflict on them. In the ultimate irony of mutual exploitation, Oglala Sioux veterans of the Great Plains Wars, were hired off the degrading confines of the Pine Ridge Agency in South Dakota, where they were forbidden to wear traditional tribal dress, hunt, dance, or participate in their own cultural practices, where they were continually harassed by missionaries, teachers, agents, politicians, and 'humanitarians,' to play themselves. Cody freed them for six months every year, providing wages, food, transportation, living space and accommodation, visitors, and exotic travel. In exchange for reenacting the popular image of native tribes dwelling in tipis, skilled in horseback riding and marksmanship and ceremonial dance, attacking settlers cabins, stagecoaches, pony-express riders, and wagon trains, and killing George Armstrong Custer at the Battle of Little Big Horn, they got to do just that. *If a man loses anything and goes back and looks carefully for it, he will find it.*

The list of Buffalo Bill's 'Show Indians' read like a Who's Who of Native history: American Horse, Geronimo, Flying Hawk, Red Shirt, Kicking Bear, Chief Blue Horse, Hollow Horn Bear, Lone Bear, Young Man Afraid of His Horses, Whirling Horse, Sitting Bull. *I will remain what I am until I die, a hunter, and when there are no buffalo or other game I will send my children to hunt and live on prairie mice, for where an Indian is shut up in one place his body becomes weak.*

Chief Iron Tail managed the Indian Police, and became one of Bill's best friends, feted by European aristocracy, and shooting elk and bighorn together on annual hunting trips. His poker hand was legendary among U.S. Army officials, and his head still graces one entire side of my Buffalo nickel collection.

All of this savagery his did not go down well with the paternalistic policies of the Bureau of Indian Affairs, primed for aggressive assimilation. Thomas Jefferson Morgan, its new commissioner in 1889, publicly attacked and threatened Bill with the loss of his bonds, and aspiring Indian performers with the withholding of land allotments, annuities, and tribal status. The following year the Bureau held an inquiry, to challenge the morality of Indian employment in show business. The Indians gave a masterful presentation, turning the hearing into a pointed denunciation of Bureau policy, by comparing conditions in Buffalo Bill's Wild West with those on the Pine Ridge agency.

Rocky Bear remarked that he worked in a show that fed him well, "That is why I am getting so fat." He said, rubbing his cheeks. "I am getting poor." only by returning to the reservation. If the Great Father wanted him to stop appearing in the show, he would stop.

"But until then, that is the way I get money." He showed his inquisitors a purse filled with $300 in gold coins.

"I saved this money to buy some clothes for my children." He said. There was silence. *You can trust the government, ask any Indian.*

Buffalo Bill's Wild West toured Europe eight times between 1887 and 1906, giving hundreds of shows to millions of fans. Cody gave command performances for royalty, including two for Queen Victoria, and one in an ancient Roman amphitheater for Pope Leo XIII. He brought the Old West to Great Britain, France, Italy, Germany, Austria-Hungary, Poland, Bohemia, Belgium, the Netherlands, Spain, the Balkans, Romania, and the Ukraine. Or at least his version.

Wild West show performances had little in common with frontier life, but the entertainment spectacle was taken for the real thing. Buffalo Bill's Wild West became America's Wild West, the 'authentic' national narrative of American exceptionalism. It may not have been accurate, but as an American cultural export, it was unquestionably genuine.

The finale typically portrayed an Indian attack on a settler's cabin. Cody rode in with cowboys to defend a settler and his family. The legendary frontiersman can take on anything in the world, without the need for any of the other people in it. The 'can do' superiority of American history and society, became the 'can do no wrong' unerring, unfailing, faultless, flawless Manifest Destiny, the many subsequent arrogant misadventures, and the mythical core of U.S. foreign and domestic policy. Life is a rodeo, and Buffalo Bill's show was the original, and the template for all that followed.

It made Buffalo Bill Cody the most recognizable celebrity on earth, and a very wealthy man. In 1879 he penned his autobiography, *The Life and Adventures of Buffalo Bill.* Six years later, he founded his own town, the one named after him, and it eventually built the museum, that Robyn and I were running to get through.

It was an impressive effort. The Native American exhibit hall was an authentic portrayal of the Indian experience, more than anything that Bill had created in his performances. There were sun dances around sacred cottonwoods, and Pretty Shield's sad reminiscence of her nomadic Crow childhood, before the Bureau corralled her life. *Moving made me happy.* There were elaborately beaded papooses, now empty, and elaborate beaded baseball caps, now empty. And there was a depiction of the trade and disease and missionaries and war and loss of buffalo that had ultimately sentenced their way of life to oblivion. *When I was a boy, the Sioux owned the world. The sun rose and set on their land; they sent ten thousand men to battle. Where are the warriors today? Who slew them? Where are our lands? Who owns them?*

Outside, and we needed some air, was a

magnificent statue of Sacajawea, and a live captive golden eagle, both with the same grim countenance. Quaking aspens quivered.

In 1886 Buffalo Bill purchased a 4,000-acre ranch and an eighteen-room mansion.

He died of kidney failure in 1917, at his sister's house in Denver. Still covering his options, he had been baptized into the Catholic Church the previous day. He received a full Masonic funeral, and was buried on Lookout Mountain, in Golden. Tributes came in from King George V of Great Britain, Kaiser Wilhelm II of Imperial Germany, and President Woodrow Wilson. The country that had formed him, the country he had formed back, would name a dam and reservoir after him, and put his face on two of its postage stamps.

But the Lone Ranger Code of Conduct would be eating at Buffalo Bill, long before its fictitious existence became real for me and the other impressionable young buckaroos, in the Paramount theatre Saturday matinees. *You can wash your hands but not your conscience. Sooner or later, somewhere, somehow, we must settle with the world and make payment for what we have taken.*

Cody would live long enough to see dramatic change in the real Wild West. The buffalo herds he hunted, the ones that give him his superhero name, were threatened with extinction. Barbed wire wound its tendrils through the open plains. He began to speak out against hide hunting, and campaigned for a hunting season.

The Indians he had scouted against, the ones he

had depicted in his shows attacking stagecoaches and wagon trains and being driven off by rescuing cowboys and soldiers, became increasingly impoverished, interned on their reservations. He called them 'the former foe, present friend, the American.' *Every Indian outbreak that I have ever known has resulted from broken promises and broken treaties by the government.* In the frenzied face of coal and oil and natural gas exploitation, and the irrepressible greed of big ranching and farming cabals, he began to support conservation efforts. "I don't believe that Buffalo Bill Cody could settle with the world and make payment for what he had taken." I said to Robyn. "I don't believe he could have received the redemption he was seeking."

"Why not?" She asked.

     "Its a path of pilgrimage. " I said.
     "To where?" He asked.
     "Not so much to where." I said. "As to what."
     "To what?" He asked.
     "Authenticity." I said. "The American West was
      The Sacred Land- the gold rush towards truth."
     "What's the truth?" He asked.
     "The achievement of redemption." I said.
     "How do you get that?" He asked.
     "By living the authentic life, by living in Nature,
      and by facing death with dignity and courage."
     "Sounds very existential." Said Carolyn.
     "That's where the truth lives." I said.

"Because." I said "Although in one sense he lived the authentic life by living in Nature, and by facing death with dignity and courage, there was this other thing."

"Which was?" She asked.

"Water and truth are freshest at their source." I said. "Bill made his fortune by bottling it, and slapping on his own label."

"So?" She asked.

"No way to redeem the bottle." I said.

Even in death, Buffalo Bill didn't find total peace. His final disposition remained conflicted, his once great fortune diminished. In 1948 the Cody chapter of the American Legion offered a reward for the 'return' of the body. In response, the Denver chapter mounted a guard over his Lookout Mountain grave, until a deeper shaft could be blasted further into the rock. The wolves.

For me the most impressive object, in the Buffalo Bill Center of the West Museum, was his Wheel of Fortune. It had a design with a diamond, a heart and a club, and a spade. Shadow lines radiated out from and beyond the perimeter posts. When you spun the wheel, you would get a date from an event in Buffalo Bill's life. It was, like roulette, a game of chance. *I have killed, robbed, and injured too many white men to believe in a good peace. They are medicine...*

"It's a calendar." Said Robyn.

"It's a calendar." I said.

We had a wheel that would take us from here to there; he had a wheel that would take him from there to the stars.

        Buffalo Bill's
            Defunct
                who used to
                    ride a watersmooth-silver
                                stallion
        and break onetwothreefourfive
        pigeonsjustlikethat

        Jesus
        he was a handsome man
                        and what i want to
            know is
            how do you like your blueeyed
            boy
        Mister Death
                            ee cummings

                    *   *   *

> "Why do you not want schools?" The
> Commissioner asked.
> "They will teach us to have churches." Joseph
> answered.
> "Do you not want churches?"
> "No, we do not want churches."
> "Why do you not want churches?"
> "They will teach us to quarrel about God."
> Joseph said.

It's a long road that has no bends, but there wasn't one of those to take us there. Charles Kurault had called it the most beautiful drive in America.

"I'm not sure you'll be able to get through." She had said, the Occidental Hotel proprietress with the grey hair, in Buffalo the previous evening. "Shoshone National Park is on fire." We were already concerned about the Idaho flames of the Beaver Creek Fire blocking our trail to Ketchum, and this was another rocking horse worry, that wouldn't get us anywhere.

"It may still be closed." Said Buffalo Bill's admissions desk giant. "But you can't hurry up good times by waiting for them."

And so we were on our way up and out of Cody, along U.S. 120 to the junction of Wyoming 296. The one road away from trouble, is straight and narrow, and this wasn't it either. We rose into puff white and powder blue, beside a pink orange sandstone layer cake escarpment frosted with white icing, tilted like it had slid off a sage baking pan. The earth turned to reveal the floating purple majesty of the Absaroka Mountain anthem, sloped walls of the green

Shoshone National Forest falling towards and across us. There had been fire. In hard times the Shoshone subsisted on the tiny tubers of a small low scabland perennial with white and deep pink and rose flowers. The French trappers called them *racème amer*, from where we got our own appellation. *Bitterroot.* The man the highway was named for, had shown Lewis and Clark how to survive on them. The Lemhi Shoshone believed the small red core in the supper taproot had special powers had specials powers to stop an attack. They would be proven wrong.

The layer cake turned into a pillbox and the wilderness melted into meadows as we continued the turn. Robyn stopped to talk to two ancient bikers, an elderly couple with head bandanas and sunglasses, rebalancing the important appendages of their Harleys, her sidecar, his white beard. We drove north, past the open veins of a massive orange Aztec temple massif, immobilized by its grass foundation. Clouds moving overhead cast shadows over the pine profiles of prominences, either breasts or anthills, depending on perspective and passion. The wagon curved up, following switchbacks over summits of ochre crumble, which looked into deep lichen valley on the other side. We pulled over at a metal monument set among the white rock and spindle pines, far above the undulating viridescence below, and the far pavilion peaks beyond.

It was an alloyed couple on two metal horses, a rust and white man riding in front, with his bow and quivered arrows, and a white and rust woman riding behind, with her papoose.

"They're heading away from where we're going." Robyn said.

"We're looking for." I said. "They're running from."

The Chief Joseph Scenic Byway, in true American fashion, was one of those national monuments named in regretful respectful retrospect, after a profound and unjustifiable governmental atrocity, which had neutered and neutralized the subject of the memorial, and rendered him historically irrelevant. The Chief of the Nez Percés got 47 more paved miles of commemoration than most of his contemporaries, but he would have preferred the bitterroots of his Wallowa winding water homeland to an asphalt river ribbon to exile.

As usual, the whites got it wrong from the beginning. French Canadian fur traders encountered a tribe of more than 70 permanent winter villages spread over a seventeen million acre area surrounding the Snake, Salmon and Clearwater River Basins, extending from the Bitterroots in the east to the Blue Mountains in the west. They were the largest tribe on the Columbia River Plateau, and covered a considerable part of what is now Washington, Montana, Idaho and Oregon, with a population of around six thousand. The trappers named them the Nez Percés, the 'pierced noses,' mistaking them for the Chinook further down the Columbia basin. The Nez Percés didn't pierce their noses or wear ornaments. They called themselves Cúpnitpelu, the *People Walking*

Single File Out of the Forest, a reference to the time before they had horses.

The *Nez Percés,* were migratory and traveled in seasonal rounds, according to where food was most abundant at any given time of year. Their Wheel of Fortune spun them through about 300 temporary camps, as far east as the Great Plains of Montana to hunt buffalo, and as far west as the west coast to fish salmon. The *Nez Percés* kept horse herds, and gathered camas roots and berries in season.

On September 20, 1805, while crossing the Bitterroot Mountains and low on food, William Clark became the first Euro-American to encounter them. His experience was exceptional. *These Indians are anti-belligerent and have some other qualities that are rare and commendable.* Not only were they well fed, but Clark entrusted their horses to Walammottinin, chief Hair Bunched and Tied, who would become the father of Chief Lawyer, the *Nez Percé* that would preside of the Wheel of Misfortune seventy-two years later. Lewis and Clark recovered their horses upon their return from the Pacific. The many kindnesses extended would soon be forgotten, and the white men that came later would be different. One of them, Jacob Miller, made the observation in 1839.

"All these Indians seem to bear the impress of a doomed race." He said. Their story was the same story as would be told by them all.

The earth is our mother. We cannot sell you our mother. The chief the highway was named after still best tells their story.

'My name is In-mut-too-yah-lat-lat (Thunder traveling over the Mountains). I am chief of the Wal-lam-wat-kin band of Chute-pa-lu or Nez Percés (nose-pierced Indians). I was born in eastern Oregon, thirty-eight winters ago. My father was chief before me. When a young man, he was called Joseph by Mr. Spaulding, a missionary. He died a few years ago. There was no stain on his hands of the blood of a white man. He left a good name on the earth. He advised me well for my people. Our fathers gave us many laws, which they had learned from their fathers. These laws were good. They told us to treat all men as they treated us; that we should never be the first to break a bargain; that it was a disgrace to tell a lie; that we should speak only the truth; that it was a shame for one man to take from another his wife, or his property without paying for it. We were taught to believe that the Great Spirit sees and hears everything, and that he never forgets; that hereafter he will give every man a spirit-home according to his deserts; if he has been a good man, he will have a good home; if he has been a bad man, he will have a bad home. This I believe, and all my people believe the same...The first white men of your people who came to our country were named Lewis and Clarke. They also brought many things that our people had never seen. They talked straight, and our people gave them a great feast, as a proof that their hearts were friendly. These men were very kind. They made presents to our chiefs and our people made presents to them. We had a great many horses, of which we gave them what they needed, and they gave us guns and tobacco in return. All the Nez Percés made friends with Lewis and Clarke, and agreed to let them pass though their country, and never to make war on white men. This promise the Nez Percés have never broken. No white man can accuse them of bad faith, and speak with a straight tongue. It has always been the pride of the Nez Percés that they were the friends of the white men. When my father was a young man there came to our country a white man (Rev. Mr. Spaulding) who talked spirit law. He won the affections of our people because he spoke good things to them. At first he did not say anything about white men wanting to settle our lands. Nothing was aid about that until about twenty winters ago, when a number of white people came into our country and built houses and made farms. At first our people made no complaint. They thought there was room enough for all to live in peace, and they were learning many things from the white men that seemed to be good. But we soon found that the white men were growing rich very fast, and were greedy to possess everything the Indian had. My father was the first to see through the schemes of the white men, and he warned his tribe to be careful about trading with them. He had suspicion of men who seemed anxious to make money. I was a boy then, but I remember well my father's caution. He had sharper eyes than the rest of our people. Next there came a white officer (Governor Stevens), who invited all the Nez Percés to a treaty council. After the council was opened he made known his heart. He said there were a great many white people in the country, and many more would come; that he wanted the land marked out so that the Indians and white men could be separated. If they were to live in peace it was necessary, he said, that the Indians should have a country set apart for them, and in that country they must stay. My father, who represented his band, refused to have anything to do with the council, because he wished to be a free man. He claimed that no man owned any part of the earth, and a man could not sell what he did not own. Mr. Spaulding took hold of my father's arm and said, "Come and sign the treaty." My father pushed him away, and said: "Why do you ask me to sign away my country? Is it your business to talk to us about spirit matters, and not to talk to us about parting with our land." Governor Stevens urged my father to sign his treaty, but he refused. "I will not sign your paper," he said; "you can go where you please, so do I; you are not a child, I am no child; I can think for myself. No man can think for me. I have no other home than this. I will not give it up to any man. My people would have no home. Take away your paper. I will not touch it with my hand..." Eight years later (1863) was the next treaty council. A chief called Lawyer, because he was a great talker, took the lead in this council, and sold nearly all the Nez Percés country. My father was not there. He said to me: "When you go into council with the white man, always remember your country. Do not give it away. The white man will cheat you out of your home. I have taken no pay from the United States. I have never sold our land." In this treaty Lawyer acted without authority from our band. He had no right to sell the Wallowa (winding water) country. That had always belonged to my father's own people, and the other bands had never disputed our right to it. No other Indians ever claimed Wallowa.In order to have all the people understand how much land we owned, my father planted poles around it and said: "Inside is the home of my people- the white man may take the land outside. Inside this boundary all our people were born. It circles around the graves of our fathers, and we will never give up these graves to any man." The United States claimed they had bought all the Nez Percés country outside of Lapwai Reservation, from Lawyer and the other chiefs, but we continued to live on this land in peace until eight years ago, when white men began to come inside the bounds my father had set. We warned them against this great wrong, but they would not leave our land, and some bad blood was raised. The white men represented that we were going upon the war-path. They reported many things that were false. The United States Government again asked for a treaty council. My father had become blind and feeble. He could no longer speak for his people. It was then that I took my father's place as chief. In this council I made my first speech to white men. I said to the agent who held the council: "I did not want to come to this council, but I came hoping that we could save blood. The white man has no right to come here and take our country. We have never accepted any presents from the Governm ent. Neither Lawyer nor any other chief had authority to sell this land. It has always belonged to my people. It came unclouded to them from our fathers, and we will defend this land as long as a drop of Indian blood warms the heart of our men." The agent said he had orders, from the Great White Chief at Washington, for us to go upon the Lapwai Reservation, and that if we obeyed he would help us in many ways. "You must move to the agency," he said. I answered him: "I will not. I do not need your help; we have plenty, and we are contented and happy if the white man will let us alone. The reservation is too small for so many people with all their stock. You can keep your presents; we can go to your towns and pay for all we need; we have plenty of horses and cattle to sell, and we won't have any help from you; we are free now; we can go where we please. Our fathers were born here. Here they lived, here they died, here are their graves. We will never leave them." The agent went away, and we had peace for a little while. Soon after this my father sent for me. I saw he was dying. I took his hand in mine. He said: "My son, my body is returning to my mother earth, and my spirit is going very soon to see the Great Chief Spirit. When I am gone, think of your country. You are the chief of these people. They look to you to guide them. Always remember that your father never sold his country. You must stop your ears whenever you are asked to sign a treaty selling your home. A few years more, and white men will be all around you. They will have their eyes on this land. My son, never forget my dying words. This country holds your father's body. Never sell the bones of your father and your mother." I pressed my father's hand and told him I would protect his grave with my life. My father smiled and passed away to the spirit-land. I buried him in that beautiful valley of winding waters, I love that land more than all the rest of the world. A man who would not love his father's grave is worse than a wild animal. For a short time we lived quietly. But this could not last. White men had found gold in the mountains around the land of winding waters. They stole a great many horses from us, and we could not get them back because we were Indians. The white men told lies for each other. They drove off a great many of our cattle. Some white men branded our young cattle so they could claim them. We had no friend who would plead our cause before the law councils. It seemed to me that some of the white men in Wallowa were doing these things on purpose to get up a war. They knew that we were not strong enough to fight them. I labored hard to avoid trouble and bloodshed. We gave up some of our country to the white men, thinking that then we could have peace. We were mistaken. The white man would not let us alone. We could have avenged our wrongs many times, but we did not. Whenever the Government had asked us to help them against other Indians, we have never refused. When the white men were few and we were strong we could have killed them all off, but the Nez Percés wished to live in peace. If we have not done so, we have not been to blame. I believe that the old treaty has never been correctly reported. If we ever owned the land we own it still, for we never sold it. In the treaty councils the commissioners have claimed that our country had been sold to the Government. Suppose a white man should come to me and say, "Joseph, I like your horses, and I want to buy them." I say to him, "No, my horse suit me, I will not sell them." Then he goes to my neighbour, and says to him: "Joseph has some good horses. I want to buy them, but he refuses to sell." My neighbour answers, "Pay me the money, and I will sell you Josephs's horses." The white man returns to me, and says, "Joseph, I have bought your horses, and you must let me have them." If we sold our lands to the Government, this is the way they were bought…" I only ask of the Government to be treated as all other men are treated. If I can not go to my own home, let me have a home in some country where my people will not die so fast. I would like to go to Bitter Root Valley. There my people would be healthy; where they are now they are dying. Three have died since I left my camp to come to Washington. When I think of our condition my heart is heavy. I see men of my race treated as outlaws and driven from country to country, or shot down like animals. I know that my race must change. We can not hold our own with the white men as we are. We only ask an even chance to live as other men live. We ask to be recognized as men. We ask that the same l law shall work alike on all men. If the Indian breaks the law, punish him by the law. If the white man breaks the law, punish him also. Let me be a free man- free to travel, free to stop, free to work, free to trade where I choose, free to choose my own teachers, free to follow the religion of my fathers, free to think and talk and act for myself- and I will obey every law, or submit to the penalty. Whenever the white man treats the Indian as they treat each other, then we will have no more wars. We shall all be alike- brothers of one father and one mother, with one sky above us and one country around us, and one government for all. The the Great Spirit Chief who rules above will smile upon this land, and send rain to wash out the bloody spots made by brothers' hands from the face of the earth. For this time the Indians race are waiting and praying. I hope that no more groans of wounded men and women will ever go to the ear of the Great Spirit Chief above, and that all people may be one people.'

Chief Joseph, An Indian's View of Indian Affairs, North American Review, April 1879

It is humbling to realize that Chief Joseph wrote these words, as gently as they appear, after an ordeal that would have made them impossible for any lesser mortal. A man like that, you dedicate your book to.

On June 15, 1877, Joseph took 800 men, women and children, the faithful that had refused to give up their land to white ranchers, for coerced relocation on a captive reservation, and ran to seek new sanctuary. Following the Battle of the Big Hole in Idaho, they fled from the US Calvary, east through Yellowstone, and briefly captured several tourists, before heading north up the Clarks Fork River.

They made a valiant attempt to reach the camp of Sitting Bull in the Grandmother's country, almost two thousand miles across four states and two mountain ranges, in an epic flight to freedom. Two hundred *Nez Percés* warriors defeated or held off the pursuing troops, over 2,000 soldiers of the U.S. Army, in 18 engagements, during which more than 100 soldiers and 100 *Nez Percés* (including women and children) were killed. The Army ROTC Manual still contains a footnote. *In 11 weeks Joseph had moved his tribe 1600 miles, engaged 10 separate US commands in 13 battles and skirmishes, and in nearly every instance had either defeated them or fought them to a standstill.* On October 5, 1877, only 30 miles from the Canadian border, the majority of the surviving *Nez Percés* were finally stopped, after the six-day Battle of the Bear Paw Mountains in Montana. In his surrender to General Howard, Chief Joseph sent an extraordinary message through his soldiers, expressing dignity in defeat. It was one of the greatest of American speeches.

'Tell General Howard I know his heart. What he told me before I have in my heart. I am tired of fighting. Our chiefs are killed. Looking Glass is dead. Toohoolhoolzote is dead. The old men are all dead. It is the young men who say yes or no. He who led on the young men is dead. It is cold and we have no blankets. The little children are freezing to death. My people, some of them, have run away to the hills, and have no blankets. No food; no one knows where they are- perhaps freezing to death. I want to have time to look for my children and see how many of them I can find. Maybe I shall find them among the dead. Hear me, my chiefs! I am tired; My heart is sick and sad. From where the sun now stands, I will fight no more forever.'

Despite promises made to allow them back on

their lands, the Nez Percés tribe was floated on flatboats down the Missouri to bottomlands of malaria and malaise. A quarter of them died over the winter. The survivors were herded into railcars in the heat of the following summer, and transported to the hot plains of 'Indian Territory,' where they died more slowly. In September 21, 1904, Thunder traveling over the Mountains was pronounced deceased by an agency physician, who listed the cause of death as a 'broken heart.'

Just over a hundred years later, an auction house in Reno sold his shirt for almost $900,000. It was made of two deerskins, cut in half behind the front legs. The two back hides were joined at the shoulders to form the front and back of the shirt, and the two front skins were folded to make the sleeves. The retained forelegs extended below the open armpits. It was shaped to honour the spirit of the animal.

"That's a pretty special shirt." Said the auction organizer.

Robyn and I continued on the same Clarks Fork that Chief Joseph had retreated along, down a curve of variegated green hills into a clay valley of winding switchbacks, pines on the inside and hoodoos on the horizon. We were flying under the blue and white puffs through a mountain desert, grey mesas and valley floor invaginations, crevices lined with pines and exploding parasols of yellow flowers. A singular sedimentary strata sombrero strutted a thick rock brim and a sloped rakish ribbon hatband of green forest. Into mist rose a mountain of

Commagenean hoodoo gods, Antiochus and Apollo guardians standing vigil over the Beartooth Highway. *Nothing lives long Only the earth and the mountains.* We skated down past a spindled peak in the shape of a heart rhythm, with a repolarization wave that took us below the clouds into scattered pines, and the Northeast Gate of Yellowstone National Park.

'The only good Indian is a dead Indian.'
General Philip Sheridan

*   *   *

'It's a howling wilderness of three thousand square miles, full of imaginable freaks of fiery nature.'
Rudyard Kipling

Since Kipling described it a century and a half ago, not a lot had changed. We arrived at the entrance late afternoon, through the 'Coolest Town in America,' Cooke City, although the thermometric justification for the honorific was not immediately at hand. There was a dead cat that had definitely reached advertised temperature, and a more foreboding sign of counter-contraceptive chic. *Love them Both- End Abortion.*

Robyn and I rolled through the gateway, into the Lamar Valley, and 'America's Best Idea,' the first national park in the world, and one of the planet's most massive supervolcano calderas, larger in area than Rhode Island and Delaware combined. It boasted 10,000 geothermal features, half of those on earth, 300 geysers, 290 waterfalls of over 15 feet high, one of the largest high-altitude lakes in North America, and up to 3,000 earthquakes annually. Yellowstone is the most prodigious remaining nearly intact ecosystem in the Earth's northern temperate zone, the most famous, finest, megafauna location in the Continental United States.

Some of it was immediately in your face. The first buffalo we encountered, all beard and tail and furry penis and horns with shaved hindquarters, walked down the centerline of the road, and up to my wagon door, checking ID. He was massive, and he wasn't alone. Behind him were sage meadows full of the oldest and largest public herd of bison in the States, free of cattle genes and inhibition and full of brucellosis and piss and vinegar. Yellowstone was the only place in the country where they had lived continuously since prehistoric times, poached down to two dozen animals by 1902, and recovering so well by 1996, that over a thousand were culled. One of *one of the great triumphs of American conservation* was fogging up my window, before deciding to lose interest.

"Clearly, we were wasting our time at the

National Bison Range." Said Robyn. "They were all vacationing in Yellowstone." And she was right. All around us in the meadows on the valley floor, inside quaking aspen and white bark perimeters from where the lodgepole pines climbed the slopes, sitting and sleeping and wallowing and heads down eating, were the buffalo of my Old West authenticity.

Black clouds darkened the rolling yellow hills to grey, and turned the sagebrush into a scouring pad. *I got peace of mind and elbow room, I love the smell of the sage in bloom.*

Yellowstone is mostly subalpine forest, with 1,700 species of native vascular plants, including 7 conifers, 199 exotic plants, 186 lichens, and 406 thermophiles. All sixty-seven original fauna species that ever inhabited Yellowstone are still there- 7 ungulates, 2 bears, 322 birds, 16 fish, 6 reptiles, and 4 amphibians. Two species were threatened, the Canada lynx and grizzly bear, and one endangered.

Since 2005, when Mackenzie Valley wolves from Canada were reintroduced, to some unwelcoming howling from local ranchers, the ecosystem has seem some interesting changes. As the elk population of the northern herd began to drop, the beavers, reliant on the same willow, entered a dam building renaissance. The white pines had come back in a flourish, along with the animals that depend on their pine nuts for food. Grizzlies put on five pounds a day, just from the 50% fat they contain. The pine squirrel is as happy as a dead pig in the sunshine. But it's a bird that the tree actually waits for. The

Clark's nutcracker can hold a fifth of its body weigh in pine nuts under its tongue. It deposits ten seeds in every cache it marks with a stone, thirty thousand across a hundred square miles. Even under the snow it will remember where he left seventy per cent of them, which suits the white bark pine just fine because the other third that escape his memory become disseminated new white bark pines. Which suit the elk as well, because now, they're looking for new forested areas to evade the thirteen new wolf packs looking for them. However, even though there are still in excess of thirty thousand elk in the park, and the southern herd migration continues to be the largest mammalian migration in the US, the fate of the balance between the elk and the wolves and the rest of the ecosystem had become imperiled by several factors. In 1995, Yellowstone was placed on the List of World Heritage in Danger 'from the effects of tourism, infection of wildlife, and issues with invasive species.' The invasive species is the western pine beetle, the infections are diseases from local domestic livestock and the real wolves are regional realtors and developers.

In 1871, a year before President Ulysses S. Grant signed The Act of Dedication law that created the park, Ferdinand Hayden presented his Geological Survey to Congress, with a warning what would happen, if the bill failed to become law. *The vandals waiting to enter wonder-land, will in a single season despoil, beyond recovery, these remarkable curiosities, which have requited all the cunning skill of nature thousands of years to prepare.*

From where Robyn and I emerged at Mammoth Hot Springs, in 'one of the remote places on earth,' we were at least a single season too late. The 'most famous, finest, megafauna location in the Continental United States,' was overrun with the most prolific megafauna top predator, shopping in its stores, filling up its gas tanks, checking into its hotels, and trying to find parking so it could elbow its way through the lines to the embattled visitor information desks inside its concessionaires. In the same month, a year before Robyn and I joined the line for information, almost a million people had come to the park. From the size of the queue, they had forgotten what they were told the first time. When it was our turn, I took pity on the tired-looking elderly woman in the ranger hat behind the counter, and asked her an easy skill-testing question.

"Where's Mammoth Hot Springs." I said. It wasn't a completely foolish query. The place seemed less of a national park than a national proving ground, and everyone there was trying to prove something. I was just looking for the hot springs. She pulled out a map. On one side was the megafauna map, showing the three hundred miles of paved roads accessible from the five different parks entrances, and the locations of gas stations, stores, campgrounds, and the 2,238 hotel rooms and cabins available in the nine hotels and lodges. None of them had a vacancy. On the other side was a simple drawing. She drew an 'X' where we were, and another 'X' where we could, if we were smart enough, find the hot springs. I thanked her, one of 3,700 dedicated employees of the howling wilderness.

We drove through the suburbs to the most remote of the three parking lots of Mammoth Springs. It made no difference. We emerged from our wagon into a geothermal hajj, swirling through the cauldrons of crusted calcium in a molten multitude. I caught a blast of Hindi off to my right, with a single phrase of well-enunciated English. *Dormant hot springs cone.* The world had come to visit a planetary hot spot.

The boardwalks led us into glaring calcite snowfields, glaciers of Greek alabaster terraces, talc quarry ponds with protruding lips, like those at Pammukkele or the Tarawera pink and white terraces, now an exploded memory, Himalayan crystalline salt pitcher plant patios of frozen bone waterfalls, in greens and oranges and pinks, all the steam from which ate the clouds above. Dead trees and their petrified skeletal branches protruded through the white ash surrounding Mammoth Mordor marble temples. We walked a ghostly silence by a white and ochre striated slope, a Nez Percés quilted blanket dropped in flight, and another melting vanilla ice cream sundae boiling with chunky caramel sauce and golden brown meringue, a skin disorder plateau of unstable sulfur crust, tide pools of hot brown fimbria and crystalline crustaceans, and a tall rock gnome like a chess piece of an eleven million year old tectonic board game. It was the perfect superheated Superman fortress of anything but solitude.

We followed a couple of head visors and too short shorts, part of whose daily caloric intake may have been pilfered from the tiny dog on the leash. In this megafauna menagerie, it was better to half starve than be eaten. He wouldn't have lasted a day without them.

"Almost there now." I said, taking the sharp turn off the highway.

"Is this the secret swimming hole on the Yellowstone River that our Montana Ale Works waiter told us about in Bozeman?" Asked Robyn.

"The very same." I said. But of course it wasn't a secret, so close the Mammoth Springs, and so far from Bozeman. Still, it was a celebration, of free hot running water and pools of Boiling River happy. The French trappers had named the river Roche Jaune, from the native Minnetaree name, Mi tsi a-da-zi. *Rock Yellow River*. But there were other Wild West colours, of yellows and greens and grays and chalk and browns and pale blues. We moved occasionally, to adjust our temperature, along the grass and flowers that grew on the midstream islands. Robyn's smile soldered the rapids to the white rocks to the shore sage to the sloped hillocks to the bare mountains speculated with pines to the setting sun in the sky. We soaked, almost at the end of our day.

Robyn drove us back into Montana, through the Roosevelt Arch, to Gardiner. It was made of wind and flies. Nancy greeted us at the door of her Gardiner Guest House. She had just returned from the market in Bozeman, shopping for next morning's breakfast.

"Did you really come all that way today?" She asked. We nodded. She shook her head the other way, and showed us where the homemade cookies were. Nancy was originally from Maine, but her ancestors had come from further north. "Pur Laine." She said. *Pure wool*, as the original Quebecois settlers describe themselves. She introduced us to Jeff and Brandy, the Texans across the hall we would share our bathroom with. It was all good. I asked her where a good place to eat might be. I could tell from her answer it wasn't nearby.

"I like The Raven." She said, defending it like the first part of the sentence could have been '*Except for the food...*'

"It's good." Said Jeff and Brandy. You plant a tater, you get a tater. We went off to The Raven.

"I wouldn't expect much." I said to Robyn. "We're a long way from a Michelin star." The blowflies came inside with us, gone with the wind. Insect strips hanging from the ceiling had already caught their limit. The waitress was pleasant enough, but she was our second clue. A big bulky bottled blonde with a button nose, and with what could have been her mother's horn-rimmed glasses, she poured her daily special welcome into our water glasses, as she wiped down the booth.

"Tonight we have a salmon encrusted with pine nuts with a vanilla buerre blanc sauce and pineapple coulis." She said. "It's kinda like Indian. And for dessert we have a huckleberry crème brulee."

I had the bison sirloin, for twenty-eight bucks. You can put your boots in the oven but they won't come out as biscuits. It came black, an unimaginable freak of fiery nature, with Barbecue sauce.

"It appears that everything including the toothpaste in Montana is drowned in BBQ sauce." I said. There was white toast with diagonal grill marks, yellow zucchini mush, and something that resembled potato salad. You plant a tater you get a tater. The waitress returned to inquire.

"Is everything alright here?" She asked. Never miss a good chance to shut up.

"We are rough men and used to rough ways." I said, smiling with mouthful of buffalo gristle.

"Oh good." She said. I don't rightly recall if we had dessert, or if we bought a candy bar next door, but on our way to the candy bar, we met Jim Cole and his moustache. Jim was eighty if he was a day, and dressed head to toe in buckskin, looked as hungry as a toothless coyote. He was selling leather, which he had burned into patterns of grizzlies, bighorn sheep, bull elk and bison.

"Looks a whole lot tastier than my dinner was." I said. He laughed.

"I come with the restaurant." He said, and told us of his life as the artist-in-residence for nine years at the Old Faithful Inn, and as music teacher for a hundred voice choir in Missoula for a quarter century. I asked him why he chose to live in Montana.

"I was in Hawaii once." He said. "But I didn't

want to swim." Jim was retired, and we retired, via the convenience store.

"My friend and me got a hankerin' for Switzerland chocolate and a good smoke." I said. We had a *Snickers*.

Late in the night, Robyn asleep, I looked out, through the crab apple trees, into the dusty back street of Gardiner. The wind was up, and the window open just enough. The leather and feather Indian dreamcatcher over the bed, spun slowly, like a wheel of fortune.

*   *   *

Buffalo Bills
Jackson, Wyoming

'For it is my opinion that we enclose and
celebrate the freaks of our nation and our
civilization. Yellowstone National Park
is no more representative of America than
is Disneyland.'
John Steinbeck, *Travels with Charley*

Uranium. Steinbeck was wrong. A halo only
needs to drop a few inches to become a noose.
Yellowstone, the authentic, would become
Disneyland. And Disneyland would become
America. And America would become a theatre
of manufactured experiences, a virtual video
game, the myth-making machine of a lost
generation, dominant hand out, searching for
the signal, missing on the open range.

"We call it a drive-by shooting." Said Richard, at
breakfast next morning, referring to the way the
license plates and telephotos hurtle through the
park. Richard was Nancy's husband, a local fly-
fishing guru, holding forth at the head of the
breakfast table. Nancy served up omelettes and
fresh muffins, and fruit. The Texans, and
another couple from Colorado, heading to Mount
Rushmore, had joined us.

"We'll be there by tonight." He said. Richard
ignored him, and continued his dissertation.

"During the construction of the post office in
Gardiner in the 1950's." He said, "They found a
Clovis obsidian projectile point dating from

eleven thousand years ago. Yellowstone arrowheads have been found as far away as the Mississippi, which gives you some idea of the traffic." I made an observation about the traffic.

"Three million visitors a year." Richard said. "Two million in July and August and a million the rest of the year." I sucked in my breath.

"Hell." He said. "That's the same number of campers that stay in the seventy-nine Jellystone Park Camp-Resorts each year, if you'd rather sleep near a Borscht Belt imitation of a bear, than the real thing."

"I think I'd rather sleep near Yogi." Said the woman from Colorado.

"Hello, Mr. Ranger, sir!" Said her husband. "I loved the cartoons as a kid, and wondered about the location of Jellystone, and *pic-a-nic* baskets."

"Disney ruined us more than Hanna-Barbera." Said Richard, speaking to Robyn and I.

"Your bucolic swim in the Yellowstone last evening has become a Casey Jr. Splash n' Soak Station. America is a Magic Kingdom of Manifest Destiny, the 'Happiest Place on Earth.' Disney World is laid out like a wheel of fortune, with Cinderella's Castle at the hub, and spokes out to a Walt Disney World Railroad perimeter of inauthenticities. The first stops are Liberty Square, the Liberty Belle Riverboat, and the shops of Main Street, USA, with an emporium of souvenirs, a confectionary of sugared sweets, and at least three food outlets selling ballpark hot dog and fries, and other fare. Frontierland is a chimera of the Old West, with romanticized versions of cowboys and Indians, rivers, mountains and fauna. Animatronic grizzlies play banjos and washboard bass in the Country Bear Jamboree. 'Thunder traveling over the Mountains' Chief Joseph had become the *rigor mortis* reincarnation of Big Thunder Mountain. Once, when Disney saw a Frontierland cowboy walking through Tomorrowland, he built a series of *utilidor* tunnels to keep his version of America's past from intruding on his vision of America's future. Adventureland represents the mystery of foreign lands, like Tokyo Disneyland, Disneyland Park Paris, Hong Kong Disneyland, Shanghai Disneyland, and now the Nintendo video game, *Adventures in the Magic Kingdom.* Then there's Disney's Wilderness Lodge, Disney's Fort Wilderness Campground, and Fantasyland's Many Adventures of Winnie the Pooh and the Enchanted Forest."

"And the real authentic future?" Asked Robyn.

"The real future is Disney's Tomorrowland." Richard said. "At least that one's accurate. The Seven Dwarfs Mine Train roller coaster ride." He turned to the duo from Denver.

"All you'll see, on your way across Wyoming, is gas well, gas well, big ass oil rig...gas well, gas well, big ass oil rig..."

"A man's got to have more than that." I said. "He needs something to believe in. Whatever happened to 'take only what you need and leave the land as you found it?'"

"You give people a choice between truth and beauty." Richard said. "They'll take beauty every time. That's why they let Disney get rid of the dirt and the bugs and the danger, and the need for redemption." The guy from Colorado was getting antsy.

"Slap some bacon on a biscuit and let's go." He said. "We're burnin' daylight." And we all shook hands, and went our separate ways.

Robyn and I kissed Nancy goodbye. She gave me some home baked ginger cookies, 'in case the glove compartment's hungry.'

We headed back south through the Roosevelt Arch. *For the benefit and enjoyment of all the people.* Robyn and I drove by herds of elk bums in the faint dawn light. The hawk that flew his loop de loop in front of our wagon was a hot damn. And there was more of that further south. The alpine lakes and pines and waterfall and river would have felt at home in my Northwestern Ontario birthplace, except for the lazy buffalo lying on the warm sulfur caldera crust, the hills and jets and baths and lagoons and horizons of vapour steaming over green and boardwalks and dead sticks and trees, on yellow mud panoramas and brown mud flats and bubbling mud volcanoes, cauldrons of copper and hot ponds of blue opals and white opalescence, streaked banana and avocado jelly moulds, and the deep sapphire nuclear heavy water pool trapped in snow white crystal crunch we photographed our profiles on. Robyn and I were first domesticated in Rotorua, New Zealand and it was almost the same, but for the pines and buffalo. And the tourists.

The largest active geyser on earth, the Steamboat, awaited in Norris Basin. It erupted while we were still high on the hill that would take us there, and we still had to look up. It exploded at the epicentre of the world's largest supervolcano, the one that was threatening to do it again. The Yellowstone caldera had erupted three times in the last 2.1 millions years. The first was the most violent, ejecting almost six hundred cubic miles of planetary material into the atmosphere. The second, a tenth of that, was still large enough to cause a significant impact on world weather patterns, and cause the extinction of numerous North American species. The last occurred just over half a million years ago, a thousand times more powerful than the 1980 Mount St. Helens eruption, creating a caldera a kilometre deep and 75 by 45 kilometres in area. Since this last supereruption, there have been at least thirty smaller cycles that have filled in the concavity with ash and lava, flattening the bowl into the platelike landscape that Robyn and I were standing on.

There were earthquakes, hundreds of them, at least six with a Richter magnitude of six or more, in historical times. One in 1959 came in at 7.5, killed twenty-eight people, and caused large cracks in the ground, and geysers to erupt. Earthquakes came in 'swarms,' 250 over four days in 2008, and as many over two days, in 2010.

The Norris Basin was closed temporarily in 2003, because of increasing water temperatures, new fumeroles, heightened geyser activity, and the discovery of a structural dome of swelling magma six miles underground beneath the surface, a 'pancake-shaped blob' of molten rock the size of Los Angeles, pushing toward the earth's surface. On March 10, 2004, a biologist discovered five dead bison that had inhaled toxic geothermal gases. Two years later geologists reported that the flow of the Mallard Lake and Sour Creek Domes had risen faster in the previous three years, than at any time since records began in 1923. Experts have informed the public that there was no increased risk of a volcanic eruption in the near future.

"So there's no possibility of another eruption?" Robyn asked.

"Possibility is a big word." I said. "An age-of-the-universe word. Probability, however, is a word just waiting to bushwhack you. If Yellowstone goes off again, and some people think its not that far away, there will be a layer of ash ten foot deep a thousand miles away. You'll see lava in the sky, and millions of people will be homeless."

We continued our drive south, toward the most famous geyser on earth, the one you could set your watch by. There were areas still black from the previous season's fires.

"These weren't the worst ones." I said. "In 1988, a third of the park burnt down. On 'Black Saturday', August 20, 1988, they lost more than 150,000 acres, two of the twenty-five thousand firefighters, 120 million dollars, 345 elk, 36 deer, 12 moose, 6 black bears, and 9 buffalo.

"But that's the way this ecosystem works." Robyn said. Lodgepole pine cones open only with fire, and their seeds are held in place by a resin that the flames melt and disperse. The Douglas fir thick bark protects the inner part of tree, and the grasslands had a natural burn cycle of a quarter century. Fire is a part of nature."

We came across a sign, better suited to a turnpike than a park. *Gas... Food...Lodging... Right Lane.*

"It seems like an overpass." Robyn said.

"It is too!" I said, and our wagon pulled off into a spiral, through a series of numbered parking lots that would have been better attached to an automobile plant. There were about that many cars, from all over America. I found the Old Faithful Inn, and the clock on the wall that indicated the time of the next gusher, and Robyn found the shops. The rock fireplace was four stories high, backdropped by lodgepole and beam and centred by an elk skull and two Arts and Crafts lanterns.

The amphitheatre outside, surrounding the geyser launchpad dome was big enough to host the second coming of Christ and, when Old Faithful arrived on cue, there was that much water that it mingled into the white clouds hovering above. *Bubble bubble whoosh.*

"About as much water as our oil well hit in Texas." I said, a story better left untold. The one that should be told was coming after us, however. Not long after our visit, Barack Obama shut down the National Park Service for two weeks in a de facto neo-monarchical violation of what even the English recognized as a Charter of the Forest in 1219, two years after King Henry III signed the Magna Carta. The Park Service morphed into the paramilitary wing of the Democratic National Party, and spent more money trying to close down the great outdoors, than they would normally do in keeping them open. Mark Steyn had it right.

'The most extraordinary story is the tour group of foreign seniors whose bus was trapped in Yellowstone Park the day the shutdown began... pulled over photographing a herd of bison when an armed ranger informed them, with the insouciant ad-hoc unilateral lawmaking to which the armed bureaucrat is distressingly prone, that taking photographs counts as illegal "recreation." "Sir, you are recreating," the ranger informed the tour guide. And we can't have that, can we? ordered back to the Old Faithful Inn, next to the geyser of the same name, but forbidden to leave said inn to look at said geyser. Armed rangers were posted at the doors, and, just in case one of the wily Japanese or Aussies managed to outwit his captors by escaping through one of the inn's air ducts and down to the geyser, a fleet of NPS SUVs showed up every hour and a half throughout the day, ten minutes before Old Faithful was due to blow, to surround the geyser and additionally ensure that any of America's foreign visitors trying to photograph the impressive natural phenomenon from a second-floor hotel window would still wind up with a picture full of government officials. The following morning the bus made the two-and-a-half-hour journey to the park boundary but was prevented from using any of the bathrooms en route, including at a private dude ranch whose owner was threatened with the loss of his license if he allowed any tourist to use the facilities.'

The geyser Nazis had repealed the Charter of the Forest. An English peasant had enjoyed more freedom on the King's land in the 13th century than a freeborn American did in a public national park in the 21st. The Japanese and Australian tourists that had come to see the authentic 'land of the free' missed it. The truth didn't live here any more.

The metaphors chased us through the southwestern portion of the park. We crossed the Continental Divide three times, the Snake River flowing off to the Pacific on our right, the Yellowstone on our left, streaming to the Atlantic via the Gulf of Mexico. The signs on the shoulders ordered us to slow down. *We saw wildlife from afar, Until we hit them with our car.*

There was one more national freak to celebrate, before Robyn and I ejected out the bottom of Yellowstone.

"It was just about here." I said, stopping at the top of a steep slope. "Shoshone Point. The last stagecoach holdup of the Old West. Forty of them, actually. The man was as sharp as a mashed potato, but even a blind pig can find an acorn once in a while."

In 1876, the year Wild Bill Hickok was assassinated, holding his poker Dead Man's Hand in Deadwood, a 23 year-old petty criminal left there for Idaho, where he got to reading a story about the James-Younger gang. Edwin Burnham Trafton resolved to become a criminal of no small notoriety, but he remained an inept amateur, and ill-equipped for the task. He always got caught, his prison sentences approached a century, and his only luck came because of his likability, in the form of latent leniency.

In 1889 he was sent to the Idaho State Penitentiary in Boise for rustling cattle, returned for robbing a store in Rexburg, and again for stealing more cattle. On one occasion Ed tried to set up another man. He wrote out a suicide note, signed the man's name to it, and headed to the cabin to murder him. But Ed was captured creeping by the owner, who got to read his own fabricated suicide note. A decade later, Ed concocted what he thought was an absolutely foolproof plan to rob his mother of ten thousand dollars. She had him arrested and sent to the Colorado State Penitentiary. No reporters took any notice, possibly because of Halley's comet, passing overhead.

In 1910 a U.S. Mail carrier opening came available for 'a good, honest, trustworthy man,' in Yellowstone. They hired Ed because he knew the area. When Yellowstone was dedicated as a national park, it meant that any crime committed within its boundaries would be a federal crime, which, one would think, would be some kind of deterrent. When tourists arrived at Yellowstone, they were required to leave their firearms with park rangers. Automobiles were prohibited in the park. Instead, a regular schedule of stagecoaches, drawn by a team of four horses, was established, to carry up to eleven passengers on a four-day tour.

On July 29, 1914, Ed Trafton, still on parole, robbed all 40 stagecoaches of the Yellowstone Stagecoach Company in a morning. When the first stage arrived, Ed ordered the driver to pull it behind a rock outcropping where it would not be visible to the other approaching coaches. Wearing several layers of extra clothes and a black mask, he ordered the passengers to disembark and place their valuables on a blanket he had spread on the ground. Ed told them his 'partner' was covering them from a nearby rise, and that he wanted 'cash only.' He asked the women to 'hide their jewelry,' refused to take one young girl's money because she was 'too pretty to rob,' and returned one elderly lady's cash because 'you look like you need it more than I do.' His hijinks and joking earned him the sobriquet of 'The Merry Bandit.' Ed even pulled down his mask for photos, and one victim later made the comment that it was 'the best 50 bucks I ever spent.' Ed's assembly line got away with three thousand dollars from 165 passengers. But no one paid much attention, because of the breakout of World War I.

Less than a year after the robbery, his wife turned Ed into the local police in Jerome, Idaho. It seems that Ed, while constructing an armoured car to use in the planned kidnapping and ransom of the president of the LDS Church, was also having an affair with the neighbour's wife. No one read about his sentence to five years in Leavenworth, possibly because of the sinking of the Lusitania.

When Ed got out of prison, he went to Hollywood in an attempt to sell his story. In 1924, he died with his boots on, while eating an ice cream cone. They found a note on his body. *This will introduce Edwin B. Trafton, better known as Ed Harrington. Mr. Trafton was the man from whom*

Owen Wister modeled the character of 'The Virginian. Ed also claimed that he rode with Butch Cassidy and the Sundance Kid in the Wild Bunch, but it is a matter of record that he did build Wister's cabin, when the author moved to Yellowstone in 1912. The verdict, like most things associated with Ed Trafton, is still awaiting authentication, and redemption.

* * *

'It will feel better when it quits hurting.'
Cowboy Proverb

Reemerging into Wyoming, I began to realize that something was terribly wrong. Something was wrong, even before all my money fell into Jackson Hole.

There was little hint of it along the John D. Rockefeller Memorial Parkway south of Yellowstone, although I'm sure he had a hand in it. There was no insinuation of it in the clouds, billowing over the large rock breasts of the Tetons, looming almost fourteen thousand feet above us, although there was some kind of big American thunder battle going on. Some of the rocks in the range were almost three billion years old, but what was wrong was much younger than that. The bighorn sheep-eating

Shoshone used to climb to 'The Enclosure' on the upper slope just below the peak of Grand Teton, for vision quests, before the fur ran out.

Whatever fur still existed would be ahead of us, in the enclosures in Jackson, along with what was left of the vision. Some of it may have still existed at Jenny Lake, but I couldn't be sure, because we couldn't find a place in the parking lot. Or maybe that was why the epiphany occurred, about what was wrong.

Below the thousand pristine acres of Jenny Lake alpine water, were a thousand less-than-pristine acres of parking lot, full of SUVs and RVs and ATVs and other acronyms, and luggage racks and bike racks and ski racks and board racks. The authenticity they had all come to see, was destroyed in their droves.

Tourists still swarm from Wild Bill Hickok's real gravesite to the modern patch of kitschy Americana downtown Deadwood, or to the town of William Cody, who transformed Hickok's tragedy into farce. Behind the Ben Cartwrights, the Daniel Boones, the Huckleberry Finns, the Roy Rogers, and all that dirt road manufactured charm and innocence, is an industrial machine.

The American dream is an assemblage of Orwellian infrastructure, artfully concealed behind a Rockwellian romantic human façade, the space within which we render technology invisible to our senses, while retaining its instrumental capacities.

The Rockwellian veil is the new substitute for authenticity, for living in Nature, for facing death with dignity and courage. There is no requirement for truth, or redemption. We live in a manufactured innocence, a studiously maintained aura of the small-town heartland ideal.

The proportions of the Orwellian heartland defy our spatial intuition. Its pace of evolution defies our sense of time. Humans are blissfully unaware of how much steel surrounds them wherever they go. The real America has become a land of cryptic conversations between radio-frequency ID scanners and software and passing railroad cars, serially numbered energy-efficient widgets manipulating infinite data, completing the veil and sealing the last reality leaks. The interfaces have thickened and acquired intelligence in proportion to our desire to convert Orwellian reality into Rockwellian innocence.

Of those still too poor to do all their shopping in Whole Foods, there are still visceral encounters with back-end realities like the factory farm-processed pink slime world of Tyson Fresh Meats and Cargill Foods.

The veil may still be imperfect, but the special effects are improving. The arms race between technological forces pulling us out of Eden, and the camouflaging forces striving to return us to a simulation of it, is entering its endgame. Marketing narratives are becoming more sophisticated, and American pop culture continues to recycle the long-term memory of Rockwell's sensitivity.

There are also new enemies of affirmation and redemption, the political progressives who seem exist only to deny bourgeois principles of innocence, loyalty, courage, virtue, self-sacrifice, love, faith, community, or achievement of any kind, are ascendant. Their myth of the nonexistent American yesteryear has itself assumed mythic status by now.

However the sentimental Rockwellian myth persists because it is useful and necessary to maintain the industrial equilibrium and momentum.

But those who want a more seamless illusion must pay more. In 1899, the economist Thorstein Veblen wrote in *The Theory of the Leisure Class*, described the birth of this deceit in the pastoralized estates of the rich.

Which is how Robyn and I came into Jackson Hole, the most complete Rockwellian veil vale in America, an artificial heartland Eden so impeccable that only the superrich could afford to live there.

Teton County is the wealthiest in the country. Wyoming has no personal or corporate income tax and relatively low property taxes thanks to mining revenue. Even the artificial hearts are Orwellian. Former Vice-President Dick Cheney had a single one-off special defibrillator manufactured by Medtronic with the Wi-Fi feature deactivated, so no one would be able to kill him online. One late night television host was less kind. *What better place for a guy who has had four heart attacks than... thin air, rugged hiking and all-beef dinners? Why don't they get some snow for him to shovel...*

Robyn and I drove onto the lined pavement of North Milward Street, beside the stream, to the

Inn on the Creek. We were made welcome by English and German and Swiss and Welsh flags and shutters on a Tudor beam and riverstone façade, flowerpots, Lindsay, and two ducks. Five months earlier, I had trouble booking the place. *Thank you for your interest in Inn on the Creek. Sorry we are booked for the nights you are interested in. Unfortunately, we do not take a waitlist in case of cancellations. We would like to invite you to stop by the property while you're in town to take a tour.* A week later I took advantage of a cancellation, and booked a 'creek-side' room. *Broke is what happens when a cowboy lets his yearnins get ahead of his earnins.*

We headed down to the Town Square statue of John Colter on a bucking bronco, and the elk-antler U-shaped arches at each corner of George Washington Park. Ski hill topiary topography rose in the background. Rows of Rockwellian shops lined the square, lined with SUVs and their luggage racks and bike racks and ski racks and board racks. *Hide Out Leather Apparel, Turpin's & Co., Pendleton, Alaska Fur Gallery, Wyoming Outfitters, Jackson Mercantile, Rare Gallery, Wyoming Country Outfitters, Belle Cose, al-ti-tude.* Robyn posed for a photo, hiding behind a bronze cowboy named 'Slim,' and then said she would meet me later. There were illusions of the Old West- a complete Conestoga wagon on a storefront roof, the *Saddle Rock Family Saloon* complete with cigar store Indian and Uncle Sam, wagon wheels on the outside of the benches on the boardwalk, fractal white Christmas lights, horses and stars and lanterns and pines and stained glass, and mountains and an Indian headdress and fire hose. A bronze Mark Twain, Tom Sawyer and Becky hovered over a bronze park bench. There was a big bronze moose, a bronze Indian bronze Winnie and Pooh in a hidden corner enclave. Redford and Newman sported Wyoming t-shirts as Butch Cassidy and Sundance in one shop window, near a building mural of a young girl riding a bucking bronco carpet. *Davies Reid Rugs Made for the American West.* A re-enactment of a gunfight occurred in the late afternoon. There was an undertaker, a hangman, and big-bellied gunfighter. The guns, all Colt Single Action Army issue, were loud. *A gun and three of a kind always beats three of a kind.*

Gunslingers in the Old West took advantage of the empty chamber by stuffing it with a rolled-up $5 bill. If they came out second best in a duel, they could still pay for a decent burial. A red stagecoach with black horses and yellow-rimmed wagon wheels rolled by. I wandered into a shop selling Mexican onyx rock sheet panels, backlit to show off their orange hearts. In another, was a real triceratops skull, on sale for $458,000.

I told the salesclerk I was looking for something a little more compact, and wandered into the watch place next door. The owner was from Lima, but any innate disposition to negotiate had been thoroughly expunged. I had selected a new tough guy timepiece and asked about a discount.

"It's only a watch." He said. "Harrison Ford lives

here. He has over three hundred." I had no reply to that. Even with a whip in one hand and a lightsaber in the other, there was no way I was getting a discount. Besides, I had to check it out with Robyn.

We met in time for our reservation at the Snake River Grill. This would be the most shi shi place on our trip. I had seen people lining up in late afternoon, while I was trying out the triceratops. Under the red and gray and black and white siding, and the logo of an Indian riding a Snake River cutthroat bareback, we entered a world of tinkling glass and clanking cutlery and popping corks and hubbub. Our waitress's name was Berry, and how could it not have been. Berry had served Harrison Ford, and told us about his three hundred watches. It must be hard to keep a secret in Jackson. The clientele were sporting a few watches themselves. And a good percentage of the precious stones of the planet. An elderly black guy with a turquoise stud earring was seated with a blonde a third his age, at the next table. He never looked at anything but her torso. She never took her eyes off the menu. *Each man is good in the sight of the Great Spirit.*

Berry did us proud. I had the buffalo carpaccio with giant Spanish capers and arugula on toast (and a sixty dollar buffalo steak), and Robyn had a grilled shoestring potato-encrusted halibut, as good as anything I've cooked at Kenny's cabin in Barkley Sound. Berry nodded, as she poured out a 2010 Domaine Boissonnet Gigondas.

"You get it." She said. I looked over at Turquoise.

She had ordered Dom Perignon. The emptier the barrel, the louder the noise.

Robyn and I said goodnight to Berry, and retired to the extravagant comfort of our creekside room, back at the Inn. We had lived a day of Rockwellian splendor, blissfully unaware of the Orwellian infrastructure that had made it all possible. But the bridle was about to come off the nightmare.

Trucks. There were trucks. Not just the odd downshifting gearbox or the rattlesnake hiss of an occasional airbrake, but the full cacophony orchestra of the industrial cathedral, rig after eighteen-wheeler after transport after tractor-trailer after flatbed after pickup. Even the plumbing groaned all night, in protest. There is a time for many words, and there is also a time for sleep. But there hadn't been much of either, next morning at breakfast. All the guests were cheerfully discussing their plans for the day, and the owners and staff were cheerfully egging them on. Casey, the owner pouring our fresh-squeezed Rockwell, asked how we slept. He was the astute one. His wife presented me with our Buffalo bill, with the same eye contact that Turquoise's escort had demonstrated in the Grill, the previous evening.

Casey came running after us, on our departure.

"Y'all like Champagne?" He asked. I nodded. He was back in a minute with a bottle of Domaine Carneros.

"Sorry about your sleep." He said. Nice guy, Casey, although real Champagne would have been better. In the end it appears that Casey lost more sleep than we did.

'It was nice to meet you both and I am sorry about your lack of adequate sleep at Inn on the Creek... The noise aspect is variable from guest to guest with the vast majority expressing a contented night's rest. As proprietor of Inn on the Creek I attempt to ask every guest: how did you sleep? This pertinent question allows me to evaluate the responses and make improvements for our guest's experiences at the Inn... This summer Jackson is experiencing a major highway reconstruction project that effects tourists and locals alike. And to add to the bustling nature of Jackson is the revival of the construction industry that has been dormant the past four years. Personally I never felt that I would welcome back all the noises associated with construction... for your desire to sleep with the window open and the use of no fan or a/c I can empathize. My wife and I live on the slopes of Snowking Mountain, one mile from the Inn, with no a/c, prefer the windows open for the fresh wonderful mountain air but use a fan to quiet the outside nightly activity of hooting owls, screech owls, the coyotes howling, our dogs barking at the wandering moose and deer, and yes late night traffic noise from the valley below. I like the wilderness sounds! So back to the noise issue. I honestly feel that had you nighted at other Jackson lodging establishments along the same route with your windows open and no "white reduction noise" efforts that you would have experienced similar discomforts. Closing windows and using a fan definitely reduces outside noise issues. I would say the majority of our guests utilize those techniques and succeed in securing a restful night. That being said, I know this offers you no appeasement. Can I stop traffic from 10:00 pm to 7:00am?'

No, Casey, you can't. The Orwellian is inexorable, the Rockwellian fragile, the world noisier, the sign on the Inn that morning prescient. *Vacancy.*

Before we left Jackson, Robyn wanted to have 'another look round.' We stopped into an art gallery of track lighting and Old West memories.

> Woodrow F. Call: There's durn people makin'
>   towns everywhere.
> Gus McCrae: And it's our fault, too.
> Woodrow F. Call: Our fault?
> Gus McCrae: Well, we chased out the Indians,
>   didn't we? Hung all the good
>   bandits. Did it ever occur to you
>   that everything we done was a
>   mistake? You and me done our
>   work too well, Woodrow. Hell, we
>   killed off all the people that made
>   this country interesting to begin
>   with, didn't we?
>   Larry McMurtry, *Lonesome Dove*

Perhaps not all the people. The diva dressed in leather and silver and turquoise behind her desk was interesting. Above her oversized Stetson hung two pink and purple cartoons of cowboys and cowgirls, playing pool and pinball.

"Just looking." We said, in reply to her inquiry. The quickest way to double your money is to fold it over and put it back into your pocket. But I did buy the watch and, while I was doing that, and not paying attention, Robyn left and returned, with a short rope, a sweet smile, and a hot brand.

"You have to see this." She said. Of course I did.

She took my hand and led me down the boardwalk, providing a glimpse at how painful this was going to be. We entered another gallery, another dimension. He had half glasses, and half a smile.

"Turpin." He said. "Ron Turpin." I was thinking Dick, as in highway robbery.

"You from Vancouver Island?" He asked. I nodded.

"I used to be a guide there." He said.

"Really." I said.

"Yep." He said. "Shot a lot of bears in your back yard." There seemed to be a lot of that going around. I was wearing my *Preserve BC Wildlife* t-shirt. *But it isn't hunger that drives millions of armed American Males to forests and hills every autumn, as the high incidence of heart failure among the hunters will prove. Somehow the hunting process has to do with masculinity, but I don't quite know how.*

"You must have a disabled brother in Bozeman." I said. For a flicker of a moment, he looked annoyed. Ron used to take his pleasure in the destruction of the rare and beautiful, but somewhere along the carnage, he was reborn as a sculptor, and a missionary. Ron carried his message to China, but I suspect there was too much noise for his signal.

"I'm a Christian now." He said. Oh joy. He pulled out the bronze.

Robyn likes frogs. I had to admit that this one was masterfully done. I asked him how much. He told me, like he was lining up on a bear. I offered him less, but I had no negotiating room.

Anything I did now would only make me look tighter than the bark on the tree outside in the sidewalk.

"It isn't worth fussing about unless the bone is showing or you ain't got no feeling in it." He said. I bought the frog.

"God bless." He said, as we were leaving. It was too late for all that. All my buffalo bills went ballistic in Jackson; my money had lasted about as long as a rattler in a cowboy's boot.

On our way to the exit, Robyn and I went by the Cowboy Bar's tan and blue and tin and neon bucking bronco marquis, to visit the old Wort Hotel. Inside the men's room was blonde cartoon cowgirl cleavage on a wooden rocking horse, with a feather duster for a tail. But the only authenticity in Jackson came in the form of the bronze couple hugging at foot of stairway, wrapped around the banister at the bottom of the staircase with the big elk head on the fireplace at the top. At first it looked like an embrace of joy, until you looked down, at the broken bronze wagon wheel beside them.

*   *   *

'Never work for a man who has electricity in his barn. You'll be up all night.'

Anonymous cowboy

The energy to where Robyn and I were headed was all Orwellian nuclear. It wasn't in Victor, *The End of the Trail*, home of the Knot Pine Supper Club, and the Big Hole BBQ. It wasn't in the Snake Range Targhee National Forest, *Land of Many Uses*. Nor in the Swan Valley, an *Idaho Gem Community*. Nor was it along the Big Lost River, nor the Four Winds Saloon nor the Big Butte in Butte City. Before Robyn and I found the energy, we would avoid engaging in the twenty-seven prohibited activities, at the rest stop overlooking the Snake River, and pass through endless amber waves of grain and green groundswells of potatoes, combines and dust devils and windmill farms, and the smell of a dead skunk. As we swerved around the dead porcupine, a bird bounced off our windshield. *Manage Wildlife.*

"Once I lose my mind completely, I can concentrate on fly-fishing." I said.

We pulled into Arco up South Front, and took a left onto West Grand. *First loan free. Future Home of the Lost River Medical Center. No Fireworks.* But there had been, of course. The first clue was a restaurant we passed. *Pickles Place- Home of the Atomic Burger.* A second arrived with Kaolin, the owner of the Deli Sandwich Shop.

"The #20 all meat combo on a white bun is the local favourite." She said. Robyn and I ordered an eight-inch submarine, and asked her to cut it in half. Not all the numbers were big in Arco. The 2010 census recorded 417 households, with a median income of $27,993. One of its only physical features was Number Hill, the face of a rocky promontory where every Butte County High School class had painted its graduation year on the face since 1920. Kaylyn had three sons, each at a different Idaho university. She told us some of the history of her town.

"It was the first city in the world to be lit by atomic energy." She said. "Even if it was for only five minutes." Originally known as Root Hog, the town had materialized at the crossroads of two stagecoach lines, along the Big Lost River. The civic leaders applied to the U.S. Post Office for the name of 'Junction,' but the Postmaster General chose to call it after a German inventor of radio transmission vacuum tubes. Kaylyn didn't mention the other history, the scary one.

In 1957 the Army began constructing the SL-1, an experimental prototype nuclear reactor designed to produce electric power for remote Arctic stations. It was conceived as a 3MW boiling water reactor that used highly enriched uranium fuel and standard components transportable by air, and requiring a minimum of on-site construction. Simple.

The reactor building was quarter inch steel, almost forty feet wide and fifty feet high. Access was by ordinary doors. The system operated at three hundred pounds per square inch, with a small core assembly of forty fuel assemblies, which gave the central rod an abnormally large reactivity. A sixty-ton crane, with a five-inch steel shield and a nine-inch thick lead glass window to protect the operator, controlled it.

The SL-1 was shut down on December 21, 1960, to repair a problem with sticking control rods that had plagued the reactor for the previous two months. Its restart occurred on a Tuesday, January 3, 1961. It was cold in the Idaho desert that day, about 27-Celsius degrees below zero.

At 9 pm, three plant workers entered the reactor compartment to reattach the control rods to their drive mechanisms. When Army Specialist John Byrnes, 27 years old, manually lifted the eighty-four pound main central control rod, it became stuck in the extreme cold and, in breaking it loose, he accidentally withdrew it 26.25 inches, 3.25 inches too far. Actually, Byrnes didn't withdraw it the final 3.25 inches. At 23 inches the exposed rod emitted a huge integrated neutron flux, instantaneously sending the reactor prompt critical. The core fuel rod took only 100 ms to travel the final 3.23 inches. Fuel material reached explosive vaporization temperature, fuel plates swelled and cladding failed. The core power level peaked at 20,000MW for 4milliseconds, forming the large steam bubble that lifted the surrounding mass of water at 50 meters per second. The resultant pressure wave water hammered into the core head 34 milliseconds later, ejecting the head shielding at 10,000 pounds per square inch of pressure, and propelling the pressure vessel out of its support structure at 160 feet per second. The entire five-ton reactor vessel and the upper control rod drive mechanisms jumped ten feet skyward, to collide with the overhead crane and the ceiling of the reactor building, before settling back into their original positions.

Specialist Byrnes was killed instantly by the steam and water that sprayed him onto the floor. The 26 year-old shift supervisor, Navy Seabee Construction Electrician First Class Richard Legg had been standing on top of the reactor vessel. The withdrawn central control rod impaled him through his groin and exited his shoulder, launching him into the air, and pinning him to the ceiling.

The third man, a 22 year-old trainee named Richard McKinley, was later found alive, but he died en route several miles to nowhere, and was returned to the SL-1 hot zone. The nurse who accompanied him was found to have received a significant radiation dose and years later diagnosed with some disease believed to have resulted from her exposure. Even if the three men had not died of traumatic injuries, their radiation exposure from the nuclear excursion would have still left them with no chance for survival. The body of Specialist Byrnes was left on the floor for another day until a recovery operation could be planned; that of Electrician First Class Legg would dangle from the ceiling for another six days.

The corpses, once removed, were emitting over 400 rad/hr, too hot for a normal burial. All were entombed in lead-lined caskets, sealed with concrete, and placed in metal vaults with a concrete cover. Other remains buried in the

Idaho desert may or may not have been human. The radioactive gold 198Au from Byrnes's gold watch buckle and copper 64Cu from a screw in his cigarette lighter later confirmed that SL-1 had indeed gone prompt critical.

It was the world's first (and the only American) fatal reactor accident. The cleanup of at least 35 acres of poisoned scrubland continues to this day.

"Did you know that the reactor would go critical if the central control rod were removed?" A scientific inquiry had asked, after the accident.

"Of course." Replied the reactor operators. "We often talked about what we would do if we were at a radar station and the Russians came. We'd yank it out."

The ambulance used in the transport of Richard McKinley was later decontaminated, and driven for several years at the Eastern Idaho State Fair.

It's a Feeding Frenzy.

*   *   *

My new watch was solar-powered, benign in comparison to the other energy endemic to this part of Idaho. Robyn and I were heading through a lava field to an active wildfire zone, missing the light, feeling the heat.

Two surrogate napkins came off the paper towel

dispenser on our table, as we said goodbye to Kaylyn. We steered southwest along US 20. The repeated taste of the pickles from the four inches of local favourite #20 all meat combo on a white bun remained resistant to an entire roll of mints. The windshield began to resemble a war zone. "The bugs bleed a lot here." Robyn said. Several barren miles of flat Snake River plain desert, sprinkled with sage and yellow Antelope Bitterbrush, and dense yellow-white eruptions of Rubber Rabbitbrush, transformed into the broken black basalt and cracked cake-crusts of asphalted lava fields. Volcanic silhouettes floated on the hazy horizon. We had entered a region of utter desolation. The most recent eruptions occurred over two thousand years ago. The Shoshone who lived through them, created a legend that spoke of a serpent on a mountain which, angered by lightning, coiled around and squeezed the mountain until liquid rock flowed, fire shot from cracks, and the summit exploded.

The white settler migration that lived through the Shoshone attacks on their wagon trains, had altered their Oregon Trail route through the northern part of this black wasteland, in a diversion known as Goodale's Cutoff.

In 1924, Robert Limbert, a sometimes taxidermist, tanner and furrier from Boise, named the cobalt Blue Dragon lava flows Craters of the Moon. *It is the play of light at sunset across this lava that charms the spectator. It becomes a twisted, wavy sea. In the moonlight its glazed surface has a silvery sheen. With changing conditions of light and air, it varies also, even*

261

while one stands and watches. It is a place of color and silence. Limbert expressed regret at having taken his dog on his expedition 'for after three days travel his feet were worn and bleeding.' Our own feet were not far behind, as Robyn and I were wearing only sandals to explore the caves and lava tubes and cinder crags. The sides of our feet would heal slowly from their lacerated encounters with the tiny purple-blue pieces of obsidian volcanic glass, but we would heal.

Three weeks after Robyn and I lost us for a while in the Craters of the Moon, two other hikers would lose themselves forever. Boise physician Dr. Jodean 'Jo' Elliott-Blakeslee, age 63, and her 69 year-old hiking partner, Amy Linkert. Any possibility of timely rescue was frustrated by the same Nobel prize-winning Barack Obama government shutdown that blocked the Australian and Japanese tourists from taking photos and 'recreating' at Yellowstone's Old Faithful geyser. All but three of the Craters of the Moon National Monument's nineteen employees were furloughed, and the family of the missing physician was forced to issue a plea for volunteer searchers. The buffalo bills were bigger now than when Apollo astronauts trained here forty years ago. Children can earn a Lunar Ranger embroidered patch in just a few hours. They should get it while it's going. Geologists predict the area will experience its next eruption within the next hundred years. Think of the money they'll save.

Robyn and I filled up in Carey, where they

seemed mighty proud of their ethanol-free premium gas. We knew we would likely hit traffic after our shortcut on Picabo Lane onto Highway 75, going north through Hailey, Ezra Pound's hometown, towards Sun Valley. We didn't count on bumper to bumper. But it was coming south, the other way. It was leaving.

There was another complication on the horizon. One of the planned stops, *back through the States on the way home,* was a hajj to the last home of one of my minor deities, the place where he blew his brains out. Hemingway had lived in Ketchum, and Ketchum was in the news. The Beaver Creek Fire had become a state-wide inferno visible from space, the smoke filled and obscured the sun in Sun Valley, homes were evacuated, wolves were chasing sheep trying to escape, and Salmon, Idaho was becoming Smoked Salmon, Idaho. If the rains came, there would be floods... *We all got pieces of crazy in us, some bigger pieces than others.*

Being crazy doesn't make you wrong. The Great White Shark Hunter S. Thompson had it right. *'Crazy' is a term of art; 'Insane' is a term of law. Remember that, and you will save yourself a lot of trouble.*

Robyn and I were arriving in the Wood River Valley on the second last day of the Beaver Creek fire, twenty two days after a lighting strike northwest of Hailey ignited over a hundred thousand acres of the Sawtooth National Forest. Beaver Creek was the largest fire the region had ever seen. The weather had been hot, dry, and windy but the arsonists had been alien life forms and topography. Epidemic infestations of Mountain Pine Beetle had devastated vast tracts of forest, and created large woody fuel falls on the ground. Cheat grass, which grew in sheets, had displaced the patchy growing native grasses, and became a continuous rapid burn conduit for any fire. The wind created an inferno that created its own wind, which created an inferno that created its own wind. It blew the fires faster up the slopes, and gravity compressed and focused the flames to burn faster down them. In a world of perfect storms, the Beaver Creek Fire was converging on immaculate.

Mass evacuations of homes and businesses had occurred, and firefighting teams were flown in from all over the continent. They brought helitankers and helicopters, and specialized firefighters called 'hot shots.' Two weeks before Robyn and I headed up the valley, Butch Otter, the Governor of Idaho, declared a state disaster.

The air was still smoke and haze, the ground a layer of soot and ash, and the smell was of smolder and sap. The setting sun looked like the moon, and the moon had become Mars red.

We drove up Main Street in Ketchum, across River Street, to Kentwood Lodge. *Best Western.* We got a warm welcome at the front desk, and a rough-hewn open poster bed with an Indian blanket upstairs. I asked if the fire had affected bookings. She looked at me like I should have known better than to have asked.

Robyn and I unloaded our packs, had a swim in the empty pool, and headed down Main Street, under the haze and the *Wagon Days* banner, to the first of Hemingway's old haunts.

The Casino was the perfect dive, jukebox, pool tables and pinball machines where the slots stood in Hemingway's day (when gambling was legal), big drinks for cash only, curses, and odours of cigarette butts and tragedy. It was different now, than when he came for his first drink in the evening. We continued to the Sawtooth Club, the swankier place he patronized for dinner, and got the last table upstairs, in the shadow of Bald Mountain.

I hadn't had any alcohol for two weeks now. This evening was a kind of homecoming, literary and liquid.

"Are you sure you're ready?" Robyn asked.

"One way to find out." I said. And we ordered, a glass of Turley chardonnay to start, and one of pinot noir to go with her duck, and another of cabernet sauvignon for my lamb. For tomorrow would be the last day of the Beaver Creek Fire, and the first of our Wagon Days. Through the windows of the Sawtooth Club, the underside of all the grey clouds in the Ketchum evening sky blazed crimson. Robyn asked me what I thought. "We're smack dab in the middle of something good." I said. "Good Lord willing and the creek don't rise."

*   *   *

Wagon Days
Ketchum, Idaho

'Hitch your wagon to a star.'
Ralph Waldo Emerson

Carbon. Labor day morning in Ketchum began scorched earth ghost town macabre. The Wagon Days banner was more visible, but the celebration it advertised seemed to be missing.
Robyn and I meandered up Main Street, along the closed storefront façades. We looked at the listings in a real estate agent's window.
Two charming cottages built in 1950 situated on 0.27 of an acre. Close proximity to the river and Downtown core. $725,000.
"They're just shacks." Robyn said.
"Not here." I said. "This is another pastoralized estate heartland of the very rich. Here, like in Jackson, you pay more for the seamless Rockwellian illusion." Across the street from the Pioneer Saloon, an older couple was setting out a row of director's chairs along the curb. We went over to inquire about the festivities.
"You're just a bit early," She said. Anne was a well-dressed elegant lady in her early sixties, with a Sun Valley sunbeam smile, short silver hair and a long silver and turquoise and fringed leather Western pedigree. The black pearl necklace was an incidental ornament to her kindness.
"Where are you from?" Asked her husband. Fred

was a remote Eastern transplant, but his roots were deep enough that he likely knew everyone who normally lived in Ketchum, if it was possible to live normally in Ketchum. Anne was the local Sotheby's Real Estate rep, the company that sold Napoleon's library. On 22 May 2002, Sotheby's sold Norman Rockwell's painting of Rosie the Riveter for $4.96 million, and Anne's sale profile wasn't likely far behind. They invited us to a luncheon Anne was hosting at her office, and their linear sidewalk inner circle for the Big Hitch Parade that would follow.

Robyn and I headed up Fourth Street to the Town Square, where the traditional eight-dollar all-you-can-eat Papoose Club Pancake Breakfast was already in full swing. *All proceeds benefit local youth.*

Also in full swing was the fiddle band in the background, the jowls of the first crossbow bouncing on his violin under his cowboy hat, through the smoke of the hundred of sausages behind the big wagon wheel doors of the big black barbeques. Toes in the boots of the Stetson pensioners at the front tables tapped in rhythm. Clone cowboy campfire cooks with white cowboy hats, blue and white striped shirts, Levi's, and red aprons manned the griddles, flipping flapjacks and feeding the frenzy. Firefighters ate free, and got extra big helpings, having achieved redemption for living the authentic life in Nature, and facing death with dignity and courage.

My paper plate was heavy with pancakes and sausages and bacon and eggs, and the orange juice in my other hand was searching for a place to land. All the picnic tables in the square were full, except for the one directly ahead of me. Only one man sat eating breakfast there in the dappled light, but I could see why he had it all to himself.

So old, he was Old West. Under his oversized grey felt Stetson, was a bushy white beard, and a penetrating set of clear blue eyes. He wore a leather vest with a marshal's badge, a blue bandana, and the same striped shirt, blue jeans and boots as the cowboy clones. I approached cautiously.

"Is anyone sitting here?" I asked.

"You see anyone?" He said. You can always tell a cowboy but you can't tell him much. He motioned me to take a seat.

"How old are you?" I asked.

"Older than the mountains with twice as much dust." He said. "I've seen eighty go by." I told him I thought that was pretty old.

"It's not about how fast you run, or how high you climb." He said. "It's about how you bounce. Out here, you live a long time. Even horse thieves have to hang five minutes longer than anywhere else." I introduced myself.

"Ivan Swaner." He said. "Pleased to make your acquaintance." But his gnarled handshake told me he was less pleased than I was, until Robyn arrived with Anne, and Ivan lit up.

"Ivan, you've got your breakfast on your moustache." Anne said. "Ivan is our local raconteur, historian and man-about-town. Too old to set a bad example, but old enough to give good advice. He went to school in a one-room schoolhouse, and remembers when 'going south for the winter' meant Twin Falls, and when skis were 'snowshoes,' used by the ladies to get around town. He was the deputy sheriff of Ketchum for fourteen years. They used to call him Ivan the Terrible."

Ivan wiped his beard.

"Sit down." He said to Anne, and then he started, his moustache dancing with the food and the telling of it.

"The Alpine had a red light on top of it, and when there was trouble, they would turn it on and we would go break up drunken fights or whatever it was." He said. "You can't drink coffee on a running horse. The one I've been riding through this life could buck a man's whiskers plum off. There are only two seasons in the valley, July and winter. I remember how much wood I had to cut, to get through January of 1951. It were minus fifty-four degrees, and the words froze clean out of my mouth." Ivan had hit his history button.

"In 1880, the town founded here was called Leadville. The Post Office renamed the place after a local trapper, David Ketchum. But it wasn't about fur trapping, it was about lead and silver. Isaac Lewis, the father of Ketchum, gave his son, Horace, ten thousand dollars to start any business he wanted. In 1884 Horace formed the Ketchum and Challis Toll Road Company, constructed a road over the steep Trail Creek Summit, and built a chain of massive wagons to run them. Each one could carry ten tons of ore on a mountain track no wider than itself, careening around hairpin turns, teetering along sheer ledges on giant six-foot wheels, making fourteen miles a day."

"There's more horse asses than horses." Horace had said. "I prefer mules to men." His Lewis wagons were daisy chained together and pulled by a team of draft mules, selected for strength and stamina and temper. Their muleskinner used a hundred-foot jerk-line to control and rein in the twenty animals it took to pull the convoy. He drove a majesty of metal and wood and beast. At the height of mining activity the Ketchum Fast Freight Line employed 700 mules and 30 wagons to haul 700,000 pounds of raw ore to the Philadelphia Smelter on Warm Springs Road, annually. Between 1880 and 1885 approximately $12 million worth of lead and silver left the valley. In 1902, rail service to Mackay and Challis arrived, and the Lewis wagon trains became obsolete. Horace died two years later. *Wagon tracks went away across it, so far that you could not see where they went; they ended in nothing at all.*

The Chinese had come with the building of the railroad. A Chinatown grew up on River Street in Hailey, with a population of hundreds.

"They had to live underground, or they'd be killed." Ivan said. On September 8, 1883, Sheriff Gray and his deputies raided the subterranean opium dens, making the first ever drug bust. He arrested 8 Chinese and a white man, and confiscated $350 in opium, pipes and smokers paraphernalia. At the trial, two days later, two

Chinese were fined $20 and another $5. Nine months later, Kuck Wah Choi, known locally as Ah Sam, was found guilty of murder in the first degree and sentenced to be hanged by the Sheriff until dead. On September 18, 1885, in accordance with the Judgment, Ah Sam was hanged in Hangman's Gulch. A fire wiped out Hailey's Chinatown in 1920, when a still, owned by a bootlegger named Monkey Frank, exploded. The fire uncovered many underground tunnels, containing opium bottles, hats, wire, and the remains of banks that the Chinese used.

In the 1890s, after the mining boom turned bust, sheepmen drove their herds north through Ketchum in the summer, to graze in upper elevations of the Pioneer, Boulder, and Sawtooth mountains. By 1890 there were a reported 614,000 sheep in Idaho, and by 1918, 2.65 million, almost six times the state's human population. Every fall, sheep flowed south into the town's livestock corrals at the Union Pacific Railroad's railhead, connecting to its main line at Shoshone. They brought money and giardia and the Trailing of the Sheep Festival, which still graces the Ketchum calendar each October.

The 1930s brought the Great Depression. Public work relief projects proliferated during the Civilian Conservation Corps CCC days of FDR's New Deal. Bugsy Siegal's girlfriend, Virginia Hill, Queen of the Mobsters' Molls, hung out in Ketchum, paying for goods and services with hundred dollar bills, sent to her in shoeboxes, before Bugsy ended up perforated with bullet holes on her couch. In 1936, the Union Pacific opening of their ski resort brought Hollywood culture to Sun Valley.

"Who were some of the celebrities that skied up there, Ivan?" Anne asked.

"Well, there was Marlene Dietrich and Lauren Bacall, Clark Gable and Humphrey Bogart, Lucille Ball and Desi Arnez, Bette Davis and Rita Hayward, and Gary Cooper and Ernest Hemingway." My head came up.

"Did you ever meet Hemingway, Ivan?" I asked.

"I used to drink with him." He said.

"How was that?" I asked.

"He was better." He said.

"Did he talk about much?" I asked

"Liquor talks mighty loud when it gets loose from the jug." He said. "But you can't drown your sorrows; they know how to swim."

"How come you survived and he didn't?" I asked.

"I stayed on the wagon, and Hem fell off." He said. I asked Ivan what he thought of the man.

"Some people thought he was a son of a..." He said. I thought he was a regular guy."

"You know he won a Nobel Prize in literature?" I asked

"That may have happened." Said Ivan. "But I ain't got no recollection of it."

Anne asked if we had visited Hemingway's house. I told her we were planning on seeing it the following day.

"It's easy to find." She said. "You just follow Warm Springs Road to East Canyon Run. Number 400." Getting to Hemingway's house would be easy. Getting inside would be impossible. I knew this from my correspondence with the Director of Communications of the Idaho Conservancy, who took two months to communicate her refusal.

Thank you again for your interest in the Hemingway House. Unfortunately, we will not be able to accommodate your request. Due to the high number of requests we receive, our staff can only schedule a few during the year that best meet our conservation goals for the property. I asked her if it was possible to provide the criteria that would accommodate a visit. *No, we cannot provide the criteria as it is part of an internal document.*

"No use diggin' for water under an outhouse." Said Ivan. "Anything you might had found inside Hem's place is likely long gone." Anne asked if we were planning on travelling up the valley to Stanley. We told her it was also on our list for the next day.

"Make sure you stop at the North Fork Store." She said. "That's where Marilyn Monroe was filmed in the movie *Bustop*." Ivan's blue eyes brightened conspicuously.

"Ever been married, Ivan." Robyn asked.

"Nope. Single, footloose and fancy-free." He said. "Getting shot and getting married are bad habits."

"You must have had some bad habits." I said.

"Every dog has a few fleas." He said. "But if a man knows anything, he ought to die with it in him." I asked Ivan for his thoughts about Lewis and Clark

"The Salmon River stopped them cold in their tracks." He said.

I asked him about Custer.

"General George Armstrong Custer was a pompous, egotistical, self-centered..." He said. "He was a goldilocks presidential wannabe murderer, meaner than a skilletful of rattlesnakes." I asked him where all the Indians went.

"Well, there were Indians, and I remember the days of their Trail Creek powwows, but they seem to have all disappeared." I asked him how Ketchum had changed.

"Our minds used to be cleaner than our fingernails, but we've been invaded by all those California developers, with their wide open wallets and wide open mouths. And Arnold Schwarzenegger and Tom Hanks and Bruce Willis and Clint Eastwood. Horseshit stays on the outside of boots, not Birkenstocks." Anne told us that Ivan was in the Big Hitch Parade.

"Its the largest non-motorized parade in the USA." He said. "You can catch me hanging off the second wagon." I asked why they cancelled the Blackjack shootout this year.

"One year a guy lost his arm when his gun misfired." He said.

Ivan was finished his breakfast, and his history lesson. He wiped his beard on his sleeve, and got up to leave.

"Where are you going now, Ivan?" Robyn asked.

"I'm going to see a man about a mule." He said.

*   *   *

'O, ha le Through the air I fly upon the air Towards the
sky, far, far, far,
O, ha le There to find the holy place, Ah, now the change
comes o're me!'

Geronimo's Medicine Song

They were chained up in a line, way out Sun
Valley Road. Robyn and I stopped inside the
mustering area behind the 1887 red barn to pet
the Bactrian camel and her new calf, and hiked
the rest of the way. In this most wagon time of
Wagon Days, we had the Lewis ore mother lode
haulers all to ourselves. Built in 1889, these
goliaths were the biggest, toughest, most
impressive vehicles that ever traversed the Old
West. The mammoth steel-rimmed wheels, seven
feet tall and four inches wide, supported a ship
of wood and leather and metal and canvas
sixteen feet long and fourteen feet high. Capable
of carrying nine tons of cargo inside their
monstrous 250 cubit foot interior, the wagons,
even empty, weighed a trail-crushing 6,400
pounds, as much as a heavy duty pickup truck,
with four times the payload capacity.

The brake blocks were three-foot massive carved
wedges in front of the rear wheels. Rough locks,
short-link chains or iron bars with chains looped
around the *felloe* rear wheel segments, and drag
shoes which allowed the wheel to "ride" in the
shoe slot, helped slow the descent on especially
steep grades, while preventing the tires from
wearing a flat spot in one area while skidding
down a slope. The wagons were loaded using a
calculation of one ton per animal. The big mules

were expected to pull a payload equal to their mass, the origin of a phrase we still use. *Pull your own weight.* The strength of these wagons was undeniable, but the beauty of their survival, the blood metal patina and the weather worn wood planks were all Old West. *Two woods diverged on a road, and I- I took the one less traveled by, And that has made all the difference.* Wild mustangs ran their enclosure on our way back down the road. It was thunder. I stopped to pet the white nose strip of one, on the fence line. A loudspeaker announced the beginning of an event, off to the right side of the road. A green Chevy truck pulled up to park along the fence. The decal on the rear window read 'Old Timer.' The old timer himself, navigated out of the drivers seat, dressed in his Wagon Days best, black Stetson and pants, and white shirt with pink and black suspenders.

"Ladies and gentleman." Announced the megaphone. "Welcome to Festival Meadows and the performance of the Eh-Capa bareback riders, here to demonstrate the horse-riding and jumping techniques of the Native Americans, without the benefit of saddles or bridles." We looked out at a montage of beaded headbands and wampum belts and black pigtails, white girls native only to Boise, with fringed buckskin costumes a size too large for their size and authenticity. The only boy wore a flaccid headdress of black and white feathers, trimmed with a red that could have come all the way from China. Single coloured handprints claimed the haunch of each horse. They rode in loose formation, punctuated by applause prompted by the megaphone.

"They make it look easy, don't they?" He said. "I can't parallel park that well." He announced the new queen of the troupe, who would 'reign for a year,' and solved the mystery of the group's appellation.

"The Eh-Capa riders, ladies and gentlemen, took their name from the Apache, and then spelled it backwards." *Ehcapa. Apache.*

Geronimo would have agreed that they had it backwards. *I was born on the prairies where the wind blew free and there was nothing to break the light of the sun. I was born where there were no enclosures.* In his medicine song, Geronimo flew through the air to the far sky to seek the holy place of change. In their reenacted performance on the Festival fairground, the Boise club was practicing synchronized stasis.

The little girl with the made-up eyes and lipstick, and the green pompom on top of her long blond hair, hung off the fence rail beside us. She turned to her mother.

"Mom." She asked. "What do Indians eat?"

"Same as us, Sweetie." She said. But we knew the correct answer. *Bitterroot.*

Robyn and I followed the big bums and short skirts and purses and cowboy boots of the rich cowgirls walking back into town to shop for expensive Italian shoes. *This is where the grumpy bear lives with his honey.* Robyn found herself looking through a rack of clothes, each clearance item on sale for $700. A Mexican man swept the floor beside her.

"Too much." I said, in Spanish. *Demasiado.*

"Oh, yeah." He agreed, without breaking stride. The banner near the ceiling wasn't helping. *Nothing last forever, so live it up, drink it up and laugh it off.*

"Where did you get your boots?" Asked Robyn of the woman filing through the $900 rack.

"Online." She said. The Internet had become a physical space. I left Robyn to roam the town.

"I'll meet you at Sotheby's for lunch." I said, having never said that before. I strolled by a cartoonish anthropomorphic statue of a hot dog squirting ketchup on his frankfurter head, a sign on a fence thanking the firefighters, and an evocative painting of an Indian wrapped in a Hudson Bay blanket. I found a wine shop that would carry the citizens of Ketchum from the guttural to the highest palatal pitch of exaltation. The $700 rack was locked, behind glass. On my way to Anne's for lunch, I encountered the first indication that Hemingway had been anywhere near the town. Outside the bookstore was a digitized portrait of the man, the one with him wearing his fisherman's sweater. Beneath it was a large mutant Dalmatian with natural pink eyes, and artificially pink-painted toenails. It was as if someone had left a pig's head at the door of a temple. Robyn was waiting at Anne's reception. The courtyard was full of Rolexes and rawhide, silver and turquoise, spandex and cowboy hats, Perrier and Payette beer, and hot dogs and chocolate ganache. It was America in full celebration.

'With the greater part of rich people, the chief enjoyment of riches consists in the parade of riches.'

Adam Smith

If you're not in the parade, you watch the parade. That's life. At 1 pm on Labor Day, Robyn and I were sitting with Anne and Fred, drinking Perrier, inside the Sotheby's director's chair enclave in front of the North Main Street sidewalk, across from the Pioneer Saloon. We were smack dab in the middle of something good.

The Big Hitch Parade started with four girls with black cowboy hats on chestnut mares carrying four big American flags. More than a hundred museum-piece coaches, buggies, carriages, carts, stages, and wagons would come around the corner of Sun Valley Road. More oxygen would be displaced with American flags than was swallowed by the Beaver Creek Fire. An army of pooper-scoopers on roller skates would weave through the parade, keeping shovel score of their potty shots for the amusement of the crowd. Buffalo Bill would have been humbled.

Troop 192 thanked the firefighters in their open wagon. Two pumpkin coaches were followed by wagons full of cowboy hats, pulled by black and white patched piebalds. A cowboy galloped by, standing with one foot on each horse saddle, each having an huge American flag trailing high in the wind.

The Bactrian camel rider looked ridiculous in his Stetson, with his belly drooped over the front hump of his mount, but most eyes were on the baby camel calf that followed. Four pretty girls with Miss Whatever banners and chaps and cowboy hats and tinseled bridles and flags went by, with Miss Idaho Senior America in her Cinderella pumpkin coach behind. A herd of donkeys trailed the troupe of Apache backwards girls.

"Look." Said Robyn, pointing to a big sombrero doing rope tricks. "A cowboy from Mexico."

"In Mexico they're vaqueros." I said. "Or charros. In the Southwest they're cowpunchers, buckaroos out West, and cowboys in the Heartland."

"What are those ones called?" She asked. A group of Peruvian riders with Chilean flat hats rode by on small horses.

"In Peru they're morochucos or qorilazos." I said. "In Chile, they're huasos."

"But they're all cowboys really." Said Robyn. I nodded.

"Just a man with guts and a horse." I said. Girls in lace went by in a two-wheeled cabriolet, followed by a surrey with a fringe on top, Clydesdales and more mules, and marching brigades of firefighters with axes and yellow shirts and red fireman hats and waders and suspenders. Before the pause, a U.S. Mail stagecoach, bristling with fringed buckskin and rifles, led an antique water wagon pulled by six black horses.

The pause turned the corner first. Another filled it, and then a hesitation, and then a mounting din of excitement. And then, like the buffalo in

Moise, they came. Twenty mules on a jerk line spilled around the Sun Valley Road corner onto Main Street, USA. The six shackled ships that slowly curved around the time and space behind them, came as tall as the buildings they obscured. The rattle of metal, the groan of old joints of wood and men, the shouts of muleskinners and marshals, all grew as loud as the history that uncoiled in front of us. Oh, how they came and turned. The Lewis wagons were alive again, the most daring of the descendants hanging on and off the sides. Robyn and I waved to Ivan, dangling from the second one, sporting deerskin gloves and a ribbon, like he had won first prize at the fair. Ribbed white canvas amanita caps covered the tall wood slatted stems of their ore cribs, and the gravity-pounded iron rims and red spoked wheels. Anne turned and smiled her sunbeam smile.

"Wagon Days." She said.

Robyn and I fell off the end of the parade for the live music back at the Casino, but it was crowded and smoky and the dirty Rockabilly band was loud and only partly true to their name of Old Death Whisper. We left them as they were in their song titles, *Pissed* and *Loaded*, *Always a Stranger* in a *Wasteland*, *Stacking Bones* in *Days Long Gone*.

We had a steak and a bottle of 2009 Dunham Syrah in the Pioneer Saloon that evening. It was the second of Hemingway's old haunts, and we sat beside two big men, a dairy farmer and a physician, visiting from Twin Falls.

I asked the farmer how many cows he had.

"Five thousand." He said. "The first farmer was the first man. All historic nobility rests on the possession and use of land."

"Emerson." I said. "We're here for Hemingway."

I asked the doctor what he specialized in.

"Pain management." He said. I asked him how Obamacare was affecting him.

"Definitely more pain." He had looked after Rita Chretian, the woman lost in the Nevada desert for seven weeks because of a faulty GPS. The skeleton of her husband, Albert, was later found eleven kilometres from their vehicle, over half a kilometre into the snow line.

"She survived on trail mix." Said the doctor. "He died on the trail."

I asked them if they had come for Wagon Days.

"Nope." Said the dairy farmer. "We're duck hunting."

"Death in the Afternoon." Said the pain doctor.

"Hemingway used to let the ducks' heads fall off." I said.

"We don't let the heads fall off." He said.

Robyn and I finished the first of our Wagon Days at the Western street dance in the square, on dusk. An old couple played cards next to us. The bluegrass banjo got our feet tapping and, when a tall thin cowboy with an oversized Stetson and a handlebar moustache got up to dance, so did we. The band sang of Billy Antrim, Billy the Kid. *How can I be an outlaw, I guess I'll never understand... and my life is wondering how long an outlaw has to ride.* Some cowboy guessed that Jimmy Webb had written *Wichita Lineman.* You could tell by looking at him that he would've known. No man can walk out on his own story. The next morning Robyn and I planned to travel further up the Wood River valley, into what was still a fire zone. The cloud bottoms blazed crimson.

*   *   *

Across the River and Into the Trees
Ketchum, Idaho

'He had known several men who blew their heads off, and he had pondered it much. It seemed to him it was probably because they could not take enough happiness just from the sky and the moon to carry them over the low eelings that came to all men.'

Larry McMurtry, *Lonesome Dove*

Oxygen. "It wasn't only the Old West that ended here." I said. "So did the American dream. It was his most important story, but he never got to write it."

"Is that what you're going to do?" Asked Robyn. We looked out at what should have been clear Idaho skies and early morning dappled sunshine, but the haze from the forest fire flare-up had returned overnight, to hover over the Wood River Valley.

Robyn and I had followed Anne's directions, across the river and into the trees. *It's easy to find... You just follow Warm Springs Road to East Canyon Run. Number 400.*

I don't know what she expected, but this wasn't it.

"Shouldn't it be a log cabin?" Robyn asked. "Or something that embodies hunting and fishing? Idaho? Big West?"

"It's concrete." I said. "It was poured to resemble treated wood, in an imitation of Sun Valley

285

Lodge. More practical than beautiful." Orwell deposing Rockwell.

"It's not pretty." She said.

"It was built by that kind of guy." I said. "A tin man. It's called the Topping House."

"Is that some kind of perverse joke?" Robyn asked.

"Not at all." I said. "Bob Topping was bald fat alcoholic womanizer, and heir to a tin industry fortune. Lana Turner became the fourth of his five wives, when Bob plopped a 15-carat engagement ring into her martini. She began drinking heavily, and in 1951, tried to commit suicide by slashing her wrists."

"It seems there was a lot of that going on around here." Robyn said.

"Anytime you mix inauthenticity with living in Nature, there's no redemption." I said. "Topping built the house the year I was born, in 1953, for his last wife Mona Moedl. She was an ice skater and ski instructor, but she left him for a warmer climate in Arizona."

"It looks like a tomb." She said.

"In a way, it is." I said. "Hemingway bought it in 1959 for fifty thousand dollars. It was a lot of money back then."

This place... was a wonderful buy. I plan to live here in the shooting months, which correspond to the hurricane months and the early northers in Cuba. My health and Mary's needs a change of climate from the subtropics for part of each year.

"It was his Fortress of Solitude." I said. "An outpost on the edge of the wild."

"Are you upset that they wouldn't let you

inside?" She asked. *We cannot provide the criteria as it is part of an internal document.*

"Yes and no." I said. "I know what inside looked like." And I did. In the master bedroom were travel trunks and duck decoys on the white fireplace, and relics of his life on the tabletops and salmon-coloured wallpaper, a bronze of him as a young moustache, typing away on the dresser, and photos of the hunter, and cat lover. Towels, monogrammed with *Mama* and *Papa*, hung in the bathroom. In the second bedroom, an old Royal typewriter sat on the elevated desk where he wrote *The Garden of Eden*, and his Paris memoirs of *A Moveable Feast*, standing in the early hours. But the typewriter was a prop. The real one was in Chicago. You can still buy it for a hundred grand. The rising peaks of the Sawtooth Range outside the window were still real. *The mountains we ride past will outlast everything we know.*

Down the red-carpeted staircase was a monstrous painting of two bloody workers, skinning a bull in a Spanish slaughterhouse. Unlike the white light and tropical temperament we had seen in his Cuban house, the living room was long and low and dark and cold and angular. A wooden console-mounted radio and television cathode ray tube, and the three-cushion turquoise ottoman were Eisenhower era, as principle was being dislodged by privilege. The old magazines weren't his, but the two gazelle heads mounted on the grey stone fireplace, and the caribou antlers and box of Remington shotgun shells were. Yousuf Karsh's portrait of him hung above the hearth, hair all silver, beard all full, cable-knit sweater rolled up his neck in the Havana heat, a sepia sea captain time capsule refugee staring over the wheel, wandering into a strange port, and wondering if he had found refuge. His eyes gazed out the wall-sized window, across the river and into the trees, to the massive houses and condos that, like the tall cottonwoods, had taken root and sprung up, and invaded the flood plain below. Development had incarcerated the stony course of the Big Wood River within its banks. The wilderness had been tamed, packaged and sold. The authenticity had been sanded and polished, until it was unrecognizable.

The empty bottle of Bordeaux on the bookshelf was from the extraordinary vintage of 1961. I'm not sure why it should be there, as like the soul of the man who left that year, it hadn't been released yet.

Hemingway had spent hardly any time in Ketchum, eight months, off and on, mostly unpleasant. He boasted of never having missed a sunrise, and the one on July 2, 1961 was glorious. Mary was still asleep. At seven o'clock, in pajamas and bathrobe, he descended the Spanish steps, down to the basement, after retrieving a set of keys from the kitchen. The hum from the freezer may have muffled his entry to the storeroom. He emerged with a box of ammunition and the English-made Boss 12-gauge he had bought at Abercrombie & Fitch, to shoot pheasants. There was nothing special about the eight by five foot brown linoleum mudroom entranceway that should have made it a tabernacle. It was just another vestibule, like the labyrinth of the inner ear, or the part of the mouth outside the teeth, or the forehead the shotgun's loading chamber was pressed against, that no more brilliance would emerge from, or like where you go to wait for the redemption that would now never come, because you didn't face death with dignity and courage. Or maybe you did. The local Catholic priest called it an accident. One of the altar boys fainted at his funeral.

"So if that was the 'yes' part of your regret for not getting inside," Asked Robyn. "What was the 'no' part?"

"The typewriter." I said. "It's not real. And I wanted to feel it through his hands."

'Perhaps he found what he came here for, but the odds are huge that he didn't. He was an old, sick and very troubled man, and the illusion of peace and contentment was not enough for him. ... So finally, and for what he must have thought the best of reasons, he ended it with a shotgun.'

Hunter S. Thompson, *What Lured Hemingway to Ketchum?*

*   *   *

'Writing is a private, lonely occupation with no
need for witnesses until the final work is done.
Once writing has become your major vice and
greatest pleasure only death can stop it.'
                                    Ernest Hemingway

Across the river and into the trees, in the
morning shadow of Baldy Mountain, Robyn and
I found the three tall spruce trees. The wild
sagebrush scrub in the foothills behind us still
threatened to push through the wrought iron
gates, and reclaim the grass that had been
trimmed into a cemetery. The horizontal grey
marble slab was as plain and simple as his
prose. *Ernest Miller Hemingway July 21 1899
July 2,1961.*
Behind one of the spruce tree trunks, was a
chaotic mound of pens and pencils, and empty
booze bottles.
"It's a shrine." Said Robyn.
"Uh-huh." I said.
"To what?" She asked.

> "Authenticity." I said. "The American West was
> *The Sacred Land*- the gold rush towards truth."
> "What's the truth?" He asked.
> "The achievement of redemption." I said.
> "How do you get that?" He asked.
> "By living the authentic life, by living in Nature,
> and by facing death with dignity and courage."
> "Sounds very existential." Said Carolyn.
> "That's where the truth lives." I said.

"So where's his truth?" She asked. "Where's his

redemption?"

"His truth, his meaning, came out of his suffering, physical and psychic." I said. "What is to give light must endure burning."

He knew war. On his first day in Milan, as an 18 year old ambulance driver, he was sent to 'collect the fragments,' the shredded remains of the female workers in a munitions factory explosion. A few months later he experienced *a flash, as when a blast-furnace door is swung open, and a roar that started white and went red*, when an Austrian mortar blew shrapnel through his legs. The surgeons couldn't tell him in English if his legs were coming off or not. In 1922, he witnessed the atrocities in the Greco-Turkish war incineration of Smyrna. In 1937, he saw the last stand of the Republican Army in the Spanish Civil War, at the Battle of the Ebro. He was present at the D-Day landings, the heavy fighting in the Hürtgenwald forest, and hospitalized with pneumonia at the Battle of the Bulge.

There was physical trauma in peacetime as well. In 1928, he pulled a glass skylight down on his head in a Paris bathroom, mistaking the chain as the one for the toilet. He got another forehead scar and a smashed knee in a car accident in 1945. Africa was unkind. In 1933 the amebic dysentery he contracted prolapsed his large intestine. In 1954 the plane he had chartered in the Belgian Congo hit an abandoned utility pole, crashed into heavy jungle, inflicting a serious head wound. Another plane he boarded the next day exploded on takeoff, and Hemingway received severe burns, two cracked vertebrae, a kidney and liver rupture, a dislocated shoulder, and another concussion, this time a skull fracture leaking cerebral fluid. He was caught in a bushfire a short time later, sustaining second degree burns to his legs, torso, lips, left hand, and right forearm.

But as bad as his physical injuries had been, the psychic trauma was worse. The first woman he fell in love with was his nurse in Italy. In January of 1919, Agnes von Kurowsky, seven years his senior, agreed to marry him. Three months later she wrote to tell him of her engagement to an Italian officer. In 1928 Hemingway wrote his father to tell him not to worry about his financial difficulties. The letter arrived moments after he had committed suicide. Hemingway had to move from Paris back to Toronto. He converted to Catholicism. On May 10, 1933, his books were burnt in a Berlin bonfire as works of decadence. His literary friends began to die- Yeats and Fitzgerald and Joyce and Gertrude Stein. In 1961 Castro expropriated 'Mr. Way's' Finca Vigia Cuban home, confiscating all its contents, including his library of five thousand books. Hemingway sank into despair. He sought refuge in the last safe place associated with 'the good years,' where he had come to hunt and fish and raise hell in the local bars. His best work came from standing on something solid, like an Idaho hillside, or a sense of conviction, where courage and independence offered a code of survival. All his themes could come together here- love, war, wilderness and loss. Ketchum was supposed to be Hemingway's Big Two Hearted River. But he hadn't come to Rockwell, he'd come to Orwell. The peace and contentment he sought was illusory. The era of and need for grace under pressure was gone. The Age of Exploration was over. The archetypical hard boiled tough guy hero, the Nick Adams he had written about and always pretended to be, was not only obsolete, was a sick and sclerotic and stress-stricken man. There would be no redemption in Ketchum.

After fifteen electroconvulsive shock treatments at the Mayo Clinic administered 'in an aura of secrecy,' he was 'released in ruins.' With the best of electrical intentions, they had fried his memory and fractured the rest of his mental aptitude, the remainder of whatever the alcohol had otherwise left intact.

"Wasn't it just the booze?" Asked Robyn.

"Not quite." I said. "Hemingway had hemochromatosis, a disease characterized by the inability to excrete iron from the body. The excess gets deposited in visceral organs. His bronze tan and diabetes and hypertension and headaches and depression were likely from this."

"But he still drank heavily." She said. "Write drunk; edit sober."

"Funny thing about hemochromatosis." I said. "Not only do more alcoholics have hemochromatosis, but more people with hemochromatosis, like more writers, are alcoholics."

"More writers are alcoholics?" Robyn said.

"Once drunk, a cup of wine can bring 100 stanzas." I said. "That was the Chinese poet Xiuxi, in the third century AD. Think about it. Dylan Thomas, John Cheever, Poe, Faulkner, Hart Crane, Tennessee Williams, Truman Capote, Dorothy Parker, Ring Lardner, Raymond Chandler, O Henry, Jack London, Delmore Schwartz, F Scott Fitzgerald, John Berryman, Jack Kerouac, Charles Bukowski, the list is its own legend." *The victim of a malodorous disease which renders him abhorrent to society and periodically degrades him is also the master of a superhuman art which everybody has to respect and which the normal man finds he needs.*

"So why did Hemingway blow his brains out in Ketchum?" She asked.

"He fell off the path of pilgrimage." I said.

"To where?" She asked.

"Not so much to where." I said. "As to what."

"To what?" She asked.

"Meaning." I said. "All men come to fear the world as they grow older. What terrified him most was not losing his life but losing his mind. Losing the ability to write. Losing his purpose in life. For him, it was an existential vacuum. In the end Hemingway may have not have shot himself so much out of despair as of defiance, to prevent becoming one of T.S. Elliot's hollow men. He and Elliot had a tangled relationship. *A damned good poet and a fair critic; but he can kiss my ass as a man.* And maybe that was it in Ketchum, where *The Sun Also Rises* finally met *The Wasteland*. Eventually, and for what he thought was the best of reasons, in this valley of dying stars, in this hollow valley, this broken jaw of our lost kingdoms, he ended it with a shotgun. *This is the way the world ends This is the way the world ends This is the way the world ends Not with a whimper but a bang.*

'Canada never had a Wild West. Largely, perhaps, because as soon as anyone came over from across the border and started to Wild West around, the North-West Mounted Police very quietly and firmly put him away where he wouldn't harm any one. Now the States had a Wild West. It was as good as the movies portray. It had faro, dice, wide-open towns, bad Injuns, red eye, gamblers in frock coats, Bill Hart bad men, discriminate and indiscriminate killings, and all the jolly features. In place of the Redskins biting the dust it is now the commercial traveler that bites the dust. Where the elk once roamed, the Elk now roams, but with him are the Mason and Odd Fellow. Thus, to coin a phrase, the old order passeth, giving way to the new.'
Ernest Hemingway, *The Toronto Star Weekly*, November 6, 1920

*   *   *

'The song of the river ends not at her banks but in the hearts of those who have loved her.'
Buffalo Toe

We headed north along the Sawtooth Mountains through Chocolate Gulch, into the fire zone. A wooden Smokey bear waved nervously from the roadside. *Fire Danger Extreme...Only YOU Can Prevent Forest Fires.* But we had arrived too late. Robyn posed on the fence under the North Fork Store sign, Marilyn Monroe's last bus stop, and the wrong kind of girl waiting for redemption in the snow, at Grace's Diner.

On our port side the Salmon River flowed grey blue. *I asked Ivan for his thoughts about Lewis and Clark "The Salmon River stopped them cold in their tracks." He said.* They had called it the River of No Return. Big raptors hovered over the valley it ran through, hawks and falcons and harriers. A golden eagle perched nonchalant, on the wooden gate of the Galena Pioneer Cemetery, indifferent to the few tiny plots marked out with stones. There was only one headstone. Francis Marion Willmorth, the local livery stable and hotel owner, dead at fifty-two.

We pulled into Smiley Creek Lodge for gas. On four wagon wheels was a log sign with a wind vane nailed on the top. *Restaurant Lodging Groceries Licenses Deli Gas LP Gas RV Spaces.* A flock of the largest sheep in the world stood near an ugly carving of a deformed standing black bear holding a green and pink salmon, surrounded by rock markers in the same pattern as in the pioneer cemetery. A mutant bloated dog by the same artist, stood frozen in front of him. The bear and the dog had the same eyes. There were tepees and chainsaw sculpted bear chess pieces. If rustic was as far away from civilization as it could ever be, any step you took was on the way to Paris. The owner came out of the main log cabin.

"Gas?" He asked. I nodded.

"Cheaper in Stanley?" I asked. We were driving to Stanley.

"Yep." He said.

"I'll take ten bucks." I said.

"Fill it to five bucks." He said, and walked away. We went inside to pay. A chainsawed cowboy with a chainsawed pot belly stood guard over the World's Greatest Candy Necklaces, on sale for a buck fifty. Bottles of Indian Creek pinot noir were a bit more. The place was packed for breakfast. For less than ten dollars you could chow down on a Basque Scramble, or some Snake River Kurobuta ham, the *Kobe Beef of ham*. I went to the toilet. The graffiti was rustic. *Shoot all the wolves and fuck all the tree-huggers.* It wasn't France.

Robyn and I went out back to look at the tepees.

"Forty bucks a night." Said an old guy in a baseball cap. "Mighty comfortable. Course there's only one toilet in the camp, and those sheep make a hell of a racket all night long, but mighty comfortable."

We easily vanished into the thickening haze from the fires. Robyn asked me what I had expected to see through the smoke.

"I didn't know they were going to burn the forest down." I said. A long ribbon of telegraph lines took us into Custer County, over Fourth of July Creek, and the turnoff to Redfish Lake Lodge, the *Jewel of the Sawtooth National Recreation Area... Stay with us and sleep like a log.* There were log cabins. The 'nostalgic' bar was called the Redfish Rustic Lounge, guaranteed to 'capture the charm of the resort.' Tuesday, Wednesday, and Thursday nights had 'Happy Hour with Jen.' There was taxidermy. A motionless phalanx of wireless guests sat along the veranda, laptops supplicated to the signal. Deer heads hung on the log walls over the wagon wheels, inside the beach boundary. *No animals beyond this sign.*

A few miles further, we pulled into Stanley, the last stop before the Salmon River headed west. A spinal column of grey ridges backdropped the sparseness. Stanley was more street than structure. The Sawtooth Hotel and the Kasino Club *est. 1938* were deserted. Log cabins were decorated with plastic window boxes containing plastic pansies and plastic American flags, crossed in synthetic salute. There were old wagons everywhere. Hobos randomly parked their moneyed massive migrant motor homes in the desolation. One gypsy's collection of big boy toys had so convincingly disproved the 'can't take it with you' theorem, that his RV was hitched to a truck pulling a trailer containing a canoe and a motocross bike. A man can never have too much mobility.

Robyn bought a pair of cowgirl boots in the only place open, and we turned back towards Sun Valley. There was no more big wood on the Big Wood River, and no more foxes (or other animals) beyond the Fox Creek Ranch signpost. But there were monster homes of concrete and copper, flagstone monuments to excess, architectural hybrids of Tuscan villa and Japanese airport.

"Big money, honey." I said. "The world's first chairlifts were installed on Dollar Mountain in 1936." We pulled into the parking lot of Sun Valley Lodge.

"Three years later Hemingway wrote *For Whom the Bell Tolls,* in suite 206." But the room was occupied, and we couldn't afford to breathe the air anyway. The signs of that were everywhere, and brazen. *Diamonds- sometimes it's OK to throw rocks at pretty girls. Eat. Pray. Love.* But there were still remnants of the man in the corridors of the rich and famous. The last thing he ever wrote was on June 15, 1961, a letter of 219 words to a nine-year old boy. It was on a hallway wall. Most people just walked by.

Dear Fritz,
I was terribly sorry to hear this morning in a note from your father that you were laid up in Denver for a few days more and speed off this note to tell you how much I hope you'd be feeling better. It has been very hot and muggy here in Rochester but the last two days it has turned cool and lovely with the nights wonderful for sleeping. The country is beautiful around here and I've had a chance to see some wonderful country along the Mississippi before and it is really a very beautiful country and there are plenty of pheasant and ducks in the fall. But not as many as in Idaho and I hope we'll both be back there shortly and can joke about our hospital experiences together. Best always to you, old Timer from your good friend who misses you very much. Mister Papa. Best to all the family, am feeling fine and very cheerful about things in general and hope to see you all soon. Papa

Just up the passageway was a photo of him and Gary Cooper, carrying their guns. Hemingway used his for the last time less than three weeks after he had written his letter. Fritz died six years later of heart failure. He was fifteen.

The Sun Valley Inn played inadvertent host to my sudden urge for another kind of purge, in a temple so luxurious it transformed a simple ablution into a rite of purification. Robyn and I ate chicken and drank white wine beside the white swans in their ponds, and the fountains on their lawn, and walked wondrous among the offerings of the annual Silver Car Auction, from 250 'gallant' collectors and dealers. And then there was the banner, strung between the exclusive shops. Sitting Bull. *It is strange that the Americans should complain that the Indians kill buffaloes. We kill buffaloes...for food and clothing...to keep our lodges warm. Your young men shoot for pleasure... What is this! Is it robbery? You call us savages. What are they?*

It was all downhill from there. But the air would rarify again, ever so ephemerally on the descent, just off Trail Creek Road. When it was dedicated in 1966, it had been chosen for its natural state, 'as when the Indians roamed this part of Idaho.' If they were roaming now, they'd be roaming the seventh hole of the Trail Creek Golf Course. And here of course were the metaphors. Here was where Orwell was fishing for his little white golf balls, lost in the same creek that Rockwell would have fished authentically. The Hemingway Memorial statue was of bronze, but looked fashioned of clay.

'Best of all he loved the fall
the leaves yellow on cottonwoods
leaves floating on trout streams

and above the hills
the high blue windless skies
...Now he will be a part of them
forever.'

"What do think unmade him?" Asked Robyn.
"The same things that made him." I said.
"Hemingway was the product of twentieth
century warfare." *I was always embarrassed by
the words sacred, glorious, and sacrifice... I had
seen nothing sacred, and the things that were
glorious had no glory and the sacrifices were like
the stockyards at Chicago if nothing was done
with the meat except to bury it.*
"God died on Flanders' fields." I said. "And the
West lost the will to live because of it. The First
World War used up all the pretty words.
Hemingway's life and narrative was all about
that, the aftermath of that, and the end of
Victorian romantic prose. The truth of that both
made and unmade him. He was the pilgrim
Jeremiah of injustice, the Kilimanjaro summit
frozen leopard, and the Old Man of the Sea,
willingly jeopardizing life itself to be true to his
own nature, and catching only the skeleton of
what might have been possible, because of the
sharks."
Our last evening in Ketchum. It was only
appropriate that we spent it where he spent his
last evening. He liked the French food at Michel
Christiani, as we would. There was a 1930's
Town and Country Cadillac in the driveway, with
wood trim, and a beautiful vase of sunflowers in
the foyer. Our waitresses name was Maria
Teresa, with double hair like the Habsburg

queen. She ran a real estate agency on the side, and would have been delighted to find us a Rockwellian refuge.

"We're good." We said. "We're just here for Wagon Days. And Hemingway."

Maria Theresa told us that he had become paranoid his last night in the restaurant, and thought he saw two FBI agents tailing him, at another table. I mentioned the prices, and how Hoover's budget would have considered it a more than prohibitive indulgence. We ordered a 2010 Groth Chardonnay. *This wine is too good for toast drinking, my dear. You don't want to mix emotions up with a wine like that. You lose the taste.* Robyn retreated to a Western Home Journal, while I studied the only other couple in the restaurant. A double chin boy with a Ralph Lauren polo shirt and his bling and bone skin wife were drinking a vintage appropriate to their own.

"Oh, my God." She said. "I'm looking for the word. Stunning!" Its a wonder their pelvic bones supported that kind of height. You can't be too thin or too rich. In the bathroom were painted magpies, and a window to a French village. I almost went.

But the food arrived to rescue the experience. Truffle, prosciutto and fig salad and Idaho trout and crawfish pie, and I wondered, for just a moment, how Hemingway could have done something so stupid.

"You know." Said Robyn, as she did when it was about to get clarified. "You had a lot in common." I differed.

"Like what?" I asked.

"Well." She said. "Like the music and medicine in the family. Like the fact he disliked his name, *The Importance of Being Earnest*. Like how he mirrored his mother's energy and enthusiasm, but couldn't really totally identify. Like the musical instrument she forced you to learn, and how you played in the school orchestra. Like the fishing and camping in the woods and lakes of the Shield. Like how boring you think Toronto is. Like how you travelled and never really came home again. Like courage and independence and suppressed sentiment. Like requited love and wine and Spanish. And now you're writing."

"We're nothing alike." I said.

"Its a concern." She said.

"Don't worry." I said.

"Why not?" She asked.

"Hemingway did what he did because he ran out of the juice in his well."

"And you?" She asked.

"That Chateau Yquem in the cellar." I said. "It won't be ready for a long while."

'The well is where your juice is. Nobody knows what it is made of, least of all yourself. What you know is if you have it, or you have to wait for it to come back...As long as you can start, you are all right. The juice will come...There is always juice somewhere.'

Ernest Hemingway

*   *   *

The Road to Silver City
Silver City, Idaho

Pea Eye Parker: What Indians is it we're fightin'
anyway?
Gus McCrae: They didn't introduce themselves.
Larry McMurtry, Lonesome Dove

Silver. We lost Ketchum in the same hazy way
Hemingway had found it, although there were
signs that its current residents had found more
redemption. *Firefighters Y'all Rock.*
"Where to?" Robyn asked.
"We're going to a battleground." I said, and on
cue, we passed a public shooting range, and
whose two upright black large scale M16
replicas with a clothesline full of camouflage in
between. Friendly fire. The local black-billed
magpies were nervous.
Through the burnt hills of Hailey, we pulled in
for gas. The attendant's name was Claudia. I
asked for a favour.
"We're having trouble with the ATMs here." I
said. "They don't seem to like our bank cards.
We're heading off to a remote ghost town and I
wonder if it's possible for you to charge our
credit card for more, and give us the rest in
cash."
"Y'all want coffee?" She asked.
"Nope." I said. "Got coffee."
"Y'all want water?" She asked.
"Nope." I said. "Got water."

"Y'all want muffins." She asked.

"Nope." I said. "Got muffins."

"Y'all got propane?" She asked.

"Nope." I said. "Guess we need propane." She rang up a hundred dollars of imaginary propane, and handed me the cash.

"Y'all have a nice day." She said.

"God bless America." I smiled as we pulled away, with a full tank and wallet, and two 'giddy-up coffees from the *Breakfast Served All Day* place next door. The Indians had travois pulled by dogs, but we had wheels and horsepower.

"Pretty smooth." Robyn said. "Try to keep the coffee in your mouth."

"When you got this much fuck-you money." I said. "You can dribble all you like."

We pulled over in Bellevue to have a look in the general store. It was Sunday, and closed. *One Nation Under God.*

Not much further south, we turned west onto Highway 20, into golden fields and hay bales and telephone poles that met at our vanishing point. The lines were thick with birds.

The horizon grew beyond our peripheral vision and the Camas County towns, such as they were, had become fewer and smaller. If it hadn't been for the *Corner Coffee and Roadside Barbecue*, we would have missed Fairfield.

"So that's where they keep them." I said, as we passed the Mormon Reservoir. A makeshift base of Erickson skycrane helicopters, and the firefighters that came along with them, bustled under burnt hills. We pulled over to read a marker about the Bannock War.

"Is this the battlefield?" Asked Robyn.

"No." I said. "Ours is in tonight's lodging. The Bannock War occurred in 1878, between Indians and white settlers on Paiute land. Ours was ten years earlier, and under it."

The road announced its only curve, when the big black Fleetwood that bounced up and down in front of us went ever so slight off center, five furrowed miles before the *Hill City Store and Saloon- Come again.* But we barely had the first time. A hollowed out stone homestead and a burned out car frame were the only punctuation marks on the moonscape.

"Makes you wonder about a man's dreams." I said. "When the homes are mobile and the vehicles aren't."

We passed Goodale's Cutoff, an Oregon Trail shortcut crossing the Snake River to the Lost River, where the high widowmaker branches of cottonwood trees would fall onto Conestoga wagoneers in the night.

Before Mystic Saddle Road, we drove by Fort Running Bear, and a game crossing. *Watch for Stock.* Highway 20 turned onto West 6th Street, in Mountain Home.

For twenty years after 1860, over fifty thousand settlers crossed the Idaho desert through here, on the Oregon Trail. *Keep your summer glow with a spray tan.* By the time it had become a post office and a stagecoach stop called Rattlesnake Station. They needed another name. *Smokey Mountain Pizzeria. Cash for guns.*

It was a town of fast food, slow pawnbrokers, mini storages and maxi religion. There was the

Love Abiding Christian Church, the Open Door Community Church, and the Apostolic Church, *the Friendliest Church in town (and the last).* The reason for this lay through the *Congestion Ahead,* directly in front of us.

West 6th Street had become Airbase Road and, in the flat and dirt of it, we had not been paying attention. What looked like a tollbooth blocked our way. The attendant wore a sharp uniform.

"Identification please." He said from behind the window. Robyn handed him her BC driver's license. His head tilted, like a dog's does, when its puzzled.

"I'm gonna need to see some military ID." He said, pointing to the sign. *Mountain Home Air Force Base.* That would explain all the jet engine noise.

"We don't want to go to an air force base." She said. "We want to go to Silver City."

"Where's that?" He asked. But we obviously didn't know.

"In the wop-wops." She said. This was a Kiwi word.

"Where's that?" He asked. We were allowed to turn around, but he didn't wave. Almost adjacent to the air force base was the Bird of Prey Conservation Area. An F-15 Eagle screamed overhead.

"More like Bird of *Pray*." I said.

What had become Highway 167 slithered through a dust bowl. Some poor fool was tilling it into a soot storm with his tractor.

"There's nothing out here." Robyn said. "Even the snakes would burn and die."

"You ain't seen nothin' yet." I said. "Nothin's coming up."

"Maybe we should have renewed our vows." She said.

"Maybe we should have renewed our wills." I said.

As we came into the infinite cattle stockyard that was Grandview, I stopped to pose on top of the gun turret of an M1 Abrams tank, painted desert storm, with an American Flag and some words. *In Honour of Those Who Serve.* It was parked beside a sign that indicated a 45-mile per hour speed limit, and the *War Eagle Village Storage.*

The Mennonites selling lemonade and cookies at the T-junction seemed surprised to see us pass without stopping.

"Maybe they know something." Robyn said.

"If they knew something, they wouldn't be standing there selling lemonade." I said. We headed north, into a mouth of mesas over green cornfields, grey-white molars rising above the back of beyond.

"What's that plant?" Robyn asked. "It looks a bit unhappy."

"Sugar beets." I said. The Idaho Ecology Waste Dump went by.

"I think we've missed our picnic spot." She said. The signs didn't get any more reassuring. *Dead End. War Eagle Mines.* A brief glimmer of hope returned at Diamond Gulch, but Idaho's Governor Caleb Lyon had salted the place in 1865, and there were no diamonds in Diamond Gulch.

There was one more garden spot along the way,

before we turned off the road and went bush. The site marker told of an Oregon Trail wagon train attacked by Indians on September 9, 1860. The party of 44 consisted of four families with 21 children, some single men, and six soldiers, five just discharged, and one deserter. The first attack occurred on the high ground just west of Castle Creek when the Indians attempted to stampede the stock. The emigrants continued towards the Snake River, where they intended to fill their water barrels, but were attacked again while passing down to Henderson Flat. The wagons were circled and the fighting continued into the next day. Towards sundown, each family hitched up a cart, and left the remaining wagons and loose stock for the Indians. But the oxen were hungry and thirsty and wounded and the emigrants were forced to abandon their property and flee. The leader of the party and his wife and three of their children were killed. The survivors escaped with only the clothes they were wearing, some firearms, and a few basics. For over a week they worked their way down the Snake River, hiding in the daytime, walking at night, over 75 miles to the Towhee River crossing. Physically too weak to go on, 18 children, 6 surviving parents, and a young man waited here to be rescued. When Shoshone Indians forcefully took their firearms two weeks later, some would stay; others would leave.

Almost twenty years before he led Custer to disaster at Little Bighorn, Lt. Marcus A. Reno would discover their bodies in a crater *gleaming in the moonlight, dead, stripped, and mutilated...*

Mrs. Vanorman had been whipped, scalped, and otherwise abused by her murderers; the boys, Charles and Henry Otter, were killed by arrows, Mr. Vanorman, Marcus Vanorman, and Gleason had their throats cut, and besides were pierced by numerous arrows. They appeared to have been dead from four to six days, the wolves had not yet molested them, decomposition was going on however... Reno buried them in a common grave.

Back at the Owyhee River camp, an adult and four children had died from starvation. After much discussion (and prayer), 'those who remained resolved to eat the flesh of the recently departed with the hopes of preserving their own lives until a rescue party arrived.'

On October 24, an Army relief expedition rescued ten survivors. Captain Dent found the remains of Christopher Trimble, who had been murdered by the Indians; his body had been much disturbed by the wolves, but sufficient remained to identify it... This boy of eleven years of age, deserves special mention. He had killed several Indians in the fight... he then became a prisoner voluntarily with the Indians, in order that he might get some salmon taken to the camp... Two weeks had elapsed since his last visit; it must have been at that time he was killed.

Zacheus Van Ornum became an Indian Scout for the Army in an effort to find his nieces and nephew. The captive children had been traded or stolen by other bands. Reuben was rescued by California Army Volunteers in November 1862, in the Cache Valley of Utah, but could not adapt to 'civilized life' again. His youngest sister, Lucinda, died soon after being rescued, and Eliza and Minerva either died of starvation or were killed while captives. Out of the original forty-four, there were only fifteen survivors.

"Who was the leader of the wagon train?" Robyn asked.

"Elijah Utter." I said. "It's called the Utter Disaster."

"Is this our battlefield?" Asked Robyn.

"No." I said. "We have to go off the road now."

*   *   *

'Caution... The road to Silver City is a narrow winding dirt road. It is impassable for large trucks and other vehicles pulling large trailers. The road is normally closed by snow from about Nov. 1 to June 1.'
    Sign at the beginning of the road to Silver City

Always heed imprecise warnings. At least the Ridge Road sign had given distances. *Old Stage Road 2, Ruby Junction 19, Silver City 20.* We were going all the way.

Rutted and rough, the track began to curve between an arroyo on our right, and a precipitous canyon on our left, across the span of which rose the brooding ledges of a long escarpment. The Snake River plain dropped away behind us. Another sign, citing the applicable section of Idaho code, warned that the cost of any search and rescue operation would be uniquely ours. But we had a four wheel drive vehicle, a full tank of gas, water, and the leftover steak from our Pioneer Saloon in our French picnic bag. Damn near invincible.

We hadn't counted on the razor sharp drops into empty space, not that we could see them anyway, because of the choking clouds of dust from the mining trucks and the hunters flying by in their Dodge half-tons at Ram speed. *Spinning cookies or fishtailing is reckless.* It wasn't long before our pure white wagon, and our mouths, was completely caked in dry Idaho dirt. ATVs roared through the sagebrush along the game trails on either side. We climbed and dropped and climbed and dropped over sheer mountain cliffs. A streambed flickered reflected sunlight off the mica on its bottom. *Hey, don't litter or smash the critters, Jack.*

We were on the last mile to Silver City when a psychotic SUV driver passed us, and the truck in front of us, on a blind corner. We gave chase into town and up a hill and into what turned out to be the front yard of his holiday home. His porch was full of family, expecting his arrival. They clearly didn't expect ours. I got out and stuck into him for his thoughtlessness, before his wife opened her beak in his defense. Robyn clarified that for her. I told them I had every intention of reporting how careless he had been. But that was then, and the heat eventually comes off these things. Forgiveness is the fragrance that the violet sheds on the heel that has crushed it. (Subaru Outback, light copper metallic colour, Idaho license plate 2CU3333).

We had arrived. Silver City was founded in 1864, and named for the metal's discovery at nearby War Eagle Mountain. At the height of its prosperity, it was one of the major cities in Idaho Territory, with a dozen streets, twelve ore-processing mills, 75 businesses, 2,500 souls, and four cemeteries. Some of the largest stage lines in the West operated in the area, and Silver City had the first telegraph and daily newspaper in the territory. More than two dozen camps provided shelter, supplies and amusement for the thousands who came to the mountains seeking their fortunes. Almost a dozen cemeteries and many more remote burial sites testify to their hard and dangerous and violent lives. Between 1863 and 1865, more than two hundred and fifty mines were in operation and hundreds more were being developed, pock-marking and honeycombing the mountains, with seventy miles of laboriously hand-dug tunnels in one alone. At least sixty million dollars worth of gold and silver was taken out of the ground, in exchange for the lives that went into it.

Rugged and picturesque, Silver City was that rare example of a gold rush mining camp jewel still intact, neither refurbished into a Rockwell theme park nor obliterated by Orwellian modernization. It was crumbling but authentic, mostly because the fires that destroyed so many other Western mining towns had never ravaged it. There were no power lines nor phone lines nor gas station, nor much in the way of plumbing. The only accommodation was the Idaho Hotel, opened in 1863, still barely standing on Jordan Street.

Despite the tidy white clapboard façade of hanging baskets on a flag and elk antler-bedecked veranda, the old wooden structure sagged with more fatigue than age, from everything it had witnessed, and the ghosts of more gravitas than gravity. It carried a dark weathered wooden backpack of disorderly additions, teetering for five stories down a steep embankment, following a psychotic roofline of cobbled and corroded corrugated convergences, planks arching away from the nails still left in them, trying to escape. Most walls were crooked and some were missing altogether.

Inside the front door was a dark wood-paneled foyer. *Hot beer. Lousy food. Bad Service. Welcome. Have a nice day.*

The heavily stained wallpaper, strips of which were also peeling, had faded decades ago to the colour of dirty water. The windows were coated in a dust layer even older. The floors were so uneven we have to watch our feet. In place of period decor, there were relics, an old piano, a poker table with a cash slot and a built-in safe. Horseshoe snow cleats hung on a wall. We were trespassing in the musty air of history.

The old sign above the entrance to the saloon was no longer true. *Meals at all hours.* Inside, the dining room and bar were illuminated in a spectral suffusion from the far bank of windows, and the reflection from the heavy saloon mirror.

Free Beer... Tomorrow. The walls were loaded with historical photos, and the old bookshelf was loaded with books. One of the owners, Jerri, stood behind the till, handing out change to the daytime visiting lunch crowd, who wanted to pay and leave, before the ghosts of Silver City came out to play. She had a big red flower in her hair. Jerri and her husband Roger had purchased the Idaho Hotel in 1983, and lived 'under the stairs.' She had been a structural engineer in a former life, and then developed a reputation for the best pies in Idaho. She looked up.

"I think we're in room number four." I said, and saw a brief panic cross her face. She checked her book.

"I'm really sorry." She said. "But Roger's still making up the rooms."

"No matter." Robyn said. "We've brought lunch. Maybe we'll have a picnic on the porch and go see the town." And everyone exhaled.

Except for Kodiak, their dog, who inhaled. Robyn and I made sandwiches on the veranda, from the leftover Pioneer Saloon prime rib and rib-eye steak. Robyn also made a mistake, by offering a morsel to Kodiak, and almost lost her fingers.

"You can't trust your dog to watch your food." I said. An ATV drove up, and another. The bearded one was dressed in camouflage. Even his baseball cap was camouflage, and the gigantic Bowie knife he had on his belt could have weighed as much as it owner. The other driver was dressed more casually, with a message-stenciled T-shirt to match his camo. *It's just genetics.*

316

Robyn and I went across the street to the only shop. Inside was a handsaw, painted in a black velvet version of Silver City. There were no words. We followed the trail along the creek to the main cemetery. Here was tragedy, and irony. *Here lies an honest man Oliver Hazard Purdy Born Barre Orleans Co. New York September 12 1824 killed Bannock Indian War June 8 1878 His motto- 'Forewarned Forearmed' His creed- He was always ready for the battle when the bugle sounded. He never flinched from duty.* I wondered how forearmed Oliver had been. *Last resting place of Helene Emilia and Albert John, Beloved children of Fred & Wilhelmina Grete Sr.* One was four, and the other was sixteen months. You could feel Wilhelmina's pain through the stone. There were several headstones with Masonic symbols, and once again it seemed that Masonry was a pervasive force in the Old West. Another marked grave was simply inscribed. *Unknown.*

"Daddy, I don't want you to die." Said a little girl to her father, one row over, in a sudden epiphany.

Back across the stream we hiked a wide circuit around and through the old mountain mining town. Many of the original buildings had been lovingly restored, including the outhouses. One was two stories high, decorated with antlers, and a notice. *Shown by Appointment.* Our Lady of Tears Catholic Church, sharpened by the angular light, perched on a rocky outcrop.

We went down Dean Man Alley. *No Trespassing. Violators will be shot.* The high sagebrush desert dirt streets and camouflage fire truck and cow skulls on weathered wood and rusted tin and hanging American flags gave the place a post-apocalyptic feel. In the Land of the Free and the Home of the Brave, it was their biggest fear, their strongest myth, and their most delicious fantasy.

Some of the structures were still recognizable for the function they had performed- the stone walls and iron bars of the jail, the assay office, the bath house, the drug store, the barber shop and the meat market, the brewing vat and the Silver Slipper saloon were all here. As was the Chinese laundry and Chinese-run brothel, the *House of False Affection.* There was a story of a Chinese Polly who had been bought, sight unseen by a saloonkeeper in another part of the territory, and then won in a poker game by a man named Charlie, who eventually married her. The town's young hooligans used to torment the Chinese, by digging and covering holes in the ground. When a vegetable vendor or water carrier fell into the tiger trap, they laughed and jeered at his broken buckets and limbs.

The surviving buildings leaned into the gaps made by the ravages of terror and time. Robyn and I followed the dust back to the Idaho Hotel dining room, in the late afternoon. It was here we met Richard, a loyal employee of Roger and Gerri's, for the previous four years. He took our bottle of Inn on the Creek Domaine Carneros and put in the propane refrigerator, and allowed us to take the only table on the window side of the saloon. There was a two-chair limit on the steep side, because of the possibility of collapse, but the view and the light, and the hummingbirds around the feeder were worth the risk. I looked down into vertigo. The fire escape ladder ended far too high off the ground. *Are you crazy? The fall will probably kill you.*

And there he was on the wall, in the famous photo, if it was real. I pointed it out to Richard.

"It's called *The Gathering*." He said. "It was supposedly taken at Hunter Hot Springs, Montana in 1883." They were all there, standing and sitting and lounging about on the porch- Butch Cassidy and the Sundance Kid and Wyatt Earp and Morgan Earp and Doc Holliday and Teddy Roosevelt and Liver Eating Johnson and Bat Masterson and Judge Roy Bean and a couple of lesser mortals.

"You think its real?" I asked.

"Probably not." He said. "But I like to think it is. The Old West was the time and place that turned dust into romance."

"And romance into dust." I said.

"It was very honest." He said.

"And very American." I said.

"You read Hemingway?" He asked. Friends.

A loud coarse obese woman rolled into the saloon, bringing noise and flies. Richard attended to her as quickly as he could, and brought me a fly swatter. As dinnertime approached two couples joined us. Frank and Chris were Brits, here because of Frank's fascination with Western ghost towns. Every year they would fly over and rent a truck and fill themselves with myth and legend.

"But you have far more history than here." I said. "What happened in the American West occurred over a period of only thirty years or so."
"It was the ultimate egalitarian adventure." He said. "Anyone could make it or fail on the basis of his own ability and luck."
The other couple was from Oregon. Friz Bee was a big guy, who worked as a mental health assistant. His wife, Dawn, was a landscape architect and photographer. They had come to Silver City for the photos.
We ordered the only thing available, six orders of French Dip, and six of Gerri's famous peach and ginger pie with vanilla ice cream for dessert. Perfect crust. Richard had even found an ice bucket, and poured our faux champagne with a sommelier's flourish. It all went down fabulously.
The six of us adjourned to the steeply sloped second floor balcony on the front of the hotel overlooking Jordan Street, and the similarly steep mountainside opposite. We had missed what Roger called the 'first sunset,' and were left in the inky blue sky creeping dusk over the granite peaks. It felt lonely and desolate, and we ran out of conversation. We should have had more in common, perhaps, but sometimes, even when you're in the same place, you're not in the same place. Just on Sunset, Frank began some polemic about Zionists. *God didn't give them the land. We did.*
Robyn and I excused ourselves to find Richard. I asked him for the key to our room.
"There are no keys." He said. "There never were."

Room number four was the smallest of the bedrooms in the Idaho Hotel, and furthest away from the sailboat pump-flush washroom. But it had the biggest queen bed in the place, and I thought it would be the quietest, if the place would be full. But it was almost empty, and the single electric bulb that ran on solar power didn't provide enough light to read by. There was more from the full moon outside our window, brilliant above the mountains. Under it, Silver City was solemnly silver, the ghost town it was exactly supposed to be. Every cabin on the skyline made its strong and solid and serene presence known, under stars undimmed by any streetlight. Moonbeams and shadows reflected off the mirror in the Victorian chiffonier, mixing with the cool drafts and distant night howls of the coyotes. The night chill that came was more moody than it should have been. Floorboards creaked. We tucked up under the covers and snuggled in for warmth.

"In the gold rush days." I said. "They had a custom of sitting up with dead bodies, the night before they were buried."

"How come?" Robyn asked.

"To make sure they were dead." I said. "And to keep away the rats."

"So where's this battlefield we came to see?" She asked.

"Here." I said. "Right here."

*   *   *

We awoke to a silver monochrome morning, the mountains still purple in the chill. It was slow getting out of bed. I had a lukewarm shower down the hall.

"Coffee." Robyn said. And we wobbled down the stairs. Roger had it covered. A big volcanic pot sat sputtering on the cast iron wood stove. I asked after Richard.

"Not a morning person." He said. Richard walked into the saloon.

"Sometimes I wonder why I hired him." They both grinned. We sat at our table, the one with the two-chair limit, on the precarious side beside the windows. Sunlight infused the room with peaches and citrus, illuminating the lace curtains, gleaming off the old wood, and throwing rainbows through the bar bottles. Richard poured us coffee.

"You know about the shootout?" He asked. I told him I knew a little.

"The call it the Owyhee War." He said. "It blew up here on April Fool's Day, 1868. But it had been brewing, like this coffee, for a while. War Eagle Mountain over there was a nine thousand foot-high Owyhee Peak, veined with rich quartz seams of gold and silver."

Two separate mining interests had started at separate locations, but when they arrived on the same vein from different directions, thousands of dollars worth of ore came into conflict. Marion

More owned the Ellmore mine, and had spent a great deal of his personal fortune to develop the techniques for extracting the precious metals from the quartz. Despite some mystery about his early career, the community respected his character, and sympathized with his position. The Golden Chariot mine was owned by George Grayson and Hill Beachy, a Lewiston hotelkeeper and stage line proprietor, who disputed More's claim to the lode, and was well supported in Boise. Wealthy and determined men of mark constituted both sides. Their collision occurred more than 300 feet underground. At that depth, there were no impartial witnesses; on the surface, legal resolution would be too slow. Every silver lining has cloud.

The two mines became fortified camps of a hundred men, half miners, half fighters. Their sappers erected barricades, cut side pits, and imported cases of rifles and shotguns and pistols and ammunition. And then it exploded.

Hand grenades and Greek fire were launched into the tunnels. Any light that appeared was met with a hail of bullets. One heavy central timber upright roof support, fifteen inches wide, had been struck and pierced with two thousand rounds of ammunition, and cut nearly in half, three feet from the floor. For two weeks the battle raged, day and night, more lead than silver, deep inside War Eagle Mountain. Two men were killed and several wounded. Reinforcements arrived for both factions, from Boise and Idaho City. The sheriff went upon the ground on several occasions, but all was quiet up top.

Governor Ballard, to 'report and assist', sent John McBride, chief justice of the Idaho Territorial Supreme Court, to Silver City.

Twelve miles before reaching his destination, he was forced to abandon his stagecoach for a sleigh, because of the snow. McBride arrived at the end of the day to find that the two parties had agreed to a compromise. Hostilities had ceased. A general rejoicing ensued. Marion More invited the judge to a celebratory banquet, but McBride considered it a conflict of interest, and declined. Instead, he checked into the hotel.

> 'I called at the room of Mr. Grayson which was
> near my own, to procure such a general
> statement from him as he might desire to give.
> An hour had been occupied in general
> conversation when an outcry in the street was
> heard, followed by pistol shots. Then came a
> rush of mixed rabble and the streets were filled
> with a surging, excited crowd.'

Marion More had been shot, and two others wounded. A crowd rushed up the stairs. Beachy and his friends had come up the stairs to join Grayson, leaving More's allies on the street. The clamor of the angry mob gathering below was loud and vengeful.

> 'I opened my door and saw Beachy and two others
> busy loading rifles and fire-arms, and a man by
> the name of Sam Lockhart, a friend of Beachy,
> holding a disabled arm, from which the blood
> was dripping... voices wild with passion and loud

with threats and cursing filled the air. "Bring him out; Hang him!" were the exclamations. Beachy rapidly loaded piece after piece and remarked as he did so; "The man who comes to take Lockhart out of this hotel without a warrant, will die before he reaches the head of the stairs!"'

A group of neutral citizens requested the judge to go out on the balcony, and speak to the crowd. He managed to restore order by instructing to the sheriff to obtain arrest warrants for the arrest of Grayson and Lockhart.

'I then proceeded to the place where More lay dying. He had been shot in the breast, the ball penetrating the lungs, and he was rapidly failing. He was able to converse in a faint voice and recognized me when I took his hand and spoke to him. He said; "They have stolen the mine and now their man Lockhart has killed me." I learned from those who witnessed the shooting that More, who had been dining with his friends and had drunk heavily, although the controversy about the mine had been settled, was not at all satisfied and considered that he had been wronged. Though generally a quiet man, he was irritable when drinking and in this mood he met Lockhart and another of the Chariot party on the street. Some hot words passed between them. More was without arms, but carried a rough cane in his hand, which he raised as if to strike Lockhart. Lockhart backed away a pace or two and fired. Ben White and Jack fisher, who were with More, both drew pistols and fired, one of Fisher's shots striking his opponent's arm. White's pistol missed fire. Lockhart always insisted Fisher fired first and that he shot More after he had been struck in the arm. Fisher was wounded in the leg by Lockhart. More died in about three hours after he received his wound. Lockhart had his arm amputated but gangrene set in and after several weeks of intense suffering, he died. Fisher, who was probably more responsible for the difficulty than anyone else, fled the country. This contest, first or last, cost the lives of six men and left the whole community in a state bordering on anarchy. Governor Ballard called in the soldiers stationed at Fort Boise and one hundred and fifty United States troops...'

"That's how the Owyhee War ended." Said Richard. "And then the silver ran out."
"As must we." I said, shaking hands and leaving him with the ghosts.

*   *   *

Capital Punishment
Boise, Idaho

Counselor: Alright where?
Laura: How 'bout Boise?
Counselor: Boise?
Laura: Boise.
Counselor: Why Boise?
Laura: What's wrong with Boise?
Counselor: Have you ever been to
        Boise?
Laura: No, have you?
Counselor: No. You have a hotel?
Laura: I'm looking as we speak.
        Tomorrow.
Counselor: Boise.
Laura: Yeah, Boise.

The Counselor 2013

Arsenic. The distance to the next milepost depends on the mud in the road. If the rain continued the way we were all going, the distance would be somewhere between late and never. In their efforts to avoid it, the California quail looked silly.

"At least there's no dust." Robyn said, squinting through the wipers at the edges of oblivion. The relief was waiting for us in the yeehaw dip that took us back onto Highway 78. We drove by a new subdivision under construction. *Eagle View.* "That's the only view they've got." She said. The *God Bless America* mud flaps, on the big semi in front of us on Old Bath House Road, hung heavy with their purpose. Through alternating curves

of yellow and green harvested hay, we passed
Blue Canoe Steaks and Seafood Mecca of 'Family
Dining,' the Snake River Inn, and miles of
sugars beets and alfalfa, and high fructose corn
syrup, still in corn form. A big *Hey Hay Hey Hay
Hey Hay* truck was parked in one of the fields. A
Michigan yell and a Hokey Hey Hay.

We crossed the Snake River onto Highway 46. A
trailer, with a tiny lighthouse out front, held the
Melba Valley Worship Center, *focused on
building relationships within the Body of Christ
and in our community.* Right onto Stage Coach
Road, and across the New York Canal past Deer
Flat Road, we came to the Bethel Church of the
Nazarene. *Celebrate recovery this Thursday.* A
sign, further on, advertised a *Highway
Evangelism* telephone number.

Nampa brought us out of the Heartland, and
from the First Amendment into the Second.
*American Pawn Gun... lending on guns, gold and
jewelry- Hablamos Espanol.*

As we approached Boise, the Second
Amendment, allowing the possession of firearms,
added the Twenty-first Amendment, adding the
possession of firewater. It was an All-American
combination. The World Center for Birds of Prey
held birds of pray. Fragments of fractured tire
treads had exploded on 184 East. A Fox 9 News
SUV blew by, in a hurry. The square miles of
vehicles parked in the Camping World RV Sales
lot, more than the standing armies of most
nations would ever require, juxtaposed in
contrast with the box store down the highway.
Axiom- Truth in Fitness. In the pouring rain, the

fire danger was still 'high.'

In the 1820s, the French Canadian fur trappers that had worked their high desert trap lines here, called it *la rivière boisée*, the wooded river. The Hudson Bay Company erected Fort Boise a decade later, and abandoned it when the pelts ran out in the 1850s. During the U.S. Civil War in 1963, Indian massacres along the Oregon Trail prompted the army to reestablish a fort, near the intersection of the trail with the mining boom route connecting the Boise Basin with Silver City.

I only knew two things about Boise. The first was that the big name, high on the malodorous pulp and paper mill in my northern Ontario hometown, was Boise Cascade.

"Its the smell of money." My father used to say. To me, it reeked of noxious decay. The other thing about Boise was that it was where I got Robyn's diamond. I was going to get it in Antwerp, which is where the guy in downtown Boise sent it. It's another, much longer, story.

But there was a third thing I had found out about Boise, on our road to get there. Every year Boise ranked higher and higher on a slew of top 10 lists- the best U.S. Downtown, the best city to raise a family, the best place to retire, the best place to be a doctor, the best place for yogis and asthmatics, the healthiest, Farmers Insurance most secure place to live, the top sexually-active city. Sandpoint may have been the most beautiful town in America, but almost by every other criterion, Boise was kicking its shins.

Winters are relatively mild in Boise, summers

not too hot. Dozens of high-tech startup companies have moved to town, bringing jobs to a place that is still affordable, and safe. Older neighbourhoods have a Boulder vibe- farmers' markets and community gardens and Tibetan prayer flags and coffee shops. Boise, for where it is, is no cultural wasteland. There is a symphony and opera and Ballet Idaho, and a couple of museums. It had two thousand acres of parks and a twenty-five mile greenbelt. The hills above the town are laced with more than 135 miles of hiking and mountain biking trails, and a bucket list of mountains and ski hills and river rafting runs and fishing streams. Boise State University professor Todd Shallat may have nailed it. *It's the myth of the empty. We're all from some place else – most of us came from places that had crowds. We envisioned Boise as a frontier. God's unfinished construction project. Boise is good at providing a nostalgic idea of home, even if we aren't from here...Most people are looking for that quintessential Norman Rockwell painting, or the Disneyland main street. There are places in Boise where if you squint, you can see it.*

Robyn and I squinted down a dozen one-way streets, before we found a parking space near the Basque Block. Boise has the largest Basque community in the United States, and the fifth largest in the world. All fifteen thousand of them were parked within five blocks of the Basque restaurant we were aiming for. We put enough quarters in the meter to choke a Basque sheep, more than we thought it could chew up and swallow, in the time we had allowed for lunch.

There were strings of dried peppers and an accordion on the brick walls of Bar Gernika, but it was more Boise than Bilbao. We had a ten-dollar marinated pork loin solomo sandwich with pimientos, and a ten-dollar spicy lamb grinder with jalapeños and pepper jack cheese. The salad came with Basque Thousand Island dressing, and a Basque smilie and message on the bill. *Have a nice day.*

But that was not a given. Robyn and I made it back to the parking meter game less than thirty seconds after the end of the final quarter. There was a ticket on our windshield. It was for a ridiculous amount of money, considering how little over the time limit we were, and how far we had come to patronize this administrative seat of Idaho government. What Boise had administered to Robyn and I was a shin-kicking form of capital punishment. It left the same reek of noxious decay I remembered from my hometown. Robyn's downtown diamond dimmed with disapproval.

They can suck eggs." I said. "I'll go to prison first." It was, in fact, our very next stop. An old Basque proverb began to beat itself around my head. *The hand of the stranger is heavy.*

> 'Never put all your Basques in one exit.'
> Ernest Hemingway, seeing a Fascist plane
> bomb a bridge of fleeing civilians

*   *   *

Cotton: Let's move to Boise, I always wanted to
go there!
Babs Johnson: Boise, Cotton? Why, that might
not be a bad place!
Pink Flamingos (1972)

Going to prison is like dying with your eyes open. At the old territorial penitentiary down Warm Springs Road, you could still see every moribund moment. There may have been places in Boise where, if you squinted, you could have made out a Norman Rockwell painting, or a Disneyland main street. But this wasn't one of them.

Beyond the *Pauly Sliding Door Locking Device*, within the seventeen-foot high sandstone walls, there had once been human voices. Now there was silence, except for the echoes, and the signs. *No loafing this area. Warning guard dogs on duty.* It says a lot about a top ten town when the main tourist attraction is its penal institution. Built in 1870, this one was a beautiful Romanesque castle with turrets. If the American West had been the gold rush towards truth, the Boise pen was where the consequences arrived, where lesser achievements were redeemed, where authenticity was still about facing death with dignity and courage. In this bastion of brutality, the Nature that men lived in, was all too inhuman.

During its century of correction and chastisement, the prison housed over 13,000 inmates, up to six hundred at a time. Over two hundred had been women.

Living conditions were a contradiction, as

cramped and as harsh as morally tolerable, for the morality of the time. The sandstone the prisoners mined from nearby rock quarries as part of their penance, to form the very walls that would hold them captive, was a plentiful and inexpensive building material, but it exaggerated the internal temperature of the cells. In the hot Boise summers, the stone retained the heat, turning the lockups into stifling ovens; in winter, it held the bitter cold, chilling the inmates to their marrow. Each tiny chamber held two tiny fold-down cots. The only other furnishing was the 'honey bucket', which served as a toilet until plumbing was installed in the 1920s. The prison's ventilation system didn't ventilate, and disease and violence ruled.

Resistant prisoners were fitted with the Oregon Boot, a thirty-pound iron donut that locked around an ankle, supported by braces that attached it to the heel of a boot. It was also called the Gardner Shackle, after the Oregon State Penitentiary Warden, J.C. Gardner, who patented it in 1866, and proceeded to make a small fortune, from each employment of the device. The asymmetry of the weight kept the inmate off balance, in extreme pain and, ultimately, bedridden. To the prisoners forced to wear them, they were often lethal.

Even more recalcitrant convicts were locked into punishment cells. The first set, built in the early 1920s, was called the Cooler, and held six men in 'solitary confinement.' In the second section, each of twelve terrifying 3'x8' isolation holes built in 1926, housed a single inmate. It was known as 'Siberia.'

Robyn and I entered the New Cell House block, built in 1889, a three-tiered painted metal lattice tagliatelle cage, rising like a giant 42 steel cavity music box, from Scheherazade's Arabian Nights. Robyn entered one of the open cubicles, to pose behind the bars. She lasted as long as the photo, escaping quickly from a 'serious case of the creeps.' Which was more than those incarcerated on the third floor would ever do. The top tier was the original 'Death Row.' It was closest to the Rose Garden, where their hangings took place.

Families would picnic on the trails above the prison to watch the executions.

When less spectacle and more convenience came into vogue, the death penalties were scored indoors, on the gallows built into the second floor 'drop room' of Cell House 5, through the hold into the 'swinging room' on the first floor. Of the eleven executions in Idaho history, ten of them took place here. A hundred more prisoners died within their self-made walls, from old age and illness and murder. It was a horror house of shanks and shivs. One inmate was gang-raped to death in the shower room.

The defined crimes of the era, that put people behind these bars, ran from the archaic to the arcane- mayhem, false personation, transporting intoxicating liquor (or selling it to an Indian), sending a threatening letter, passing a fictitious check, adultery, unlawful cohabitation, bigamy, polygamy, or the larceny of domestic fowls and poultry. One Chinese man, in the enthusiastic racism of territorial Idaho, was imprisoned for months for 'an excessive appetite for chicken.'

One prisoner, James Oscar Baker, was convicted in 1885 of shooting and killing a man that got into a brawl with Baker's father at a Soda Springs saloon. He was ten years old. A second, James Whitaker, was incarcerated for nine years in 1912, for the murder of his mother who had forced him to help with the family laundry. He was eleven.

W.M. McGraw, had his rape conviction pardoned on appeal because it had been handed down 'during a sensation of female suffragette agitation.' Other convicts were of an even more scandalous provenance.

The first execution at the penitentiary occurred in 1878, a Bannock Indian named Tambiago, hung for the shooting death of a white teamster. Alex Rhoden was a drover bringing cattle to the resettled Shoshone and Bannocks at the Fort Hall Agency. Tensions were high, not only because the broken promises of the Federal negotiators to provide farming and craft training, seeds and food supplies and warm clothing, on which their very survival depended, but because of the crimes of rape and horse theft, committed by unknown white men, that went unpunished. One frustrated brave shot two drovers and, as he was brought through Fort Hall, Tambiago 'snapped' at the injustice. *The Indian who killed Rodin had no grudge against him. He simply wanted to kill a white man and Alex was the first one he saw.*

The last execution, in 1957, was of the prison's

most notorious inmate, 'Idaho's Jack the Ripper,' Raymond Allen Snowden. After a night of drinking, he murdered Cora Dean, a local woman and mother of two, so depressed by the death of her husband that she used to drive into downtown Garden City, Idaho, to drink and play the gambling machines on Saturday nights. Her body was found with 35 stab wounds, from a two-and-a-quarter-inch pocketknife. A pathologist determined that her throat had been slashed first. The blade had been pushed further into the base of her skull to probe for the spinal cord, where another quick and expert slash severed it. Detective Frank Boor remembered locking up Snowden for a night years before, because he had threatened to cut his girl friend's spinal cord. Witnesses confirmed that he was the last person she had been seen with. Snowden confessed to killing Cora and, before his hanging, to murdering two other women. When the trap door was pulled, the noose failed to break his neck. He struggled and strangled at the end of the rope for fifteen minutes, before the suffocation killed him. Other inmates would later claim to hear the moans of his ghost.

The longest sentence had been handed to Harry Orchard, who died within the prison's walls in 1954, after nearly fifty years of incarceration. Harry had been a union goon assassin. He killed former Governor Frank Steunenberg by placing a bomb in his home, and murdered seventeen others, relating his methodology in an eerily polite, calm and unhesitating manner.

The most infamous woman prisoner was Lyda

Southard, otherwise know as 'Flypaper Lyda' or 'Lady Bluebeard,' for poisoning four of her seven husbands with arsenic, to collect their life insurance. Their exhumed bodies were found to have been far too well preserved.

'O Twin Falls farms are bonnie in the middle of July,
And 'twas there that Lyda Southard baked her famous apple pie.
Her famous apple pie, and ne'er forgot will be
And for Lyda Southard's apple pie, men would lay them doon to dee.

She sprinkled it with cinnamon, a bit of allspice too
She sprinkled it with arsenic, a tasty devil's brew.
A tasty devil's brew and ne'er forgot will be,
For, Lyda Saffer's apple pie, men lay them down to die.

When they arrested Lyda, she began to cry,
It was just dessert she murmured, I never thought they'd die.
I never thought they'd die, I never thought they'd die,
It was just dessert she murmured, I never thought they'd die.

Now Lyda's got her just desserts, she's in the jailhouse strong.
Her pie crust it was short and sweet, her sentence it was long.
Her sentence it was long and ne'er forgot will be
For, Lyda Saffer's apple pie, men lay them down to die.'
Lyda Southard's Famous Apple Pie, 1921

Lyda was also suspected of killing her daughter and her brother-in-law. She was released after twenty years, and an escape down a rope made of bed sheets, after a final pardon, in 1942.
In the hundred years of use, there had been over

337

500 escape attempts from the penitentiary. Of the 90 that had been successful, most only enjoyed freedom for a few months, days, or hours. In 1901, Bob Meeks, an associate of Butch Cassidy, made a daring dash out the front door. A guard shot him in the leg, which later required amputation at the knee. In 1904, Charles Smith ran away from garden work outside the walls, and was thought to have drowned in the Boise River. Officials were quite surprised, in 1940, when he returned to give himself up.

What finally opened the doors for the prisoners of the Idaho Pen, were the conditions they had been enclosed in, the 'Pennsylvania System' of reform that had emphasized isolation, labor, and religious reflection as a means to seek penitence and remorse from the inmates. And the overcrowding. In 1971, and again in 1973, riots broke out. Prisoners burned the chapel and dining hall to the ground. The buildings that survived were left exactly as they were in 1973. The untouched cells look today as they did then, perhaps a bit more weather-beaten. Each is infused with the character of their last tenant, their 1973 calendars hanging on the smoke and fire-blackened stone walls, and their artwork and decoration and wit carved into them- some poignant, some trivial, some profane. The word 'Idaho' is writ large on the underside of an upright toilet seat. A vintage television screen sits dark and silent, where *All in the Family, Jeopardy, Mission: Impossible, Ironside, The Odd Couple,* and *The Wonderful World of Disney,* used to play.

The groans of the bones of dread and oppression remain within the sandstone walls of the Old Idaho Penitentiary. Some report fleeting glimpses of inmates tending the flowers in the rose garden.

They say there are two days you remember about prison- the day you go in and day you come out. Fortunately, for Robyn and I, they were both on the same day we had our jailbreak.

*   *   *

'If you're ridin' ahead of the herd, take a look back every now and then to make sure it's still there with you.'

Cowboy Proverb

I'm not sure what will happen to Barefoot Thomas, now that it's for sale, but for six hundred grand, you can have your own private Idaho.

Robyn and I turned down the back lane, and pulled in under a magnificent trumpet vine, flushed orange with bugle flowers and dripping with long green pods. There are nineteen native species of squirrel in Idaho, but the giant rodent on the stairs to the Carriage House was, like us, a Pacific coast invader. The Western Grey squirrel, big as a marmot, squatted on his turned-out cowboy legs, and cussed us for interrupting his snack. A young balding guy, bearded and barefoot, opened the back door of the main house. I asked him what the alien woodchuck was doing here.

"Eating peanuts." He said. Turnip tops don't tell you the size of the turnips.

Even though we had arrived early, Thomas allowed us in, to drop off our baggage. The innkeeper's resident host, he apparently had a fair bit of it himself.

Thomas had lost his father when he was four, and moved nine times before his tenth year. To compensate, he had cultivated a fine opinion of himself, and was more than happy to share. I asked him why he was barefoot. He told me he was a martial artist. I asked him about breakfast. He told me he was a master chef. I asked him about the wine on offer for the afternoon happy hour. He told me he was a supertaster. I asked him for a restaurant recommendation for that evening. He told me he was a foodie.

"I send all my clients to Bardenay." He said. "It's an amazing place." But the place we were standing in was even more amazing. The Idaho Heritage Inn had started life in 1904, as the home of Harry Falk, a member of a Jewish merchant family that owned the local department store. When Harry built the Mode Building, people came from all over Boise, to watch live models portray fairy tale characters, on decorated sets in the big store windows. Harry's own fairy tale was centred here, in his majestic living room, the incredible formal dining room, seven master bedrooms, eight bathrooms, and the Carriage House, which Robyn and I had reserved, for not much at all.

"You got a good deal." Said Thomas. "The price goes up after you leave."

"Water seeks its own level." I said. Thomas told me he was an expert fly fisherman. I asked him about trout. Trout fishing was wimpy. Thomas preferred carp. Despite his age, he appeared to be stuck somewhere between hay and grass.

"Governor Clarke Chase lived in this house in the 1940s." He said. "And then his daughter, Bethine." I wondered what kind of father would name his daughter Bethine. But then again, he had a brother named Barzilla. I wondered if Bethine and Barzilla had ever eaten at Bardenay in Boise. Bethine would marry a United States senator, Frank Church, and moved east. *I have often described my life in Washington as like Cinderella's: I was either cleaning the fireplace or going to the ball.* Thomas told me he was an excellent ballroom dancer. I asked him if he had a girlfriend. Thomas told me he was a ladykiller. He was using up all his kindling to make a fire. Robyn asked him if he had any other interests.

"I ski Bogus." He said. At first I didn't realize that it was the name of the local mountain resort.

Thomas told us he was a biochemist. Robyn told Thomas I was a medical specialist. For a brief moment Barefoot Thomas became a Doubting Thomas, before the epiphany.

"When you get all un-astonished," I said. "Maybe

you could look after our bags."

Robyn and I left him for the big sights of Downtown Boise. About half way down West Idaho Street, Robyn decided that shopping would trump sights, and we made arrangements to meet at the Inn later.

My first mission was a Governor Chase chase to his old stomping ground, under the dome of the Idaho State legislature. An Idaho State Police Black Maria was parked out front, like they were expecting me. A bronze statue of Lewis, wearing a three-cornered hat and Clark, with a rather jaunty fur cap, seemed to be asking directions from a Nez Percé. The native, Twisted Hair, is pointing west, over the head of his son, Lawyer. The work was called *The Hospitality of the Nez Percé*. Lawyer was handling the trade treasure. There was far too much symbolic irony for me to bear.

I walked by a granite headstone. *Desert Storm...Operation Home Front.* I read it wrong at first, as Stormfront, the first Internet hate website, peddlers of the same neo-Nazi ideology as their Aryan Nations brothers in The Most Beautiful Town in America. *White Pride World Wide.* Its founder, Don Black, wasn't, although he had tried to overthrow the government of Dominica, the predominantly black Caribbean island, in 1981. Perhaps he had mistaken klanship for kinship, before being nailed midship while boarding his invasion vessel in New Orleans, in the *Operation Red Dog* fiasco that would later be called the Bayou of Pigs.

I walked up the stairs of the Idaho legislature,

between two hundred Doric and Corinthian and Ionic pillars of marble dust, plaster, and scagliola gypsum and glue. Gigantic yellow nylon ribbons and bows wrapped their sentiments around each one, trying to remember if it was trying to look like a Roman St. Peter's, a London St. Paul's, or some other sinner that had kept on going. I kept on going into its five acre interior, with over an acre of artistically carved red marble from Georgia, grey marble from Alaska, green marble from Vermont, and black marble from Italy, and under the capitol dome over two hundred feet high. The Duomo that Filippo Brunelleschi had built onto the Florence Cathedral was higher than the one in Boise, but it was over a hundred feet narrower, and there hadn't been enough timber in Tuscany to build the scaffolding and forms. I looked up into the vast expanse of exquisite light and symmetry above me, and over at the state motto, on the Great Seal of Idaho. Esto perpetua. *Let it be perpetual.* For this kind of coin, it had better be. The marble washroom was transcendent.

Just as I was about to make my descent, a human appeared in the vast hemispherical space. Her echo caught me half a staircase away, asking if she could be of some assistance. I told her of my surprise, to find a mere mortal employed in what was clearly a sacred space. She laughed.

Her name was Nancy, some undersecretary of some other undersecretary, and she invited me into her office, for a cup of tea, and a human connection. She asked me why I had come, and I

343

went all Steinbeck on her.

"There are two kinds of people in the world." I said. "Observers and non-observers. I'm an observer." She asked me what I had observed. I told her it was hard to miss the dome.

"Any ranch that you can see on foot just isn't worth looking at." I said. I asked her how she liked working in the marble mausoleum. She gave me Steinbeck back.

"I find out of long experience that I admire all nations and hate all governments," She said. And then, as a parting gift, she gave me a hard copy of the Idaho Blue Book, a 450-page tome on everything Idaho. I asked her if she knew what had happened to Chief Joseph.

"It does not require many words to speak the truth." She said. We parted friends.

I wandered further into town. There were big manhole covers and colourful murals, paintings of flying pigs, of hummingbirds hovering in front of an old Victrola horn, of an Idaho potato face, with a crown on his head. A cyborg with an exposed brain drove by on a motorized unicycle. The Hollywood Market fresco held 'a Boise principle.' *Happiness is spoken here.* I bought some homemade lavender and sandalwood soap for Robyn. It was authentic.

I arrived back at the Idaho Heritage Inn in the late afternoon, in time to meet Craig, the owner. He poured us a chardonnay, from the local Ste. Chapelle Winery, named after Louis IX's 13th century court chapel in Paris.

"Not bad." I said. Not French, I thought.

"They make over 130,000 cases a year." He said.

Craig was a Vietnam veteran. We didn't talk about that, at first, until the chardonnay kicked in. I told him I loved the Inn. He asked if I wanted to buy it. I thought he was kidding.

Robyn was resting in the Carriage House. I warily dodged the air rat on the way up the stairs. The water was geothermal, and we would both reek of sulfur from the shower. It was a *Boise Cascade*. I smelled like my hometown used to.

We walked to Bardenay, and drank gin basil mojitos. I had a 14 oz. rib eye with blue cheese butter and a veal demi-glace. Robyn had a grilled Hagerman trout fillet in a balsamic reduction sauce, with capers. There were garlic mashed potatoes and chef's vegetables. I asked the waitress what kind of trout a Hagerman was. "It's a farm." She said. And I realized why Thomas caught carp.

The grey squirrel had already gone to bed by the time we arrived back in the Carriage House. The bedding, like the inn, was a bit worn, and radiated heat in the night. It was muggy, like a stormfront was coming, and quiet on the street outside our windows. I turned on the air conditioner. A cement truck engine throttled up through the gears. It was unbelievably deafening, and poured water all over the carpeted floor. In our choice between heat prostration and dehydration, or deafness and drowning, we chose the baked potato option. Lightning lit up the sky with electric blue crackling, turning what little air supply we had left into ozone, and thunder. It lasted all night long.

We had to wake Thomas in the morning. He entered Harry Falk's incredible formal dining room barefoot, eating bacon. Twenty minutes later than we had requested, he brought out his master chef Texas egg bake. It was good. He talked about creationism and climate change as we ate. We both believed in one and not the other. I asked him where he thought all the poor air quality was coming from in Boise, during the winter and summer inversions, why everything seems to be on fire during the warmer months, and how that might threaten to affect his Olympic outdoor recreational pursuits. He told me it was cyclical, and that Boise would continue to be safe.

And I pondered, as we drove down the lane and back onto West Idaho Street, how Boise was the kind of place that had traded affordable and safe for any chance to be authentically alive. It was all very comfortable, but comfort never produced an obsession for excellence or a single original thought. The absence of a true spirit to achieve a great anything was, in my mind and theirs, the ultimate form of capital punishment.

'I guess folks and horses are a lot alike. And it all depends on how they're saddle-broke whether their good or bad crops out.
                    Red Ryder, *Stagecoach to Denver*

*   *   *

Guts. Glory. Ram Rodeo.
Lewiston, Idaho

'We find after years of struggle that we do not
take a trip; a trip takes us.'
                John Steinbeck, *Travels with Charley*

Chromium. The landscape northwest of Boise
looked like the Texas egg bake that Thomas had
served for breakfast. Just past the native food
truck, and the gold and silver pawnshops, were
signs of Boise capital loss. *Pray for the USA. Sign
up for Fantasy Football. Who does your hair?*
Our wagon rode the great divide between the
cookie cutter houses on our port side, and the
tracts of trailer trash to starboard. We passed
through Eagle, and gave thanks that we were
two months too late for the World's Largest
Rocky Mountain Oyster Feed. Robyn and I
preferred our shellfish without vertebrae.
Beyond Floating Feather Road, the dead deer,
the shredded truck tire, and mansions in the
middle of nowhere, were Highway 55, and the
route up through the wild guts of western Idaho.
We crossed over the Payette River at Horseshoe
Bend, *pop. 770,* where the prospectors had
waited for the snows to thaw, after gold had
been discovered in the Boise Basin Mountains,
in 1862. The last habitation, before the river
turned to follow our road true north, was where
God had come down and pulled civilization over
for speeding. Behind the red, white and blue

347

used car lot tinsel banner that spanned the gate was a hideous derelict shingle box, with twenty-eight windows of filthy lace curtains. Three satellite dishes and two air conditioners clung to the walls. A fire had tried to end its misery. In the yard was a matte black mailbox on an old rusted oil barrel, wooden pallets and paint cans and garbage cans and a large yellow mobile road sign that could have illuminated its message, if the leaning power pole beside it could have delivered enough power. *Don't get lost! Follow Jesus!* But this was Idaho, Christ had been a crucified Jew, and he was long gone ahead of anywhere we wanted to be.

The sun lit the conical conifer candles, and turned the brown hills gold across the left bank of the river. It was still twilight in the mountains on our right. Further on up part of the road had slipped off into the rapids, reflecting radiant rising rays of white light through the trees.

"There's something about rivers and rocks." Said Robyn. The marker after the pretty town of Gardena warned us to watch for falling ones. Just past the sunflowers and the swing bridge were sheep, grateful not to be riding the trucks that rumbled by. Crowded convict cattle stood in painted metal lattice tagliatelle cages, similar to the ones we had posed in, the day before. A hawk circled fate, high enough overhead.

At Smiths Ferry, we drove by the 4D Longhorn Guest Ranch, where Frank from Silver City was planning to achieve his dudeness. At the Post Office in Cascade, we stopped for Robyn to mail a card. It was empty, except for the postmaster, and the sunflowers on the counter. I asked him where the Chief Hotel was. He asked me why. I told him I was looking for the twenty-foot tall Indian sculpture made by a fellow named Big John, which was supposed to be next to it.

"Gone." He said. "Ten years ago."

"The sculpture or the hotel?" I asked.

"Both." He said. Shame.

"But Big John also made a ram, out of barbwire, over at the Dodge dealer." He said. We drove back in, past *Dollar Bill's Casual Fine Redneck Dining*, to find it. A sophisticated work of art, the mountain sheep had rusted just enough of his fleece, to make you want to take up knitting. Cascade was the other half of Boise Cascade, as faded in my memory, as the tricolour ribbon around the tree, across from the hand-painted sign on the City Hall.

Just north of Cascade Lake was the Boulder Creek Inn, which invited us to 'Stay Here, Play Longer.' We came into Donnelly, the 'Crossroads to Recreation.' *Welcome Hunters.* The biggest sign on the trading post was for liquor, and there were metal bears, in the metal gratings around the trees along Main Street. A buggy was for sale, for $650. We followed an RV dragging an SUV dragging a boat, to the old First State Bank building's western wooden façade, and the Silver Tip Hat Company. Inside, the old man with a long white beard and a diamond straw fedora woke to the clanging bell hanging over the entrance, which announced ours.

"Randy." He said. "Randy Priest." I asked if he was a cleric.

"I've been God." He said. Robyn saw me roll my eyes. But Randy had been divine. In his son-in-law's film, *Ibid*, he had played Don the Almighty, a cosmic cowboy creator, a duplicitous trickster talking head threshold guardian, a grizzled old man with a simple gruff message for the main characters. *Inscribe some new commandments before I kill everyone.* He gave the protagonists a week to find The Book, and add four more divine directives.

"It was an experimental low budget road journey of discovery." He said.

"Like our own." I said, trying on a big Boss of the Plains hat, with a marshal's star in the middle. I looked like Hoss Cartwright, from *Bonanza*.

"So what was the first new commandment?" I asked.

"Truly see oneself." He said. "People don't see themselves, but rather the false realities they've created for and surrounded themselves in."

"Orwell and Rockwell." I said. He nodded.

"The journey becomes about finding the meaning that holds everything together, for them and the rest of humanity." I asked Randy how it was all working out.

"I don't make a killin' but I make a livin'." He said. He asked me what I did. I told him.

"That's a new commandment." He said.

"What's that?" I asked.

"Heal thyself." He said.

"That's the journey." Said Robyn. I took off the hat.

"Gotta go." I said. "Bull-riding in Lewiston tonight."

"Don't hurt yourself." He said, and settled back into his snooze, after the bell rang, for the second time that day.

A few miles north of Don the Almighty's siesta, we turned onto the shoreline town of McCall. The lake, like the river, had been named for François Payette, a French Canadian who fur-trapped the area with Jim Bridger, Peter Skene Ogden, Jedediah Smith, and other mountain men, before there were so many sailboats. The first of these had belonged to Jews Harp Jack, who gave 'pleasure rides' to visiting tourists staying at the Lardo Inn. Bright orange pedestrian flags were mandatory. You can't trust water. Even a straight stick turns crooked in it.

We passed an old log cabin, near the *Heart of Idaho* town of New Meadows, built by John Welch in 1862, after the deep snow wouldn't let him further down along the Boise Trail.

> Close beside the bubbling Goose Creek
> In the Meadows Valley fair,
> Leans low an ancient cabin,
> Crumbling, half-forgotten, there...
>
> There, the trader, Packer John,
> Spent the winter days alone,
> Trapped for muskrat, mink, and beaver,
> Built this tiny cabin home...
>
> Now this ancient cabin dozes
> In the golden summer sun,
> Living with a host of memories,
> Dreams them over, one by one.
> Bessie Baker, *Packer John's Cabin*

The backcountry went through Smokey Boulder

Road, to a picnic spot on the Little Salmon River. Above us, on the right bank, was our own Montmartre, looking more like the original Roman mountain of Mars, than what became a martyr's talking head, in Paris. We ate leftover Bardenay rib eye from the night before, in bread rolls from the Inn. There was white noise from the white water, for dessert.

Where the Little Salmon met the Salmon, nestled deep in Hell's Canyon, Robyn and I drove into *Idaho's Whitewater Capital* of Riggins. We were far enough away from Boise, that the cops drove white cars, and the commerce was country-fried. *We buy antlers.* Just after Bert and Kate's Cattleman Dining, the Seven Devils Saloon, the Big Iron Motel, with complimentary beer, iced tea and homemade cookies, was a cinderblock and plywood villa, under a column of halogen security bulbs.

"Out here?" Robyn said. "Who would need a mini storage out here?"

"Americans live in bigger houses than ever before," I said. "But their competitiveness has programmed them so powerfully to hoard, that they're literally getting pushed out of their living spaces by stuff. In their own heads they're not storing junk, they're storing the American dream- the Rockwell time when there will be a better house to move into, where they'll be able to read all those magazines and make all those recipes, where they'll find a place for grandma's bric-a-brac."

"But they never go back for it." She said.

"True." I said. "It's the first law of Newton, and

the second of thermodynamics. Inertia and entropy. It takes more energy to rent a truck and sell the stuff, than to have an automatic monthly payment come out of a bank account. Maybe even in Riggins."

The hills got bigger and browner, and turned into crenellated gravelly mountains; the river got wider and calmer, and the incident sunlight hit the sand beach at the bottom of the canyon.

A logging truck passed us, loaded with truncated trunks.

"You see any trees?" I asked.

"Maybe that's why." Robyn. said. A mining claim was on offer in Lucile, but no one was home. Dream lots were for sale on the Salmon River in Maynard Hole. *Jesus is the way, the truth, and the life.* We continued over Skookumchuck Creek, past the White Bird Battlefield site and Camas Prairie, until the mountains and the greenery and our gas ran out in Grangeville. I asked the young bubble gum cashier where we might see the ten-foot tall Idaho Country Farmer scrap metal sculpture the local icon, with his arm raised in a 'cheery hello.' She continued chewing through her answer.

"Never heard of it." She said. But the old fat farmer, in line behind us, had.

"We used to call him Ironman." He said. "Someone stole it years ago."

"It weighed over five hundred pounds." I said.

"And so did the base."

"That's why they call 'em half ton trucks." He said. On the billboard across the road were *God's 10 Commandments*, four less than Don the

353

Almighty had back in Donnelly, and at least one more than was apparently applicable in Grangeville. Clues to the statue's disappearance were hinted at, over at Groaner's Fitness, and the Blown Away Hair Salon. The Visitors Information Center was unavailable for comment. *Closed for Awhile.* We didn't have time to wait.

Wheat fields waved us past the second disappointment of the day. We had come this way, in part, because of the roadside attractions. So far, we missed a big Indian chief and a big farmer. Americans love to erect monuments to their local excessive exceptionality, with the expectation that it will put them on the map. Proportion and aesthetic beauty is the antithesis of authenticity. The only important things are that these symbols must be big, and inflame the senses. In Northern Ontario, we built like the Yanks. There was Max the Moose, a twenty-eight foot Canada goose and, in my hometown, a forty foot tall fibreglass fish. The name of the effigy, and his slogan, had been chosen from hundreds of entries. *Huskie the Muskie says Prevent Water Pollution.* But here in this part of Idaho, there wasn't enough water to pollute, and all the allegory seemed to have been abducted.

Our one last hope was further up the flatland road and amber waves of grain. Originally a way station for prospectors and mining suppliers on their way south, Cottonwood was home to the chapel of the Benedictine Monastery of St. Gertrude, said to be 'the most ornate in the state.' But although it may have been another roadside attraction, it wasn't the authentic one. The real shrine to shrewdness was 'Sweet Willie,' the World's Largest Beagle, a wooden Bed and Breakfast in the shape of a thirty-five foot dog, with a stairway to the en-suite bedroom in the Beagle's belly, and a ladder to the loft in his nose. Robyn and I parked in the Barking Lot. I made use of the adjacent giant red fire hydrant portable outhouse.

"Are we staying here?" Robyn asked.

"No, Honey." I said. "Tonight isn't the Voyage of the Beagle. It's Gold Buckle Dreams."

*   *   *

'You see, in this world there's two kinds of people, my friend: Those with loaded guns and those who dig. You dig.'
    The Good, The Bad, & The Ugly, (1966)

Mushroom clouds rose hundreds of feet into the air, from the farpoint field fires burning all over the Nez Percés Reservation. It may have had some simple agricultural purpose, but I suspected that an occasional subliminal smoke signal may have been delivered, although to whom and for what purpose at this late stage in the game, was just as hazy. The two names on the first Indian mailbox offered no clue. *Larry and Patty.*

Robyn and I encountered no other vehicles on Big Butte Road, which took us past the Big Butte Community Hall, a copse of blue spruce, erosion barriers of rolled grass, and a warning sign. *Watch for Ice.* The only two vehicles on Fort Misery Road were two trucks traveling towards us, on both sides of the highway. They were talking in parallel on their mobile phones. The smoke signal strength was no longer up to the task.

Way too far south of Lawyer Creek, we curved through the heavy equipment junkyard of Kamiah, *pop 1160.* Demolition and recycling was less than a prosperous industry, by what was parked in the lot of the Branding Iron saloon. The town was named after the ropes the Nez Percés made here to fish steelhead, when there were more, when they bred Appaloosas, and before the appellation was appropriated by María Elena Marqués who played a Sacagawea clone leading Clark Gable's Lewis or Clark clone back over the Bitterroots to Three Forks in *Across the Wide Missouri,* a 1951 'mountain men' Hollywood history. A quarter of a century earlier that when the film was set, the Nez Percé leader Hohots Ilppilp had played host to the Corps of Discovery, for several weeks during the spring of 1806. Fields of huge sunflowers, and our gas needle stuck in time were the only commemoratives. In 1895, President Cleveland, showed his gratitude by 'opening up' the reservation to white settlement. *Larry and Patty.* Kooksia had been cracked open to invasion the same year. A remote highway work camp of the Civilian Conservation Corps in the 1930's, it was appropriated by the Federal Bureau of Prisons, and converted to house Japanese resident aliens in 1943, so far into the wilderness that fences and guard towers were deemed unnecessary. When an American General was sent to arrest Chief Looking Glass eighty years earlier, just before the Nez Percé War, several trigger-happy militiamen opened fire into the settlement, killing several natives, and destroying the village. Chief Lawyer, son of Twisted Hair, and Eagle from the Light and Bird Alighting and White Pelican and Yellow Wolf and Yellow Bull and Wrapped in the Wind and Rainbow and Red Paw and Poker Joe and Five Wounds were killed in the Battles of Bear Paw and Big Hole, and their home town replaced with guns and ammo and tackle and cheap tobacco, and a different kind of Indian. I asked the station attendant, when the gas needle finally fell, where he was from.

"Chandigarh." Raj said. "The northern capital of divided Indians." He directed me to the Purple Feather Smoke Shop. Inside were shelves of cigarettes and plastic eagles and T-shirts and dreamcatchers and beadwork and irrelevant Americana knickknacks. *Having Kids is like being pecked to death.* I bought two *Outlaw* Honduran cigars.

Robyn and I had come to Kooksia to see what we thought would be the last roadside attraction. Past the Old Opera House Theater and the Western Bar Café Banquet Room and the painted wall mural of a Sasquatch, on the roof of the Western Motor Inn on Main Street, was a giant ghost white leaning Elk sculpture, pushing its antlers against the inevitable.

But we hadn't anticipated the last house on the edge of town. All of Grandma's possessions were on the lawn, instead of the mini storage. We drove by a midget tractor and tin robot driver, hundreds of American flags around the portico, an American eagle over the doorway, a helmeted scarecrow football player with lipstick on one side of the sidewalk, a basket-toting woman gardener manikin on the other, and bowling balls down both. There were pinwheels, wall-mounted flying ducks and giant butterflies, wooden tulips, window boxes and hanging baskets, a wishing well, brightly painted chairs, plastic roses and sunflowers, a stuffed cow reclining on a porch swing, a totem pole, a cement dog, spiral mobiles, open umbrellas, topiary, flamingos, rabbits, gnomes, and a welcome sign. *North Korea can kiss my proud ass.*

Moving north on the Northwest Passage Scenic Byway, beyond the Tribal Gaming Casino, was a bare rock mound, the mythical site of the Nez Percé's mythical creation.

> A monster was eating all of the animals. Coyote fooled the monster into swallowing him. Using a set of stone knives that he had brought with him, Coyote cut apart the monster from the inside to release all of the animals that were trapped in the monster. Upon emerging from the remains of the monster, Coyote cut it up and threw the

pieces all over the land, creating the Indian people who inhabit the land. Fox asked Coyote about the land around the monster, it had no people, what was he to do? As Coyote washed the blood of the monster off his hands, the drops became the Nez Percé.

They called it the Heart of the Monster. But the monster was ahead of us. Overloaded logging trucks overtook our wagon, along the white sand beaches of the Clearwater River, the Coyote's Fishnet, and an eagle's nest perched high on a telephone pole.

At the confluence of the Snake and Clearwater Rivers, the clearwater darkened into the effluent from the ugly malodorous pulp and paper mill. *"Its the smell of money." My father used to say. To me, it reeked of noxious decay.*

A Harley Davidson dealership and the strip mall signs announced our arrival in Lewiston. *Born again Resale and Consignment. Lord Jesus, I belong to you.*

We stopped to ask directions to the best place to stay in town. The landmarks provided were all fast food outlets.

"Go straight up the hill past the Denny's, and turn left at the Red Lobster." He said.

"How does a lobster get to Lewiston?" I asked.

"Lewiston is a seaport." He said. "We're the farthest inland harbour east of the West Coast of the United States." But that still wasn't the right answer.

The radio was on, and all the stations were playing country music. There's no money above the fifth fret. *Three chords and the truth* carried us all the way up to the Holiday Inn Express.

'On a highway bound for nowhere
I ran my fingers through my tangled hair
As I pulled in for another tank of freedom
With a hundred miles behind me
And a million more to go...'
Sara Evans, *Three Chords And The Truth*

*   *   *

'May your stomach never grumble. May your
heart never ache.
May your horse never stumble. May your cinch
never break.'
Old Blessing

It's the bulls and blood, dust and mud, and the roar of a Sunday crowd.

"Y'all here for the Roundup?" The desk clerk asked.

"Just today." Said Robyn.

"Well, Honey." She said. "You picked it right. Tonight's the bull riding." Our room card opened up on the yellow grey down to the Clearwater River. I pointed way over to the left side of the horizon.

"Washington State." I said. "Tomorrow we cross over."

The desk clerk waved as we left.

"Enjoy the bull-riding." She said. We promised to

try.

The arena was further up the hill, at the end of Tammany Creek Road. Parking was anywhere you could find space in an endless pasture. A battalion of Dodge Ram pickups immediately surrounded our Toyota RAV. *My truck is made by wrenches not chopsticks.*

"Welcome to the 78th Annual Lewiston Roundup!" Blared the speaker over the Gold Buckle Club at the top of the airport tower trailer stairs above the Mobile Command Center. "Ram Rodeo. Eat. Sleep. Ride!" *Eat. Pray. Love.*

Eat always comes first. Robyn came away from trying on pink cowboy hats, to a burger and a pulled pork sandwich and two Coors at one of the concession stands. Once we had our 'over 21' wristbands, the local ticket currency rolled off a spool, like beads at a Club Med. Three would get you a slab of Indian bread as big as a pizza, or five-pounds of curly fries, a serving the size of your head. This was Idaho.

Two fat boys with fat arms, in Stetsons and blue jeans and big brass belt buckles, strummed guitar and sang bad country on a trailer with huge black amplifiers. Another big boy drove by on an ATV with a message on his T-shirt. *Ohrtman for Council.* The women wore short jeans shorts and tattoos. One bleached bottle blond with long toes supplicated herself to the signal in front of the *One Smooth Ride She's Wild Vodka* banner, next to the plastic M-16s for sale.

"Welcome, rodeo fans!" Announced the MC. "Find your seats!" Robyn and I climbed into the bleachers, behind a short fat kid plowing through a platter of curly fries, and an old tattooed lady playing poker on her cell phone. It was right on dusk. A big Dodge Ram truck, lights blinking off and on, drove slowly into the arena under a moody sunset sky, the last streaks of light coming through the clouds like drone projectiles. A gigantic HDTV screen on the other side of the fairground came alive with a projection of waving American flags. High banks of carbon-arc lights on towering poles thwacked on and into your solar plexus. The truck just sat there, blinking on and off. It was a Nuremberg rally.

'And on the 8th day, God looked down on his planned paradise and said, "I need a caretaker." So God made a farmer. God said, "I need somebody willing to get up before dawn, milk cows, work all day in the fields, milk cows again, eat supper and then go to town and stay past midnight at a meeting of the school board." So God made a farmer. I need somebody with arms strong enough to wrestle a calf and yet gentle enough to deliver his own grandchild. Somebody to call hogs, tame cantankerous machinery, come home hungry, have to wait lunch until his wife's done feeding visiting ladies and tell the ladies to be sure and come back real soon -- and mean it." So God made a farmer. God said, "I need somebody willing to sit up all night with a newborn colt. And watch it die. Then dry his eyes and say, 'Maybe next year.' I need somebody who can shape an ax handle from a persimmon sprout, shoe a horse with a hunk of car tire, who can make harness out of haywire, feed sacks and shoe scraps. And who, planting time and harvest season, will finish his forty-hour week by Tuesday noon, then, pain'n from 'tractor

362

back,' put in another seventy-two hours." So God made a farmer. God had to have somebody willing to ride the ruts at double speed to get the hay in ahead of the rain clouds and yet stop in mid-field and race to help when he sees the first smoke from a neighbor's place. So God made a farmer. God said, "I need somebody strong enough to clear trees and heave bales, yet gentle enough to tame lambs and wean pigs and tend the pink-combed pullets, who will stop his mower for an hour to splint the broken leg of a meadow lark. It had to be somebody who'd plow deep and straight and not cut corners. Somebody to seed, weed, feed, breed and brake and disc and plow and plant and tie the fleece and strain the milk and replenish the self-feeder and finish a hard week's work with a five-mile drive to church. "Somebody who'd bale a family together with the soft strong bonds of sharing, who would laugh and then sigh, and then reply, with smiling eyes, when his son says he wants to spend his life 'doing what dad does.'" So God made a farmer.'

So God made a farmer. He didn't make him smart enough to realize that the Rockwell family farm had been industrialized into an Orwellian agricultural factory nightmare. He didn't make him eloquent enough to take his narrative outside the religious imagery of a Dodge Ram commercial. From the Fourth Quarter of the Super Bowl to the Empty Quarter of the Lewiston roundup arena, God made a farmer into a cynical anachronism and an angry martyr.

The night riders in the cavalcades that streamed into the arena stood on their saddles, gigantic hoisted American flags fluttering large behind them, synchronized swimmers with white cowboy hats and white shirts and black bolo ties and brown horses. They were followed by a red stagecoach with yellow wheels, the fat sheriff in the open chuck wagon, waving with his wife, more stars and bars, and Toby Keith's *Angry American.*

'American girls and American guys, will always stand up and salute.
We'll always recognize, when we see ol' glory flying,
There's a lot of men dead,
So we can sleep in peace at night when we lay down our heads.
My daddy served in the army where he lost his right eye,
But he flew a flag out in our yard 'til the day that he died.
He wanted my mother, my brother, my sister and me.
To grow up and live happy in the land of the free.

Now this nation that I love is fallin' under attack.
A mighty sucker-punch came flying in from somewhere in the back.
Soon as we could see clearly through our big black eye,
Man, we lit up your world like the fourth of July.

Oh, justice will be served and the battle will rage:
This big dog will fight when you rattle his cage.
An' you'll be sorry that you messed with the U.S. of A.
'Cos we'll put a boot in your ass, it's the American way.

Hey, Uncle Sam put your name at the top of his
list,
And the Statue of Liberty started shaking her
fist.
And the eagle will fly and it's gonna be hell,
When you hear Mother Freedom start ringing
her bell.
And it'll feel like the whole wide world is raining
down on you.
Ah, brought to you, courtesy of the red, white
and blue.'

A young cowgirl raced into the centre of the arena, saluting with a fringed deerskin glove.
"Give it all up for Queen Darryl Kirby!" Announced the announcer. Everyone gave it all up. A posse of lesser rodeo queens followed in Queen Darryl at a distance. Some of them were so thin, I thought of taking up a curly fries collection.
"Ladies and Gentlemen!" The announcer announced. "Behind every good man is an even better woman!"
"Yeah!" Said Robyn. All the other women in the bleachers gave it all up too. A group of mounted Indians dressed like cowboys rode in.
"Ladies and Gentlemen!" The announcer announced. "The Nez Percés County Mounted Sheriff's Posse!" The applause wasn't quite as spirited, as it had been for the rodeo queens, and they looked a little uncomfortable, like Warsaw Ghetto kapos. But they were just decoration for what was coming.
"Ladies and Gentlemen!" The announcer announced. "We live in the greatest country on God's Green Earth!" Robyn and I looked at each

other in agreement.

"The United States of America!" He said. "Please rise for the National Anthem!" And we all rose, as the big voice in the little girl on the podium below roared into patriotic purpose. I knew the words, having lived so long so close to the Americans and so far from their God, but Robyn had to lip sync her compliance. Everyone was too busy giving it all up to notice. A big Ram truck rode around the arena, throwing free Ram Rodeo T-shirts into the bleachers. It really was the greatest country in the world.

"Ladies and Gentlemen!" The announcer announced. "The cowboy is a patriot, but the only two things you'll see on the back of a bull are a fly and a fool." The fools were ready to go.

In between all the love and anger, Robyn and I had met the couple in front of us. Bill and Lexie had 'never missed a roundup,' and were camped in the canyon. Bill had been a bull rider for thirteen years, and related how insecure his life in the rodeo had been. A good rider could make up to a quarter million dollars a year, or nothing. He had no insurance, all his own costs, and just one bad ride could put him out of business for good. Or worse. I asked him what it was like.

"It's like a hurricane dancing with a kite." He said. "You gotta want to get off bad enough to want to get on in the first place." I asked him if he had ever broken any bones.

"Every damn one of them." He said, and then began teasing me about the Canadian contact sport of curling. "Tried that one time in

Kelowna." He said, wiping his brow, and grinning. "Never again." I told him that Robyn had ridden the mechanical bull at Gillie's in Dallas, and won. He nodded.

"The only good reason to ride a bull is to meet a nurse." He said. This time it was Lexie who grinned.

"Never approach a bull from the front, a horse from the rear or a fool from any direction." She said.

Out on the sand, the bull riders had been coming off their mounts in quick succession. The announcer announced, and ZZ Top and Alabama provided accompaniment. *Boy, you're going to make yourself dizzy... That horse didn't want to play... He needs to have his hammer cocked tonight... Now that's how that's done... Live fast. Die young.*

Indian bread and paper toweling went by, all mixed up together by the two too young boys with two too big cowboy hats. They stretched themselves tall on the wire fence, and watched the last of the men come off the hooves. The announcer announced.

"Here's to the families saying grace tonight with an empty seat at the table." He said. Cans of Coors and Pepsi rode the air.

"Let us never take our freedom for granted."

'The bulls and the clowns The ups and the downs
He's hooked on this eight-second ride
The spurs and the blood The dust and the mud
This will be his first time to ride
His one chance at stardom His one chance at Fame
She doesn't want him playin' this game
She told him no, but he just had to go
On with his rodeo dreams'

Dawn, *Rodeo Dreams*

*   *   *

Cherry Pie and Coffee
Snoqualmie Falls, Washington

Dale Cooper: Wanna know why I'm whittling?
Sheriff Truman: OK, I'll bite again. Why are you
          whittling?
Dale Cooper: Because that's what you do in a
          town where a yellow light still
          means slow down and not speed
          up.

Phosphorus. The lowest point in the state of Idaho is on the Snake River in Lewiston, where it flows out of Idaho into Washington. The Holiday Inn Express machine-made pancakes and biscuits and gravy next morning came in a close second. Nothing beats the taste sensation when maple syrup collides with ham.

It had rained hard during the night and the thunder almost shook the windows out of their frames. Robyn and I got on the road early. One brown horse stood shivering on a yellow hill. The radio played either Jesus or country, or both.

"This is the line." I said, as we crossed it.

"Idaho to Washington?" Robyn asked.

"Huckleberry to cherry." I said.

We followed an old Ford Model 'A' past the roadside attractions. There was a tyrannosaurus and a great white shark made out of beer cans, a mailbox in the shape of a log cabin, and a drop down menu of local churches chained under a big white cross. *Baptist...Assembly of God... Catholic... Christian... Episcopal... Lutheran...*

Methodist... Nazarene.

"Multicultural." Robyn said.

Welcome to the friendly city of Pomeroy. There was a Pioneer Plaza, silos belonging to the Pomeroy Grain Growers, a mural of Pomeroy Mercantile, and the Garfield County seat, a French Champagne mansion that looked more Pommery than Pomeroy. We stopped across the street, and entered Meyer's Giftware Collectibles Hardware and Sporting Goods.

"Help you?" Asked the owner, under a banner above the till. *Your Husband called... He said buy anything you want.*

"Do you have a map of Washington State?" I asked. She fished out an atlas. I told her it was a one-day wonder, and we would follow the sun. Robyn and I headed west, past a cop giving a ticket to some kid on a bicycle, a windmill, and a collapsed barn with the hay still in it. We drove through Dayton, the 'Home of the State Champions,' although the category wasn't immediately apparent. There was a bird convention on the wires that led past Sorghum Hollow Road, to a big-bellied bearded porch surfer in a baseball cap, and his plaid buddy in the rocking chair next to him.

Waitsburg billed itself as 'One of a Kind,' most likely the John Deere combine with fourteen tires that almost ran us off the road. The town of Starbuck had suffered more for its singularity. The downstream bridge built over the Snake River in 1914 collapsed the traffic. In 1929 the bank failed, the high school closed in 1956, and five years later the railroad station shut down as well.

"You'd think in a country of 350 million, you'd run into a car every once in awhile." I said.

"It's amazing." Robyn said. "You go through nothing and then suddenly, you go through even more nothing." A yellow crop duster biplane barrel-rolled above us, and almost into the bird convention on the telephone lines to nowhere. The corn, as far as the eye could see, turned into grapevines, as far as the eye could see. We crossed the Snake River.

On October 16, 1805, when Lewis and Clark came through Pasco, there was no tract housing and no signs of discontent. *Impeach Obama... Litter and it will hurt.*

Across the Columbia River Bridge were the Yakima River, and the Yakima Canyon Drive. Except for the pines and the single motorcyclist, it could have been the Nile. We pulled in to fill up at the 38.83 Food and Gas Mart. The bearded attendant had his baseball cap on sideways. I asked him why they called the place 38.83.

"It's 38.83 miles to the next gas station." He said.

"It's also a palindrome." I said. He asked what that was. I asked if he had a map of Washington State. He went into the back.

"Now that's two things I've learned today." He said.

"What's that?" I asked.

"That palindrome thing." He said.

"And the other?" I asked.

"I didn't know we don't have any maps of Washington State." He said. I told him it was a

one-day wonder, and we would follow the sun.
An oversized camper pulled out in front of us.
The oversized driver had an oversized toothpick
in his mouth. His oversized bumper sticker was
hard to miss. *Dirty Love.*
The air began to fill with moisture, and far away
clouds. As they came closer, they revealed the
rocks they were hiding inside.
"Cascade Mountains." I said.
"Douglas fir." Said Robyn. The entire right lane
filled with 18-wheelers, and then we were three
trucks wide. One of the tankers was labeled
'Inedibles.'
"Fair warning." Robyn said. "Are we stopping for
lunch?"
"Take the North Bend exit." I said. *I have no idea
where this will lead us. But I have a definite
feeling it will be a place both wonderful and
strange.*

*　　*　　*

Denise Bryson: Understand we're both staying at the Great Northern. How's the food up there?
Dale Cooper: Denise, you're in for a real surprise.
Twin Peaks

"This looks very familiar." Robyn said. "I feel like I've been here before, yet I know I haven't." The big yellow neon pentagon flattened against the acoustic ceiling tiles cast a fiery orange glow. "This is where pies go when they die." I said. "I know this restaurant." She said. "It's the Double-R Diner from *Twin Peaks.*" "It's actually called Twede's Cafe." I said. "But it's the same place." The five patrons at two tables were all very old. The sign beside the clock invited us to seat ourselves. The waitress took awhile.
"What'll you have?" She asked. Robyn ordered the garden salad. I had a bowl of chili.
"You have cherry pie?" I asked.
"Every day." She said.
"I'll have the cherry pie, and a cup of damn fine coffee."
"How do you take it?" She asked. I had been waiting.
"Black as midnight on a moonless night." I said. She rolled her eyes and spun away.
It was all pretty mediocre. I hit the men's room, after paying. The graffiti was better than the food. *Laura Palmer R.I.P... Where's Coop at?*
About a half-mile down SE Reinig Road I pulled onto the shoulder, and cranked on the iPod. The theme from *Twin Peaks* backlit the clouds above

Mt. Si, the iconic 'Welcome to Twin Peaks' sign site of the show's opening scene. The local Snoqualmie tribe has a Prometheus story about Mt. Si. According to legend the mountain is the dead body of Snoqualm, the moon. Snoqualm had ordered that a rope of cedar bark be stretched between the earth and the sky. But Fox and Blue Jay went up the rope and stole the sun from him. When Snoqualm chased them back down the cedar rope, it broke and he fell to his death. Fox then freed the sun free into the sky and gave fire to the people. *Through the darkness of futures past, The magician longs to see, One chants out between two worlds, Fire Walk With Me.* Robyn asked where I was going.

"There's nothing quite like urinating in the open air." I said.

"I can assume that the rest of the day has the same theme?" She asked. "Let me guess, Agent Cooper. We're staying at the Great Northern, right?" *One woman can make you fly like an eagle, another can give you the strength of a lion, but only one in the cycle of life can fill your heart with wonder and the wisdom that you have known a singular joy.*

"It's actually called Salish Lodge." I said. "But it's the same place."

Snoqualmie had a beautiful old train depot, a long track of old rusting steam locomotives, a mural of loaded logging trucks, and a gigantic double-spoked metal wheel with a chain it didn't need. The Chinese restaurant was named 'Got Rice' and the church had United hearts and Methodist minds.

We continued up to Snoqualmie Falls, and walked along the riverine cliff edge that gave us the best view of the waterfall. Below the moss covered bigleaf maples and Douglas fir and sword fern and salal was a waterfall over 250 feet high. If the spray from it was almost blinding, the Snoqualmie legend definitely was. Snoqualmie Falls was where First Woman and First Man were created by Moon the Transformer and 'where prayers were carried up to the Creator by great mists that rose from the powerful flow.' The mists rising from the base of the waterfall served to connect Heaven and Earth. When the falls were first nominated for the National Register of Historic Places in 1992 as a traditional cultural property for these Snoqualmie beliefs, the property owner, Puget Sound Energy, objected. It took another seventeen years for the listing to succeed. Whoever is new to power is always harsh, especially when it owns the connection between Heaven and Earth. On the rock wall, Robyn and I stumbled on a triangle made of pennies, with buttons and an egg in the middle.

The Falls flow over the center of a twenty million year old extinct volcano. Across the river were thousands of volcanic bombs and lava flows. *Water Fire Heaven Earth.* For the Snoqualmie, it was all here. The ravens were monstrous.

Robyn and I checked into the lodge. By the time Akeem had our room ready, he had changed shift with Omar. The room was small, and decorated in muted lichen and mustard. There was a set of tagliatelle-latticed doors you could crawl through, directly from the hot tub into the bed. We opted instead for the 'award-winning Spa, the soothing aromas of cedar and eucalyptus, and the healing elements of the therapeutic pools in the gorgeous, natural surroundings which reflect the calm, contemplative environment of the Pacific Northwest.' It got a whole lot more contemplative when I found the open magnum of cabernet sauvignon in the empty clubroom next door, and a guy decorated from Adam's apple to ankles in Yakuza tattoos slid into the pool beside me.

"Where from?" He asked.

"Vancouver Island." I said. "You?"

"L.A." He said. "What do you do?" He asked.

"Doctor." I said. "You?"

"I hear Seattle has a good football team." He said. And was gone.

Lori was our waitress in the Great Northern restaurant that evening. Her parents were from Calabria. She knew more about wine than the sommeliers. She suggested the lamb shank and pork belly, and asked me how I enjoyed the contraband cabernet I had siphoned earlier. We ordered the lamb shank and pork belly.

The night ended in frustration. Fire is the test of gold; adversity, of strong men. I was unable to light the wet logs in the fireplace without kindling. A Mexican woman brought some from reception, but I had used up all the matches.

"Cerillas." I said.

"Ah, fósforo." she said. She brought matches.

Robyn and I fell asleep next to the fire.

'Welcome to Twin Peaks... There are many stories in Twin Peaks — some of them are sad, some funny. Some of them are stories of madness, of violence. Some are ordinary. Yet they all have about them a sense of mystery — the mystery of life. Sometimes, the mystery of death. The mystery of the woods. The woods surrounding Twin Peaks. To introduce this story, let me just say it encompasses the All — it is beyond the 'Fire', though few would know that meaning.'

Log Lady, *Twin Peaks*

*   *   *

The Long Road Home
Nanaimo, British Columbia

'The closer you get to Canada, the more things'll
eat your horse.'

Tom Logan, *The Missouri Breaks*

Gold. There was no damn fine coffee next
morning. The machine in our room didn't work
and, to get on the road early, we skipped the
Salish Lodge country breakfast. *Enjoyed since
1916.* At thirty-four bucks, it wasn't immediately
clear which country it had been flown in from.

As we drove into and through the suburbs of
Seattle, we ran headlong into the morning
commuter traffic oozing from the vast tract
housing lava fields. The white Ram Rodeo trucks
of the West, like the cowboy hats of good guys
and bad guys on the Paramount silver screen,
had turned into BMWs and Mercedes and Audis,
as black as the coffee. And God made a software
mogul. And we arrived in their metropolis.
Rather than living authentically in Nature, they
obviously preferred a more virtual reality.

Heavy merging traffic came at us from all sides.
The pouring rain that arrived out of the vertical
axis, washed all the *Wagon Days* bugs off our
mirrors. Interstate 5 extruded us out of the
Seattle's northern sphincter, past the resort
casino on the Tulalip Indian Reservation. I
remembered the native elder tapping his stick
near the front door of the old one, years before.

He told me they were gradually getting their land back.

"One house at a time." He had said. An hour further up the highway, turned us off into Bellis Fair Mall, in Bellingham. Long the cross-border Mecca of Canadian shoppers looking to avoid the high prices and taxes in British Columbia, the mall had been owned by General Growth Properties, until it filed for bankruptcy and was forced to accept an equity investment from Canadian property company Brookfield Asset Management, looking to avoid the high prices and taxes in British Columbia. *The closer you get to Canada, the more things'll eat your horse.*

Robyn set her rangefinder, and told me to meet her in the food court in another hour. Being male in a mall is a loveless marriage of gender and geography. I found a bench at the end of store-lined corridor designed to resemble a Rockwell small town cul-de-sac. The other people on the benches looked lost, and would take no pleasure in being found. It seemed that everything they might ever think or do or become had been inexorably sclerosed by whatever they had once thought or done or been. The mobile ones were cemented to their mobiles, glancing up every so often to avoid a collision with their own lives.

My bench seat had a long view of the situation. A Moslem woman with a long beard came out of Macy's. Neither of us had known that, a year before we arrived, an ad appeared in Bellingham for a special kind of mall employee.

'Now Hiring Train Drivers for a new train ride concept at the Mall. The train will take kids/adults for a ride inside the mall... We are looking for someone that is: Non Smoker -Very outgoing and Bubbly. -Has a driver license and can pass background check and drugs test. –Love working and interact with kids and can make kids happy. -Very responsible, Hard worker and self motivated... For more details email us your resume and why you think you can be our driver.

It was called the 'Wild West Express' and, while I was taking no pleasure in being found, the winner of the job application came by, driving his locomotive, pulling a coal car, and three coach cars painted in primary colors. Not quite the picture of the job offer, his train was empty. Six months after we left, the Wild West Express became the victim of the first train robbery inside a mall.

BELLINGHAM, Wash. – It might not have been the great train robbery, but it was a brash burglary at the Bellis Fair Mall that left many shoppers shocked.
Bellingham Police say Sunday night a white, 40-year-old male used some type of cutting instrument to sever the cable that secured the cash register for the Wild West Train kiosk inside the mall. The man fled with the register and its contents to the parking lot, where witnesses say he left in a white truck.
Lieutenant Bob Vander Yacht says police are seeing more crimes like this in the Bellingham area, in which, if something of value isn't tied down it's going to be stolen.
Vander Yacht believes these crimes are due to the increase use of heroin and methamphetamine and people needing cash quickly to feed their habit.

We had noodles, in the food court, for a few dollars more. The last of our wagon days would

end as a spaghetti western, watching the train.
Dingdingdingdingdingding...

> Cheyenne: Harmonica, a town built around a
> railroad. You could make a fortune.
> Hundreds of thousands of dollars.
> Hey, more than that. Thousands of
> thousands.
> Harmonica: They call them 'millions.'
> Cheyenne: 'Millions.' Hmm.
> Sergio Leone, Once upon a time in the West

*   *   *

'The sons of the white chief say his father sends us greetings of friendship and good will. This is kind, for we know that he has little need of our friendship in return, because his people are many. They are like the grass that covers the vast prairies, while my people are few, and resemble the scattering trees of a storm-swept plain.

The great, and I presume also good, white chief sends us word that he wants to buy our lands but is willing to allow us to reserve enough to live on comfortably. This indeed appears generous, for the red man no longer has rights that he need respect, and the offer may be wise, also, for we are no longer in need of a great country.

There was a time when our people covered the whole land, as the waves of a wind-ruffled sea cover its shell-paved floor. But that time has long since passed away with the greatness of tribes almost forgotten. I will not mourn over our untimely decay, nor reproach my pale-face brothers for hastening it, for we too, may have been somewhat to blame.

When our young men grow angry at some real or imaginary wrong, and disfigure their faces with black paint, their hearts are also disfigured and turn black, and then their cruelty is relentless and knows no bounds, and our old men are not able to restrain them.

But let us hope that hostilities between the red man and his pale-face brothers may never return. We would have everything to lose and nothing to gain.

True it is, that revenge, with our young braves, is considered gain, even at the cost of their own lives, but old men who stay at home in times of war, and old women, who have sons to lose, know better.

Our great father Washington, for I presume he is now our father as well as yours, since George has moved his boundaries to the north; our great and good father, I say, sends us word by his son, who, no doubt, is a great chief among his people, that if we do as he desires, he will protect us. His brave armies will be to us a bristling wall of strength, and his great ships of war will fill our labors so that our ancient enemies far to the northward, the Simsiams and Hydas, will no longer frighten our women and old men. Then he will be our father and we will be his children.

But can this ever be? Your God loves your people and hates mine; he folds his strong arms lovingly around the white man and leads him as a father leads his infant son, but he has forsaken his red children; he makes your people wax strong every day, and soon they will fill the land; while my people are ebbing away like a fast-receding tide, that will never flow again. The white man's God cannot love his red children or he would protect them. They seem to be orphans and can look nowhere for help. How then can we become brothers? How can your father become our father and bring us prosperity and awaken in us dreams of returning greatness?

Your God seems to us to be partial. He came to the white man. We never saw Him; never even heard His voice; He gave to the white man laws but He had no word for His red children whose teeming millions filled this vast continent as the stars fill the firmament. No, we are two distinct races and must ever remain so. There is little in common between us. The ashes of our ancestors are sacred and their final resting place is hallowed ground, while you wander away from the tombs of your fathers seemingly without regret.

Your religion was written on tables of stone by the iron finger of an angry God, lest you might forget it. The red man could never remember nor comprehend it.

Our religion is the traditions of our ancestors, the dreams of our old men, given them by the great Spirit, and the visions of our sachems, and is written in the hearts of the people.

Your dead cease to love you and the homes of their nativity as soon as they pass the portals of the tomb. They wander far off beyond the stars, are soon forgotten, and never return. Our dead never forget the beautiful world that gave them bring. They still love its winding rivers, its great mountains and its sequestered vales, and they ever yearn in tenderest affection over the lonely hearted living and often return to visit and comfort them.

Day and night cannot dwell together. The red man has ever fled the approach of the white man, as the changing mists of the mountainside flee before the blazing morning sun...

The Indian's night promises to be dark. No bright star hovers above the horizon. Sad-voiced winds moan in the distance. Some grim Nemesis of our race is on the red man's trail, and wherever he goes he will still hear the sure approaching footsteps of the fell destroyer and prepare to meet his doom, as does the wounded doe that hears the approaching footsteps of the hunter. A few more moons, a few more winters, and not one of all the mighty hosts that once filled this broad land or that now roam in fragmentary bands through these vast solitudes will remain to weep over the tombs of a people once as powerful and as hopeful as your own.

But why should we repine? Why should I murmur at the fate of my people? Tribes are made up of individuals and are no better than they. Men come and go like the waves of the sea. A tear, a tamanawus, a dirge, and they are gone from our longing eyes forever. Even the white man, whose God walked and talked with him, as friend to friend, is not exempt from the common destiny. We may be brothers after all. We shall see.

We will ponder your proposition, and when we have decided we will tell you. But should we accept it, I here and now make this the first condition: That we will not be denied the privilege, without molestation, of visiting at will the graves of our ancestors and friends. Every part of this country is sacred to my people. Every hillside, every valley, every plain and grove has been hallowed by some fond memory or some sad experience of my tribe.

Even the rocks that seem to lie dumb as they swelter in the sun along the silent seashore in solemn grandeur thrill with memories of past events connected with the fate of my people, and the very dust under your feet responds more lovingly to our footsteps than to yours, because it is the ashes of our ancestors, and our bare feet are conscious of the sympathetic touch, for the soil is rich with the life of our kindred.

The sable braves, and fond mothers, and glad-hearted maidens, and the little children who lived and rejoiced here, and whose very names are now forgotten, still love these solitudes, and their deep fastnesses at eventide grow shadowy with the presence of dusky spirits. And when the last red man shall have perished from the earth and his memory among white men shall have become a myth, these shores shall swarm with the invisible dead of my tribe, and when your children's children shall think themselves alone in a field, the store, the shop, upon the highway or in the silence of the woods, they will not be alone. In all the earth there is no place dedicated to solitude. At night, when the streets of your cities and villages shall be silent, and you think them deserted, they will throng with the returning hosts that once filled and still love this beautiful land. The white man will never be alone. Let him be just and deal kindly with my people, for the dead are not altogether powerless.'

Chief Seattle, January 1854 (not published until
29 October 1887, *Seattle Sunday Star*)

*   *   *

'It's not how you're buried; it's how they remember you.'
John Wayne, The Cowboys

My dread of Canadian border crossings began when the bastards illegitimately confiscated the wine I had been storing in Washington State. True, I may not have declared the absolute full value of what I paid for it, and I may have been a little surly as a result, but any jurisdiction that has a government monopoly on an essential and erudite food group, prices the commodity into the stratosphere, is incapable of filling orders for anything other than the totally unexceptional (its a government monopoly), and limits you personal importation to two bottles, is just plain barbaric.

I had come off the plank of the appropriately named Black Ball Ferry, into the arms of these mongrels. It was a slow day Sunday, and one of the uniformed young ones was in full crime-fighting mode. What used to be Customs Canada, a civilized arm of the Federal Government, had mutated into the Canadian Border Services Agency. It often behaves, to me and other hardened criminals, with all the courtesy and fairness of the Waffen SS. The judge of one particular case that reached the BC

Supreme Court concluded that the agency had 'wrongly delayed, confiscated, destroyed, damaged, prohibited or misclassified materials imported by the appellant... errors were caused by... systemic targeting.'

The agent in the booth that we pulled alongside took our passports, and a long time to look at his screen.

"What happened off the Black Ball Ferry?" He asked. *I'm tryin' to put some bad times behind me, but sometimes they don't stay put.*

"I really don't want to revisit that, if that's OK with you." I said. He looked up.

"Sure." He said, handing back the passports. "Have a safe trip home."

Robyn and I had forgotten to fill up with gas before we crossed, and we were on dead empty.

"Take the turnoff for White Rock." I said. "There's bound to be a gas station." White Rock is a town of twenty thousand people, and as many hills. We drove along the waterfront for miles before finally asking someone where they were hiding the gas stations.

"Oh, they're not here." He said. I asked him where the citizens of White Rock go to fill up their vehicles.

"I think there's one at the top of the hill." He said.

"Which hill?" I asked.

"I think it's that one." He said. But it wasn't. It wasn't the next hill either. Or the one after that. It was the last hill. The final molecule of gasoline vaporized in disgust, as we pulled up to the pump.

The attendant was nice enough. I asked him why they put the gas stations on the hill.

"Traffic." He said.

The delay cost us a sailing wait, two hours in line at the ferry terminal. For Robyn and I to get home, we had to head west, across the Georgia Strait. We camped out in the back of the boat, hot sun shining on our faces, making us sleepy. I awoke to a lost generation, holding out their dominant hands, in supplication to the signal, missing on the open water. The way they looked past me, spoke to my age, and irrelevance. But it felt good to be invisible to the socially obsessed, reclining in my chaise lounge on the side of the gene pool, watching the blood in the water. Connections are more important than connectivity. *Always drink upstream from the herd.*

On the other side, a turkey vulture turned a lazy sky circle above the *Jesus Loves You* sign. We turned into our long gravel drive, and gave silent thanks for who we were, and when and where we lived.

A few months later, Robyn surprised me with a party, for my sixtieth birthday. I opened the front doors to a gathering of good friends. The first ones I saw, at the end of the line, were Richard and Carolyn. I hadn't communicated with them, since we left their dock at Christina Lake, across the borderland of fable. But Robyn had.

"You better?" Richard asked, handing me a glass of wine.

The evening evolved into the slow motion rituals that characterize every milestone of unwanted maturity. There were presents and speeches, and jovial repartee. Richard and Carolyn would stay the weekend. We finally got to sit down together after everyone else had left.

"So." He asked. "How was the trip?"

"Good." I said. As one does.

"Did you find what you were looking for?" Asked Carolyn.

"I think so." I said.

"What was it?" She asked.

"Buffalo steak." I said. "And huckleberry pie.

* * *

Afterword

'I'll keep rolling along
Deep in my heart is a song
Here on the range I belong
Drifting along with the tumbling
tumbleweeds.'
Bob Nolan, *Tumbling Tumbleweeds*

Plus ça change. *Star Trek* is *Wagon Train*. Gene Roddenberry, its creator, had been the head writer for *Have Gun Will Travel*, before he conceived the frontier characters traveling to worlds 'similar to our own,' and living the drama that become our legends. Some of the same lines are interchangeable. *From him to the stars, in all directions, there was only silence and emptiness.*
The West had been a religious struggle between the land of possibility and the land of possession- the invading settlers tamed it, shaved it, fenced it, cut it, dammed it, drained it, nuked it, poisoned it, paved it and subdivided it, and turned it into a theatre of faux-bucolic manufactured experiences.
In Sun Valley, where Hemingway fired his final shotgun shell, the golden ghettos of the west might as well be sealed and gated, even if some of the streets are technically open. Some places have a real estate agent for every hundred people. In Jackson Hole anything under five million dollars is a starter home.
But a house with twelve fireplaces is a home

without a hearth and America is still a nation rooted in apocalypse. The nation's foundation is tied to the End of Times. When the Puritans landed in the bitter bogs of New England they carried with them the forecast of annihilation. They hadn't come to delight in religious freedom, but to ring in the last of days. Preacher's still bible thump the rapture of it. Apocalypse is in America's DNA.

Green-eyed wolves are staring back again from behind the aspen groves of Yellowstone. There is space and meat. They live authentically in nature, and face death with dignity. There's no app for that.

'But if the book is good, is about something that you know, and is truly written and reading it over you see that this is so you can let the boys yip and the noise will have that pleasant sound coyotes make on a very cold night when they are out in the snow and you are in your own cabin that you have built or paid for with your work.'
Ernest Hemingway

*   *   *

Other Works by Lawrence Winkler

Westwood Lake Chronicles

Orion Cartwheels Quadrilogy
Orions Cartwheel
Between the Cartwheels
Hind Cartwheel
The Final Cartwheel

Stories of the Southern Sea

Samurai Road

*   *   *